FAIRHAVEN
A HISTORY

Brian L. Griffin

The complete history of that most southerly community on
Bellingham Bay, one of the four original towns that were
consolidated in 1904 to become the present City of Bellingham.

⪼⊶⊶O⊶⊶⪻

Knox Cellars Publishing Company

Fairhaven, a History

Copyright © 2015 by Brian L. Griffin

Knox Cellars Publishing Company
Bellingham, Washington USA

ISBN: 978-0-9635841-7-5

Brian L. Griffin
1801 Taylor Ave.
Bellingham, WA 98225
BrianGriffin1@mac.com

Griffin, Brian L.
History/United States/General

Photographic assistance: Jeffrey Jewell, Whatcom Museum;
Ruth Steele, Rozlind Koester, Center for Pacific Northwest Studies; and
Allison Costanza, State of Washington Regional Archive.
Front cover painting: Ben Mann (ben-mann.com).
Editorial assistance: Gayle Helgoe.
Book design, editorial assistance, and prepress services: Kate Weisel (weiselcreative.com).
Back cover photo: 1927 Harris Avenue with C.X. Larrabee II ready for action. Brian L. Griffin caricature from the 2013 mural on the Village Green, painted by Lanny Little.

Photos and images not attributed to others are from the Brian L. Griffin collection.

CONTENTS

Aerial photo of Fairhaven, circa early 1930s. Whatcom Museum.

PART TWO

Fairhaven Anecdotes & Recollections

1891 Fairhaven Birdseye. The original of this rare lithograph was one of eleven copies found by the author in the attic rafters of the 1890 home of Fairhaven lawyer Thomas Newman. Only fifteen of these are known to have survived. Collection of the author.

Preface

I find it surprising that a comprehensive history of Fairhaven has not been written until now. The story of Fairhaven is such a unique one, filled with great personalities, wild speculation, great hopes and the depths of despair. It is a long story that begins with glaciers, native peoples and Spanish adventurers long before the modern arrival of Dirty Dan Harris. It is a tale of high aspirations, human depravity, financial boom and bust, and dedication to renewal. It covers many eras of human endeavor. It is a challenging and engaging story to tell.

In 2007 I published my history of Bellingham's great waterfront park, *Boulevard Park and the Old Fairhaven Waterfront,* and necessarily included many stories about old Fairhaven. Soon after publication I was contacted by a number of Fairhaven faithful who urged me to attempt the broader story, the entire history of this charming village within a city.

Prompted by the larger research of the life of J.J. Donovan, one of Fairhaven's and Bellingham's most illustrious citizens, I have taken on the task. In the years since writing *Boulevard Park* I have accumulated a large amount of historical information useful to this effort. I have enjoyed a four year correspondence with two important observers of local history who grew up in Fairhaven in the 1920s. I have devoted an entire chapter, The Prince and the Pauper, to what I learned from those charming correspondents. One is the grandson of the wealthy C.X. Larrabee, the other, the son of a Fairhaven laborer, Roy "Rocky" Hansen.

I have received in an old cardboard box, the corporate records of the 1889 Fairhaven Water and Electric Co. They reveal the fascinating story of building the utilities for a booming city before the turn of the twentieth century. I have interviewed men who demolished the fire-ravaged Fairhaven Hotel and delivered more than a thousand truckloads of its rubble to the shoreline that we now call Boulevard Park. Most importantly, I have had the unique privilege of finding and securing for our community archives the personal papers of J.J. Donovan who arrived in Fairhaven in 1888 when its population totaled a mere 140 souls. His diaries and papers provide a never before seen view of the Fairhaven story.

Armed with this new information and supported by the invaluable archives of the Center for Pacific Northwest Studies, the Whatcom Museum, and the private museum of Gordon Tweit, I have attempted to present the entire story of this unique part of Bellingham.

Introduction

Dan Harris had it right when he named his town Fairhaven. Dan was a sea-faring man and he would have been keenly aware of those blessed places on this earth where a sailor could find rest and respite from the storms that threatened his ship and his safety.

He would have recognized the cove as a place of safe haven that day in 1854 when he wearily rowed his boat around the prominent Poe's Point into its protection and received the welcome of that early resident, the tubercular John Thomas.

The forces of nature over geologic time had created an attractive place of refuge on the eastern shore of what by then was called Bellingham Bay. The cozy harbor was defined by a high promontory of soft glacial till which protruded north from the bluffs fronting the larger bay. Then the land curved deeply to the east lowering to a sand-gravel beach which reached a quarter of a mile to the mouth of a fulsome fresh-water stream flowing through a broad valley from a lake nestled in the foothills to the east. On the eastern bank of the stream the beach now narrowed to a gradually rising bluff that curved gently to the north as it formed the eastern shoreline of Bellingham Bay. Great cedars and firs and spruce crowded the shore to the very edge of the bluff and carpeted the rapidly rising hill to the east with a mantle of green. The low marsh lands behind the beach berm had begun their formation 14,000 years before Harris stepped ashore

The small cove and the beach were perfectly protected from the prevailing southerly winds and even avoided the worst of the fierce winter northeasters that howled out of the great river gorge to the north in the English territory. Its fury was diminished by the thickly forested hills to the northeast that would one day be known as Sehome and South Hill. Only the rare northwesterly wind could disturb its calm. The cove was indeed a *fair haven*. Equally important to sea-goers was the deep water just off the beach which allowed a deep draft sailing ship to anchor close to shore, taking full advantage of the prominent point and the curve of the harbor.

No one knows when man first used the cove, but surely the Salish peoples who had occupied these lands for perhaps 12,000 years must have been attracted by its sheltering qualities. It offered abundant fresh water, the shellfish on its beach and the seasonal salmon runs returning to the creek each fall. These attributes marked it as a perfect place for aboriginal peoples. Perhaps there was a year round village there, perhaps just a seasonal fishing camp. No one knows for sure.

Local legend relates the story of Spanish explorers landing there to fill their water barrels and rest, and of an ugly confrontation with the local Indians who attacked them in great numbers. The legend tells of a great battle that was waged from the beach and up the stream bed; and even hints at a Spanish cannon and a drinking chalice found along the stream bed. Once again, the written record is unavailable. The physical evidence lost or a fable. There is no proof, there is only the possibility.

It is known that Spanish naval explorers traversed the larger bay on their way north in 1791. That voyage of discovery is well documented in Spanish naval records. They did not record problems with the natives.

The *fair haven* as first seen by the Salish tribes and Dirty Dan is vastly changed. The protective glacial moraine has been graded down flat and its alluvial soils shoveled and pushed into the marsh behind the beach berm and outward into the salt water to form more usable land. A park and a shipyard now occupy the ground it arose from. The tidal basins have been filled with the detritus of European settlement, the former salt marsh now hosts a municipal sewer treatment plant and various industrial properties. The beach is replaced by Harris Avenue and blocked from the sea by the stone fill of a busy railroad track. Only the stream remains, still running through the land into the salt water of the bay, but it too has been hugely altered. Its twin tidal estuaries filled or silted, its stream bed raised by a century of upstream siltation.

Despite the many changes, a small run of salmon and cutthroat trout still manage to return to the stream. Harris Bay remains a fair haven, now sheltering the Alaska Ferry, several Coast Guard boats, the shipyard and a small flotilla of pleasure boats anchored out or tethered to buoys.

The village that in 1889 grew to a town almost overnight might still be recognizable if Dan Harris were to return from his eternal rest. Wardner's castle still stands watch high on the hill and a handful of the old buildings from that boom time remain. The street that Harris named in his own honor still lies straight as a die up through the center of Fairhaven; but alas, both Harris's hotel on the waterfront, and the soaring brick and stone magnificence of Nelson Bennett's Fairhaven Hotel at the high corner of 12th and

Harris no longer grace the village. Even the massive Mason Block across the street has been diminished by the cutesy name, Sycamore Square, thrust upon it by its latest owner.

What would be recognizable to any old-timer would be the enterprising spirit of a new generation of *boomers* who have done so much to create Fairhaven's modern growth and economic strength.

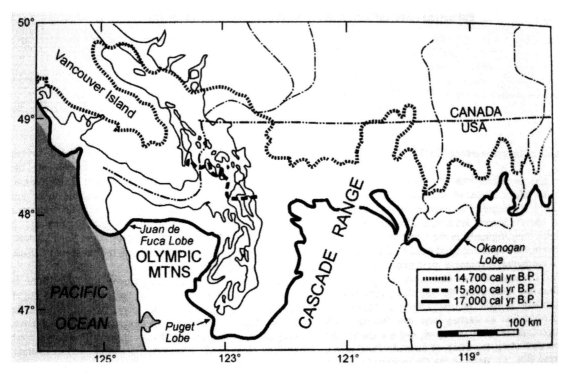

1.1. Incursion of glacier. This image shows the southern extension of the great glacier that buried the Fairhaven area under an ice sheet six thousand feet thick. It was stopped by the Olympic Mountains, although the Puget lobe extended as far south as Olympia. *Glaciation of Western Washington, Quarternary Glaciers Extent and Cronology, part 2.* Steven C. Porter.

PART ONE

➤┄◆┄〇┄◆┄◄

┅┄ ⧓◆⧓ ┄┅

CHAPTER 1

In The Beginning

L ong before Dan Harris rowed his skiff from Victoria, British Columbia, and rounded the high forested point into the protected cove, the forces of nature had been at work to create the harbor that Harris would one day name after himself.

Eighteen thousand years ago, just the blink of an eye in geologic time, a massive glacier covered Bellingham Bay. The Earth which had been warm and ice free for millions of years had entered a long cold stage ushering in the Ice Age which continues to this very day.[1] The creation of ice on the planet began with a cold phase much colder than it is today. During that frigid time, glaciers began to grow at the poles of the Earth, and they spread latitude by latitude until an ice sheet 6,000 feet deep engulfed present day Canada and much of what we now call Washington, Idaho and Montana.

The ice was so heavy that it depressed the crust of the Earth by approximately 2,000 feet, pushing much of the land on which we currently live under the nearby sea. Its ponderous movement scraped ridges and scars in the bedrock of the Earth that remain in evidence of its passing. Scars proving the glacier's north-south movement can be found on bare rock mountain tops in the San Juan Islands and Whatcom County, perhaps none more dramatic than the glacial scars at the Artist's Point parking lot high above the Mt. Baker Ski Area at a present height of 5,800 feet above the sea.

The massive glacier was stopped on its southward movement only by the Olympic Mountains. It had reached all the way to the present day city of Olympia.

---

1   Scientists consider this 'ice age' to be merely the latest glaciation event in a much larger ice age, one that dates back over two million years and has seen multiple glaciations.

Then the Earth began to warm. Over several thousand years the glacial ice melted and slowly retreated back north. As it melted, innumerable rocks and boulders that it had picked up in its earlier southward journey were deposited on the earth. Those rocks, mostly granite, can be found all over Whatcom, San Juan and Skagit counties. They are called glacial erratics—rounded stones that were broken off of mountain peaks to the north—ground and rounded by the moving glacier, and finally left behind here when the glacier melted.

With the ice receded, the Earth's crust recovered and began to rise upward to its present state, the sea was thrust back. Our glacially scarred Earth began to heal itself. Vegetative growth began to cover the scraped land.

Then the Earth began to cool again; and approximately 13,000 years ago the ice returned to Bellingham Bay. This was a much smaller glacier. It slowly moved across the bay and stopped right at the place in Fairhaven where the shipyard is now. The glacier scoured across the bay gouging out the mud, sand and gravel down to bed-rock, pushing before it a huge mound of loose material. There it stopped. The Earth had begun to warm once again. Very rapidly this small glacier melted and disappeared, leaving behind it a mound that would define the protected cove. Such mounds, bulldozed by glaciers are called glacial moraines. The material within them is called glacial till.

The moraine left by the last glacial outbreak with its bulk and height would serve for years as protection for the harbor. It is likely that as the first glaciers receded, humans began to follow the emerging shoreline toward the

1.2. Poe's Point, circa 1895. Poe's Point was logged in 1890, only two large firs survived. McKenzie Avenue was cut through to the beach. The railroad trestle had not yet been built. The Bellingham Hotel and the Hill Welbon (Taylor Avenue) Dock are seen across Harris Bay and Dan Harris's Fairhaven Hotel can be seen to the right. Whatcom Museum.

SECTION XI

U S COAST AND GEODETIC SURVEY

F M THORN SUPERINTENDENT

SHEET Nº 7

TOPOGRAPHY OF

ROSARIO STRAIT

W T

SAMISH FLATS TO BELLINGHAM

1887

1.3. Coast and Geodetic Survey of 1887. The government survey clearly shows the outline of the glacial moraine and at its eastern end, the two large tidal estuaries where Padden Creek meets the salt water. Tim Wahl collection.

south, having crossed the land bridge from the Asian continent. It is likely that they arrived on the bay shortly after the small second glacier receded. That glacier had created a welcoming place for these early immigrants.

The long extension of the moraine protruding well out into the bay created a broad cove protected from the prevailing southerly winds. Tidal and wave action gradually caused the accretion of beaches on both sides of the point behind which thousands of years of vegetative growth built life-enhancing tidal marshes. The seasonal flows of a freshwater creek meandered through the marshes, reaching the sea at the eastern extremity of the cove. Salmon and trout occupied the stream and a pair of inland tidal lagoons offered perfect protection from the storms of the sea. The glacier had created an ideal place for human habitation. A fair haven indeed. Over time, sediment was swept into this cove area by currents along the shore and runoff from the land. Gradually a sand barrier known as a *baymouth bar* formed, creating behind it, beside the running creek, two tidal lagoons or estuaries which would empty and flood with the tides. As the sand barrier grew higher, water exchange with the saltwater of the bay became less frequent, the estuaries filling with each high tide.

Eventually the protective sand bar would be extended and bolstered and connected across the creek by a bridge and become Harris Avenue, the main street of the city that would be built there.

What Dan Harris found when he arrived in 1854, what John Thomas had seen the year before when he made his homestead claim on the land, and what the Native Americans found when they first speared salmon at the creek mouth, can perhaps best be illustrated by the 1887 Coast & Geodetic Survey map printed by the Federal Government.

It clearly outlines the shape and extent of the massive glacial moraine that was Poe's Point.

In the shelter of this great hill, John Thomas would build his cabin. Atop its heights, the early settlers would bury their dead and name it Graveyard Point. Legend has it that they were simply following the lead of the Native Americans who had buried their dead at its summit for untold generations. On its western slope Alonzo Poe would stake his claim and build his cabin and many would call it Poe's Point. Eventually the 70-foot-high glacial moraine would be bisected, several roads and a railroad track hewn through its mass to create access to the waterfront. Finally, it would be ignominiously shoveled and scraped down by man's modern steam shovels and shoved into the sea to fill in behind driven piling to make more land for the shipyard that was to develop there.

But we get ahead of our story. Before all of this, before John Thomas and Dan Harris, and before the City were the people of the tribes, the first inhabitants of the lands around the glacial mound.

CHAPTER 2

The First Inhabitants

Over hundreds of years the frigid Earth began to warm and the glaciers began to retreat. As the great ice shield retreated northward it created opportunity for life to return to the coastline around the northern Pacific Ocean. As conditions changed the first humans began to migrate along the ice-free shore. Just when they arrived at Bellingham Bay is unknown, but we do know that they were here at about 3,200 years ago. They lived in a village site beside Padden Creek in the shelter of the great glacial moraine. The ancestors of today's Nooksack, Lummi or Samish tribes lived along one of the tidal estuaries that had formed in the low-lying marsh at the creek mouth and left their identifying shell middens beside at least one of those estuaries inland of the creek mouth.

In 1973 Professor Garland Grabert, and his team of what were then Western Washington College students, conducted an archaeological dig at the place where Padden Creek met the larger of the tidal estuaries. Their modest operation met with considerable success. On this site they found artifacts in a shell midden that established that Native Americans had occupied the site between 2,400 and 3,200 years ago, during what archaeologists call the Locarno Beach Phase. To put this in the perspective of European history, when Julius Caesar ruled Rome, a Native American woman broke a stone *labret* which had pierced her lower lip and discarded it in the village refuse dump beside Padden Creek.

Such dumps, now called *shell middens* by archaeologists, contain the clues that reveal the life styles of these ancient peoples. The Padden Creek midden consisted of large numbers of clam and snail shells of various species, rock oysters, crab shells, salmon and other fish bones, all discarded in the area of their lodgings. Always a surefire sign of native habitation, this midden contained a number of *cobble flakes*, rounded rocks broken to provide sharp edges which could be used for cutting and scraping. Abrading stones of sandstone were used to scrape, sharpen and polish, while wedges made of deer or elk

2.1. Labret found in the Grabert excavation. 1973. This broken labret enabled Prof. Grabert to date the human occupation of the tidal estuary to between 2,400, and 3,200 years ago. Collection of WWU Anthropology Department. Photo by author.

2.2. Obsidian micro-blade, Grabert excavation, 1973. Collection of WWU Anthropology Dept. Photo by author.

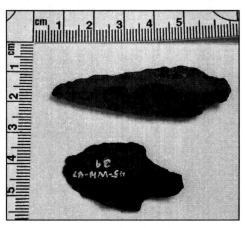

2.3. Projectile Points, Grabert Excavation, 1973. Collection of WWU Anthropology Department. Photo by author.

antlers were used for splitting the plentiful Western Red Cedar used for house planking, canoe building and many other purposes.

Of special interest was a tiny obsidian micro-blade barely 3/4-inch long made of an obsidian found only in the Three Sisters area of central Oregon. It provided stark evidence of a trading system with other tribes that even 3,000 years ago saw goods traded across the mountains, as well as great distances north and south. The most significant find, according to Dr. Sarah Campbell, Chair of the Department of Archaeology at Western Washington University, was the broken labret which had been discarded so long ago. Its presence established the antiquity of the site.

Dr. Campbell related that in the time period 2,400 to 3,200 years ago native women pierced their lower lips and inserted labrets made of bone or stone. The practice was abandoned after that period. The broken labret had rested in the midden beside Padden Creek for perhaps 3,000 years, just waiting to be found and testify to the presence of the inhabitants of this protected fresh-water campsite.

Also found at the site were nicely fashioned projectile points. The Grabert dig was a small one and of brief duration. I have learned from several sources that shell middens covered a broad area of the flat lands behind the beach berms on both sides of the Poe's Point moraine. It is clear that the area was a place favored by the Native Americans. It is not known (without further

2.4. Encampment on the beach south of Poe's Point (now first trestle). Whatcom Museum.

scientific study) whether the Padden Creek estuaries were the site of a permanent village or simply a seasonal fishing camp. Dr. Campbell mentions that the midden site at the Gates/Lee farm on Chuckanut Bay is of the same era. A Carbon 14 test was done on some of their findings there, and the site was determined to have been occupied 2,500 to 2,600 years ago. It is hoped that further digs will be conducted at these sites to better understand their prehistoric use.

To this unscientific observer it seems possible that the Padden Creek site would have been an excellent site for a permanent village. The tidal estuaries would have provided a waterway navigable by canoes. Clear fresh water in abundance flowed down the creek. In season the creek would have swarmed with migrating salmon and trout, while the stream bed would have provided easy trail access through the forest to the hunting opportunities of the fertile valley upstream. Just a short distance upstream where the valley broadens it is likely that the Indians would have found camas and other vegetative food items essential to their diet. The marshes surrounding the estuaries, and on both sides of the great moraine, would have provided the reeds which those early peoples used for clothing, bedding and mats. The surrounding forests of cedar, alder and fir would have provided for their dwelling and boat construction. Only further archaeological efforts can finally determine the use of the site.

The tribal identity of these early residents is difficult to attribute. Bellingham historian, Tim Wahl, cites a very early people he calls the

Mamosee, who called Chuckanut Bay and the Fairhaven shorelines home. He claims evidence of petroglyphs carved on large rocks which once stood on the shoreline near First Trestle, until they were disturbed and then removed for railroad construction.

The Nooksack tribe, currently centered at their up-river site at Deming, believe that their people hunted, gathered and fished the entire area from the saltwater and upriver to the mountains. Their forebears may have camped at Padden Creek.

The present day Lummi were more likely to have been inhabitants of the offshore islands in those long ago days, although they have legends which give them an early presence on Bellingham Bay. The Samish people from the lower part of the bay might also have used the Padden Creek site.

I find it of great interest that much of the larger tidal estuary that held the native campsite is still clearly evident and remains visible to the discerning eye. Despite more than 100 years of siltation from modern man's activities up stream the outlines of the estuary are still evident. Fortunately most of the surviving estuary is owned by the City of Bellingham. If the reader will begin at Harris Avenue and walk up the Park Department trail on the west side of Padden Creek, you will soon come to a significant depression in the earth, which widens out into what is now an overgrown swamp at high water times. The trail splits and follows the swamp's edges. The westerly trail leads to 6th street. The easterly trail will take you up Padden Creek. Both trails mark the northern boundary of the surviving tidal basin around which those first inhabitants lived.

As you walk the trails, let your imagination take you back in time and you can see dugout canoes pulled up on the shore, a few cedar planked houses on the bank above, and the smoke of cooking fires wisping up through the alder trees. The first and smaller tidal basin has been completely filled for many years by the developments of man. The larger basin remains with margins largely unchanged, but has been silted in by 160 years of upstream activity in Happy Valley so that the tides can no longer fill it.

I wonder if we will ever see the surviving tidal basin returned to its original state, dredged of its silt, again charged with salt water from the high tides surging up Padden Creek. Perhaps with an interpretive Indian cedar-planked house or two on its shoreline. This surviving piece of historical land could become a marvelous interpretive center, teaching tomorrow's inhabitants about the lives of those first inhabitants of long ago.

CHAPTER 3

European Exploration

Native Americans had lived on the shores of Bellingham Bay in primitive isolation for thousands of years; their existence threatened only by the occasional attack of other tribes seeking hegemony, treasure or slaves. Estimates by ethno-historians indicate a large and thriving population. It was not until the waning years of the eighteenth century that Europeans appeared and began to influence this primeval existence.

The vast regions of the northern Pacific Ocean were essentially unknown to the great European powers until the mid-1700s. Spain had discovered and settled the lands around the Caribbean, conquered the lands of Mexico and built cities on the Pacific Ocean side at Panama City, Lima and Acapulco. They were the sole European power with a role in and knowledge of the great Pacific Ocean. The English had claimed and settled much of the central Atlantic coast of the new continent and were slowly advancing settlements over the Appalachian mountains and forests in westward expansion. The other great power, France, had a tenuous hold on the northern Atlantic coastline and down the interior Mississippi valley to New Orleans. Neither of them had knowledge of nor much interest in the far northern Pacific.

It was the riches of the Orient and the commercial competition to exploit them that caused the imperial powers to finally look northward. That competition brought Europeans to the Pacific shores of North America.

As early as 1523 the Spanish Emperor Carlos—wanting to find and claim the fabled passage through the continent which separated the two great oceans—sent conquistador Hernán Cortés instructions stressing the necessity for a search for the passage that they called the Strait of Anián. If found, the imagined waterway would save months (perhaps years) in travel time from Europe to the Orient, while avoiding the dangerous route around Cape Horn in the southern latitudes. The nation that controlled such a waterway would be heir to untold wealth and power.

Spanish nobles had developed a great weakness for oriental finery. As early as 1527 Spanish galleons had sailed from Acapulco for China, carrying manufactured goods, cloth, tools, arms, munitions and Mexican silver. They returned with silks, fine China, porcelain, gold coins, cinnamon and other spices, candles and beeswax in bulk. They returned by way of Manila, as the winds and currents made the Philippines a necessary way-station between China and South America. These galleons came to be known as *Manila Galleons.*

The Spaniards had early established the sea route to China by riding the northwest trade winds to the east, but when they responded to their Emperor's orders to explore north up the coast they fared less well. In 1532 Cortés sent Diego Hurtado de Mendoza on a northbound expedition. He only reached as far as Sinaloa, somewhere near present day Mazatlan, before he and all of his men were slain by natives. Undaunted, the conqueror of Mexico outfitted two more ships. They at least discovered Baja California, but also met death at the hands of natives. Only a few survivors returned to tell of the discovery. Spain struggled periodically to explore to the north in the ensuing 200 years; but fog, fierce storms and adverse currents thwarted their efforts and discouraged their leadership. Exact knowledge of how many expeditions were launched or how far north they came is still shrouded in the secrecy with which Spain kept their knowledge of sea routes in the Pacific. Protection for their heavily laden treasure ships relied on secrecy, not armament. Their charts and reports of expeditions were often recorded on a master chart and then secreted away in the royal naval archives.

Spain's veiling of her nautical knowledge was based on a realistic fear— fear of the buccaneers that preyed on their shipping in the Caribbean. There was also the fear that sharing their information might allow a foreign nation to discover and claim the legendary Strait of Anián.

For decades, knowledge of the Manila galleons had been kept from rivals. The slow vessels, laden with treasure sailed without escort or heavy armament, easy prey for any attacker. Finally the secret leaked out to the buccaneers of the Caribbean. That terror of the Spanish Main, Englishman Francis Drake, was drawn to the Pacific by tales of the rich prizes. In 1578 Drake sailed around the Horn and laid waste to ports in Chile and Peru, seizing vessels and booty.

Off the coast of Equador he took the *Nuestra Senora de la Concepcion* laden with bullion, and from its charts gained knowledge of the Manila ships and their route. He now headed north seeking the Straits of Anián, to claim it for his Queen and to make for a quick passage home. Driven back by fog and bad weather and in need of a sheltered cove to make repairs he made a landing at a bay north of San Francisco. He performed a claiming ceremony there fixing a brass plate to a tree claiming the land for England. (In 1934, a plaque fitting

Drake's description was found at what traditionally had been called Drake's Bay.)

After spending 36 days in the bay—the ship now repaired and re-provisioned with water and food—he sailed for home crossing the Pacific, rounding the Cape of Good Hope and dropping anchor in Plymouth after two years and ten months at sea. He was feted and knighted by Queen Elizabeth. His buccaneering adventure ended Spain's total dominance of the Pacific. In fact, England then claimed rights to all of the land north of Drake's Bay and Spanish hegemony in the Pacific was threatened.

Drake's incursion struck fear in the heart of the Spaniards. Now that they had competition the Spaniards renewed their exploration with vigor and dedication.

Then, further competition came from an unexpected quarter. Europe's fourth great power, Russia—driven by the vision and curiosity of Peter the Great—sent Vitus Bering to Siberia to launch a voyage of discovery. The Tsar died in 1725, but his westward efforts lived on. In 1728 Bering discovered what is now called the Bering Sea. On his second and final voyage in 1741 Bering, with Aleksei Chirikoff, sailed from a Siberian port, across the strait, and discovered Alaska. Then Chirikoff continued down the coast of North America as far as the mouth of the Columbia River, though far out to sea. The Russians also discovered the valuable furs of the sea otter and by 1743, Russians were moving along the Aleutian Islands enslaving the Aleuts in the harvesting of furs. Europe began to hear of the Russian encroachment onto the American continent.

The Spanish, reacting to the competition awoke from their long period of quietude. Now the search for the Strait of Anián or the Northwest Passage would begin in earnest. In 1774 they sent Juan Perez north in an expedition that went farther than any previously known Spanish exploration. Perez discovered an excellent harbor that he named San Lorenzo, but would famously come to be known as Nootka Sound. Perez had gotten as far north as 54° 40'. He saw many places on his return voyage to Monterey, but he did not find the mouth of the Columbia, or the entrance to the Strait of Juan de Fuca.

It was during this time period that the fabled Spanish occupation of Fairhaven was thought to have occurred. In the 1904 celebration of the consolidation of Fairhaven and Whatcom into Bellingham, a *Chronology of Bay History* was published by the *Bellingham Herald* and it began, "1775-6 Spaniards winter at Fairhaven." The source of their information we do not know.

Now it was the English turn. In July of 1776, Captain Cook set sail for the Pacific with orders to sail to the "New Albion coast at about 48 degrees and to search north to 65 degrees for the Northwest Passage." Along the way, he discovered a group of islands in the mid-Pacific that he named after Lord

Sandwich, and which we now know as the Hawaiian Islands. Several months later he arrived at the North American coast at about 44 degrees and searched diligently northward for the fabled Strait of Juan de Fuca. He failed to find it and labeled its existence a myth. He then sailed north to Nootka Sound where he traded for sea otter skins with the natives. Later, thwarted by the oncoming winter, he turned south again to the Hawaiian Islands where he would lose his life. An unexpected, but extremely meaningful, discovery was made on the crew's voyage home. The ship stopped in China and learned that the furs that they had traded for odd bits of rusted metal and assorted gee-gaws at Nootka Sound brought fabulous prices in Canton. The fur trade that would forever change the lives of the Northwest native had been launched.

It was the fur trade which brought the attention of the world to the Pacific Northwest. The mouth of the Columbia River had not yet been discovered. The entrance to the Strait of Juan de Fuca was still a legend, not a reality. It was not until 1790 that Spanish Captain Manuel Quimper entered the mouth of the Strait, sailed its length, turned the corner at what is now Victoria and discovered Haro Strait, naming it after Lopez de Haro.

The following year 1791, Francisco de Eliza was sent from the harbor of Nooka to explore Haro Strait. He had two ships, the *San Carlos* and the sloop *Santa Saturnina*. The larger *San Carlos* stayed at anchor in Esquimalt Harbor near present day Victoria; while the *Santa Saturnina* commanded by Jose Maria Narvaez was sent to explore and chart the islands. Narvaez sailed past Eliza Island, naming it after his commander, across and through Chuckanut Bay, and then across Bellingham Bay which he named Seno de Gaston. They were most likely the first white men to have entered what would become Bellingham Bay. He then sailed up Hales Passage and well up Georgia Strait. On their return to Nootka Sound, while sailing out of the Strait of Juan de Fuca, they discovered the harbor of Port Angeles protected by its great spit, Ediz Hook.

The next summer, Eliza returned. This time anchoring his mother ship in Port Angeles. He sent two small *goletas* (47-foot schooners), off to explore. The *Sutil* was commanded by 32-year-old Dionisio Alcala Galiano. The *Mexicana* was commanded by 25-year-old Cayetano Valdez.

Again the Spaniards sailed north, passing Eliza Island as they entered Bellingham Bay. On the night of June 12th, they anchored for the night in the shallow waters off what is now the mouth of the Nooksack River. Their ships' logs report that in the early morning darkness they "constantly saw light to the south and east of the mountain of Carmelo (Mt. Baker) and even at times some bursts of flame, signs which left no doubt that there are volcanoes with strong eruptions in those mountains." The night also brought a serious emergency as they had anchored a bit too close to the shore and a southwesterly came up in the early morning. The tide was also ebbing. First the *Mexicana*

3.1. The *Santa Saturnina* in Bellingham Bay, July 1791. This carefully researched painting depicts a schooner of that day. Mayo depicts her leaving Post Point astern and heading for Hales Passage. Watercolor by Steve Mayo. Prints of this painting can be obtained from the artist.

began to ground and then the *Sutil*. The ships received some hard knocks on their hulls as they were pounded on the sand bottom, but they sustained no damage. Crisis maneuvering ensued and the two schooners were able to claw away and out of the bay where they entered Hales Passage at 4:00 PM and were immediately becalmed. Annotations indicated that they were still becalmed in the Passage at 8 AM, and such is the life of a sailor.

When they did sail out of the Passage and into the Strait of Georgia they spotted two English longboats in Lummi Bay. Captain George Vancouuver was anchored in Birch Bay and his longboats were out exploring to the south. Vancouver's log records that Whidbey, in charge of the longboats, headed back to Birch Bay upon seeing the Spaniards. Whidbey returned to enter Bellingham Bay on the 13th or 14th of June, 1792. The Spaniards would continue north to complete what would be the first circumnavigation of Vancouver Island.

These intrepid Spanish and English explorers would chart, map and claim the territory, but it would be another eight decades before the first European would come to Bellingham Bay to settle. The fur trade developed into a frenzy of activity on the coast. Sea-borne traders would buy sea otter

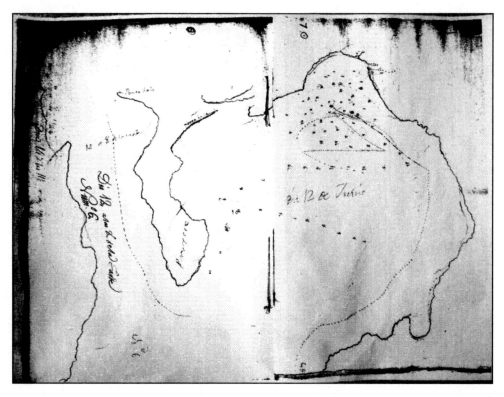

3.2. Copies from the *Sutil*'s log book, 1792. Museo Naval, Madrid. These pages depict the course of the *Sutil* and the *Mexicana* as they sailed into Bellingham Bay, anchored for the night of 12 June and sailed out the next day up Hales Passage.

pelts from the natives for ever increasing prices and sail them to China to sell them at even more rapidly increasing prices. With the money received, they would fill their ships with tea, China and silks, and then sail for home, England or New England, to sell the Chinese goods at a huge profit.

They would then purchase cheap trade goods and set sail again around the Horn for the long trip to the Northwest villages.

In the meantime another fur trade was prospering as traders and mountain men came overland from the east, trapping beaver and mink and furs of all descriptions. After the discovery of the mouth of the Columbia River in 1792, and the Lewis and Clark Expedition in 1806, the settlement of the northwest country appeared inevitable.

First came the fur traders. The American John Jacob Astor established his fur trading post at Astoria on the Columbia in 1810, ready to buy furs from any and all coming out of the mountain interior. He would also buy or trade for the furs brought by ship into the Columbia, and ship out his furs on ships returning to the east coast. His enterprise looked promising until the day in 1812 when a British Royal Navy frigate sailed across the river bar

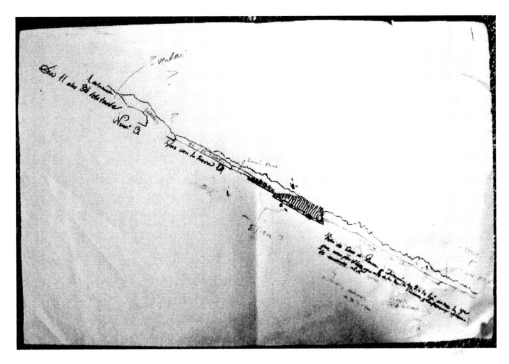

3.3. Sketch from the *Sutil's* log book, 1792, Museo Naval, Madrid. This sketch of Bellingham Bay looking north may have been done by Jose Cardero, pilot, cartographer and artist on the *Sutil*. Taken from the 15-page sketch book.

and with her 24 guns bristling, took over Astoria. The British felt they owned this land and they installed their own fur trader, the Hudson's Bay Company. The fur trading business was moved upstream and across the river to the newly constructed Fort Vancouver. There Dr. John McLoughlin would reign benevolently, doing business with whomever came upriver or down, and the Hudson's Bay Company would prevail for the next 34 years.

Then came the missionaries who, without notable success, tried to bring the white man's religion to the Yakamas, the Nez Perce, the Umatillas and the Cayuse. Almost simultaneously in the early 1840s, the great western movement began with thousands of immigrants crossing the continent to settle in the rich Williamette Valley. The lure of free land and a new beginning brought more than 1,000 immigrants over the first Oregon Trail in the year 1843. Each year more people came, struggling across the trail with wagons and cattle and more possessions than they were able to carry.

The American migration, into lands that the treaty of 1818 had determined would be occupied by both the United States and England, brought great pressure on both governments to settle the question of just whose land this was. Negotiations began and in 1846 they resulted in the Oregon Treaty, in which both nations agreed to divide the Northwest lands at the 49th parallel, just where the international border is to this day. This meant that the

English Hudson's Bay Company must abandon its post at Fort Vancouver and move north to Fort Victoria at the southern tip of Vancouver Island. The treaty called for the border line to dip south to include all of Vancouver Island as England's territory.

The United States government, now possessed of the rich lands north of California all the way to the 49th parallel, decided it would be wise to encourage settlement in their new territory. In 1850, President Millard Fillmore signed the Oregon Land Act providing for 160 acres of land for a single settler in Oregon Territory, 320 acres for a married couple. As though this was not enough incentive to move west, the year before gold had been discovered at Sutter's Mill and San Francisco was booming. The reverberations from this economic firestorm were felt as far north as the yet to be settled Bellingham Bay.

CHAPTER 4

Settlers Arrive on Bellingham Bay

There is no known record of Euro-American activity on Bellingham Bay between the Spanish and English expeditions of 1792 and the year 1852; but it is not difficult to believe that trappers from the Hudson's Bay Company at Fort Victoria, ship builders looking for spars, or casual explorers had frequented the bay so close to Hudson's Bay headquarters in those years. In fact there is an undocumented mention in George Hunsby's book, *The Birth, Death and Resurrection of Fairhaven*, which mentions that the Hudson's Bay Company's ship, *Beaver*, had landed employees on the shores of Bellingham Bay to cut spar trees in 1848. It is known that Indians had told white men of "black fire dirt" that was to be found along the shores of that bay named by George Vancouver so many years before.

It is also known that the economic boom created by the San Francisco Gold Rush of 1849, and the subsequent San Francisco fire was creating opportunity for the entire coast. San Francisco needed coal to fuel its gas lamps and warm its fog-bound homes. San Francisco needed lumber to satisfy its rollicking construction boom after the fire. There was money to be made supplying its needs. In Port Townsend at the entrance to Puget Sound eager men gathered looking for opportunities to cash in on the California opportunity.

Henry Roeder was a 28-year-old mariner who had captained ships on the Great Lakes. He was of German ancestry, a capable, determined and ambitious man. He had heard of the "black fire dirt" to be found around the bay, but he was more interested in the endless forest of Douglas Fir and cedar that grew down to the waters edge, and the waterfall that he had been told dropped to the sea from its rocky ledge far above high tide, more than enough height to power a saw mill.

It is believed that he was told of the promising falls by a Hudson's Bay employee William Pattle who offered to guide Roeder to the falls for $1,000. Pattle had his own plans for the bay. Roeder, a thrifty German, found another way. He partnered with a man name Russell V. Peabody. They located a pair of Indians who were visiting Port Townsend and familiar with the falls on Bellingham Bay. The natives called it "Whatcom," or something that sounded like Whatcom to the white entrepreneurs. The meaning of the name was "noisy waters." Roeder and Peabody hired the natives to take them to the falls in their cedar canoe. The four men arrived at the beach below the falls on December 15, 1852.

Roeder and Peabody each filed a Donation Land Claim under the Oregon Land Act. Peabody staked his claim straddling the creek, Roeder staking off his 160 acres adjoining him to the west. The cooperative Lummi chieftain, Chow-its-hoot, agreed to provide men to help and the first settlers began to construct their saw mill on the east side of the creek below the falls.

William Pattle's interest in Bellingham Bay was in its coal. He had found two like-minded friends, James Morrison and John Thomas. Just days before Roeder and Peabody landed at the falls, they had filed for Donation Land Claims along the eastern shoreline where they had found indications of coal deposits. Pattle filed first, on April 1st, 1853, claiming 320 acres for him and his wife. Their claim extended from a "blazed cedar tree on mineral point," to a point one mile north along the bay, then east 1/2 mile, thence south a mile, and finally west 1/2 mile to the starting point. Apparently the Pattle marriage was troubled and perhaps ended, since Pattle only ended up with 160 acres and his claim ended only 1/2 mile north of that "mineral point."

Morrison's and Thomas's 160-acre claims are dated the next day, April 2nd. Morrison's claim contains this statement, "this claim is made in virtue of settlement thereon or about the 1st of December, 1852." His statement would indicate that it is probable that James Morrison, not Roeder or Peabody, was the first person of European descent to settle on Bellingham Bay.

Pattle and his friends James Morrison and John Thomas were not seeking to carve homes in the wilderness, but to strike it rich by selling the coal they believed would be found on their claims. They had agreed to spread the risks and the possible rewards of their venture by a sharing agreement. They would each stake out adjoining land claims along the eastern shoreline. Even before they had filed their claims they had signed an agreement with a San Francisco syndicate to which they jointly agreed to sell their rights to the coal they hoped to find. To validate this agreement they had to dig and send 100 bags of coal to San Francisco to be tested for its quality. If the coal passed muster the men would each receive the princely sum of $75 monthly with a $2,500 bonus when the federal patents were received on their claims.

Pattle's claim was the northernmost. It began just north of present day Boulevard Park where the twin stone marker defines the old border between Sehome and Bellingham.

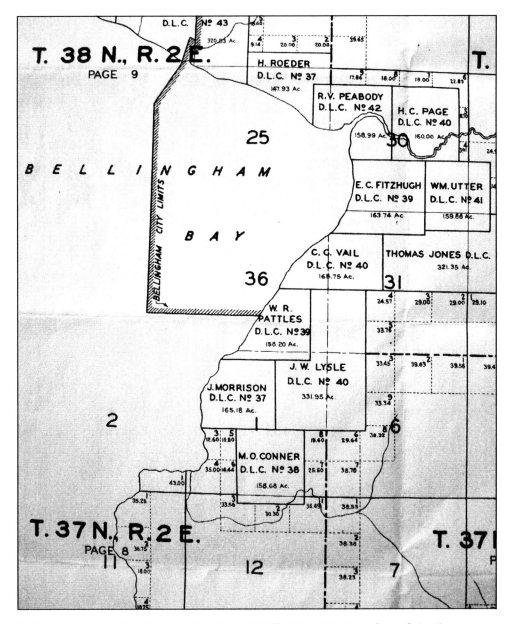

4.1. Map showing early Donation Land claims. Percival R. Jeffcott Map 1-14, Center for Pacific Northwest Studies, Western Libraries Heritage Resources. (CPNWS).

He built his log cabin on the prominent "mineral"[1] point which stuck out from the bluff, where The Woods Coffee shop now sits in Boulevard Park. It must have been on that now greatly reduced point where the "blazed cedar tree" stood, as that was the southern border of his claim. Adjoining him to the south was James Morrison, whose land began at the "blazed cedar"

---

1   The use of the word "mineral" in these early land descriptions was an indication that it was a point of rock, it was not the name of the point.

and extended south to present day Douglas Avenue. His cabin was built at the southern extremity in the acre which contained the site of the former Reid Boiler building. The most southerly claim belonged to John Thomas and began at Douglas Avenue, extending south beyond McKenzie and west around the curve of the cove, across the creek and to what is now 6th Street. Thomas started his cabin just behind the beach near the mouth of the creek.

It was to John Thomas's cabin that Daniel Harris rowed on that fateful day in 1854 when he rounded the glacial moraine and entered the cove that would later bear his name. He moved in with Thomas and it is thought, helped him complete his cabin. Thomas was not a well man. He suffered from consumption, the tuberculosis that would claim his life the next spring. He would be buried somewhere on his 160-acre claim and Dan Harris would arrange to buy the land claim rights from Thomas's relatives. Harris continued living in the cabin that he and Thomas had built and finally received his government patent in 1871.

Nineteen donation claims were made on the lands surrounding Bellingham Bay. All of them proved out to be within the 160-acre limit with the exception of that of Alonzo Poe, Mr. and Mrs. Edward Eldridge, and Mr. and Mrs. John Lysle. The Eldridges and Lysles qualified for 320 acres because of their married status. Poe qualified for 320 acres as he had been a resident of Oregon Territory prior to the enactment of the Oregon Land Act in 1850.

The Oregon Donation Land Law was a powerful incentive to settlement of the virgin territory around Bellingham Bay. Soon after Pattle, Morrison, Thomas, Roeder and Peabody made their claims, other names were added to the role, filling in the patchwork of land holdings around the bay. The settlers came from all across the country to this lonely wilderness in the north country and began carving homes and livings out of what opportunities they could find.

ALONZO MARION POE. John Thomas's immediate neighbor to the west was Alonzo M. Poe who filed on 303 waterfront acres adjoining Thomas's claim. Poe's claim began at what is now 6th street and included the glacial moraine that would be called Graveyard Point, and most of the lands down the waterfront to the south that are now known as Edgemoor. Poe was a bachelor, but because he had resided in the Territory before December 1, 1850, the Land Act allowed him to claim up to 320 acres. He was the only one of the 19 settlers who could claim the higher acreage by dint of early arrival in the territory. Because of the contours of the shoreline Poe ended up with only 303 acres. He built his cabin on the west side of Graveyard Point near the north border of Marine Park.

Alonzo Marion Poe was a remarkable young man. Born in Clay County Wisconson in 1826, he came to Oregon Territory in 1845, probably one of the immigrants on the Oregon Trail that had just opened in 1843. When he arrived he was 19 years old. He was a civil engineer and a lawyer. Poe was one of the founders of Olympia. In 1846 he was elected lieutenant-colonel of the Oregon Rangers, an early militia formed to protect the settlers from Indian troubles.

He was elected sheriff of Lewis County in 1847. He was secretary for the preliminary meeting on July 4, 1851, formed to consider the division of Oregon Territory and the creation of Washington Territory. He became the clerk of Lewis County in 1852. In July of 1852 he became the clerk of Thurston County. He served with Eaton's Rangers during several events of the Indian wars that broke out in 1855.

4.2. The only known photo of Alonzo Marion Poe, 1826-1866. Howard Buswell Photographs #684, CPNWS.

By 1854, after moving north, he was the auditor for Whatcom County. He was a member of the Territorial Legislature for Whatcom County for the 1854-55 session. He used his civil engineering skills to survey and create the first map of Whatcom County, and he was hired by Henry Roeder to survey and plat the town of Whatcom. His later sale of a number of Whatcom lots would indicate that Roeder paid him in land rather than cash.

By 1858, the impatient Poe had decided to sell his property in Whatcom County and return to Olympia. He sold most of his land holdings before he left. On the 26th of October 1858 the record shows he sold the land of his donation land claim to his brother Americus, who was recorded as a resident of Napa City, California. The price was $775. He also sold several lots in Whatcom for $200 each, and on November 24th for $100, he sold to a Samuel Howe a 1/12th interest in the Whatcom Wharf, and a 1/12th interest in all of the unsold portions of 30 blocks of residential property in the town of Whatcom. One suspects that the fee for his survey and plat work for Henry Roeder had been a 1/12th interest in the property platted. Cash was in short supply in those early days.

Poe was clearly washing his hands of Whatcom County. He returned to Olympia where at the outset of the Civil War in 1860 he owned and operated a popular weekly newspaper, the *Overland Press*. By using the fastest pony express routes, Poe was able to publish the most current news and his paper enjoyed considerable success.

By 1862 Poe's health began to fail. Hoping to regain his health he moved to the drier climate of Napa City, California, where his brother Americus lived. He married Miss Emma Hartson, daughter of a prominent banker who he had met in Napa City. Unfortunately Poe's health did not improve. He died there in 1866 only 44 years of age. His death was attributed to inflammation of the lungs. He had lived an adventurous and productive life.

JOHN W. AND MARY FRANCES LYSLE. East of Pattle's and Morrison's claims, high on the hill in the saddle between South Hill and Sehome Hill where the University now stands, was the 331.95 acre homestead of John W. Lysle and his wife Mary Frances.

The Lysles were true pioneers. Originally from Utica, New York, they had come west in a covered wagon over the Oregon Trail. They traveled north to Olympia where they hired Indian canoes to bring them to Bellingham Bay. They first stopped in Chuckanut Bay on September 24, 1854, where they spent the night with the William Cullins family, early settlers on Chuckanut Bay. The next day, in two Indian canoes lashed together, they were paddled by their Indian guides to the beach on the western slope of the great glacial mound where they became the guests of Alonzo Poe, who had just completed his comfortable cabin.

Mary Frances Lysle was 21 years old and became the third white woman to settle on Bellingham Bay. They remained guests of Alonzo Poe as John climbed Sehome Hill to stake out his Oregon Donation Land Claim. He immediately set to work clearing land and building a two room cabin. By Christmas the young family was able to celebrate in their own home in the cozy valley between the wooded crests of the two hills. Five children would be born to the family. Mary Frances lived to the age of 79, spending her final years at her home at 2215 Walnut Street, close to her beloved St. Paul's Episcopal Church.

MAURICE O'CONNER. Just east of Thomas's claim in what came to be called Happy Valley, was the 158.66-acre claim of Maurice O. O'Conner.

By 1856, the Oregon Donation Land Law had run its course. Free land was no longer available, but still the settlers and the speculators came. Now the un-allotted government land could be purchased for $1.25 an acre and there were plenty of takers.

JOHN PADDEN. John Padden bought acreage in Happy Valley and the surrounding hills, getting a dandy lake in the process. A wealthy speculator from Maine, Erastus Bartlett, would buy up hundreds and then thousands of acres, eventually partnering with Edward Eldridge to own all of the Pattle and Morrison lands and platting the first town of Bellingham in 1883.

The land rush over, the tiny population of settlers scattered around the shores of the bay busied themselves with making a living. The early interest was in finding a vein of coal that would justify a mine. Pattle, Morrison and Thomas found a promising vein at the south end of Pattle's claim near what is now the Chrysalis Inn. They mined enough coal to satisfy the 100 bag requirement and sent it off on a sailing ship to be tested. That mine came to be known as Pattle's Mine. Its coal apparently did not pass muster, as before long county records began to show that the partners were selling partial shares of mineral rights on their claims to other speculators.

Two miles up the shoreline a better vein was found under the roots of a blown down cedar tree. Henry Roeder, having spent all his capital building his saw mill acquired the mineral rights and then sold them to a San Francisco syndicate who sent their man Pierre Cornwall north to capitalize on their investment. Cornwall soon opened the Sehome Mine. Around the mine the town of Sehome would grow. The Sehome mine was successful and would provide the foundation of the economy on the bay for many years. The syndicate, represented by Cornwall, would eventually form the Bellingham Bay Improvement Company, own most of the land surrounding Whatcom, bring water from Lake Whatcom, build a saw mill, and start the area's first railroad—the Bellingham Bay and British Columbia.

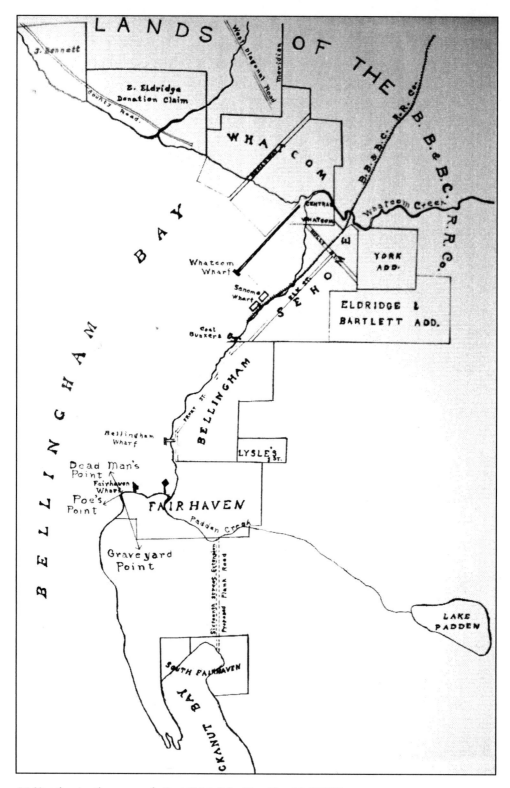

5.1. Map showing three names for Poe's Point. Galen Biery Map 4.2, CPNWS.

CHAPTER 5

Dirty Dan Harris

On an early spring day in 1854 Daniel Jefferson Harris rowed around the heavily forested glacial moraine and into the protected harbor that would someday bear his name. Harris was twenty-one years of age and a sea-faring man. He must have recognized this lovely cove as a special place of refuge from the perils of the sea. Dan had been sailing the seas pursuing whales since the age of 15. He had whaled in the North Atlantic in the beginning. In 1847 he had joined a ship bound for the Pacific Ocean. This ship, captained by Mercator Cooper, pursued whales from the South Pole to Japan and Hawaii. They sailed to Canton, China in 1852, where Dan jumped ship for another whaler bound for Hawaii and Victoria in what was now England's colony of British Columbia, Canada.

In Victoria he must have decided that he had enough of the sailor's life. Again he jumped ship, secured a rowing skiff and began the long row across Haro Strait and through the San Juan Islands to Bellingham Bay. We will never know what he was seeking or what he was expecting when he rowed around that high promontory of Poe's Point, but we do know what he found in the protected waters of the cove. He found a friendly greeting and an invitation to move into John Thomas's almost completed cabin on the beach near Padden Creek and he found a place to make his home for most of the rest of his life.

Dan accepted the offer and moved in with Thomas who had just filed his donation land claim on 146.44 acres. He probably helped Thomas with the completion of the rude cabin, as Thomas was ill and most likely welcomed the strength and skills of the husky young sailor.

Dan Harris had been born February 16, 1833, to a farming family in Southampton, Suffolk County, New York. Southampton is a very old town at the far end of Long Island where his family has been traced back six generations to 1657. In 1847, when just a lad of 15, he had joined an uncle on a whaler sailing out of Sag Harbor in the North Atlantic. Now in 1854 he would be leaving the high seas forever, settling down to build a town and eventually a personal fortune.

In the winter of 1854, not long after Dan's arrival, his new friend John Thomas succumbed to the tuberculosis which had destroyed his health. Dan was so shaken that he did not attend the simple funeral. He remained in the cabin on the beach during the ceremonies. He eventually purchased Thomas's land claim rights from his heirs. In 1871 Dan received the Patent on his 146.44 acres. Earlier he had purchased 43 acres from Alonzo Poe extending his land westward to include Poe's Point and the surrounding waterfront. On page 14 of Book G of the *Whatcom County Book of Deeds* there is a cryptic entry. "August 13, 1861, Alonzo Poe of the town of Olympia, Thurston County, for the price of $53 sells to Daniel Jefferson Harris all of that certain tract or parcel of land being the north end of the donation claim of said Alonzo M. Poe." Etc. The description includes the words "containing 43 acres." The document is witnessed by James Morrison and Elwood Evans.

With this purchase Dan Harris extended his land west to the salt water including the glacial mound that was Poe's Point. He recouped the cost for his land quickly. On December 22, 1862, just four months later, the *Book of Deeds* contains an entry indicating that Dan sold four acres of Deadman's Point to Whatcom County for $150. The county now had land for their graveyard, and Dan had a profit of $97, and 39 acres of hill and waterfront free and clear. Dan may have been dirty but he was not dumb. The property description was as follows, "that certain piece or parcel of land in the county of Whatcom W.T. known as Graveyard Point."

The great glacial moraine had first been called Poe's Point after its owner. Then after the 1857 murders of two men on the point by the northern Indians, Deadman's Point became a popular name, now it was an official county graveyard and Graveyard Point was added. The confused map maker of that old map decided to show all of the names.

In 1857, a war party of British Columbia Haida had sailed and paddled down from their home islands north of Vancouver Island to avenge a killing of one of their chiefs by white men the previous summer. They sought a "Boston Chief" for their victim and found Colonel Ebey on Whidbey Island. After slaying and beheading him, the Indians started north in their great cedar canoes. The alarm went out and the settlers on Bellingham Bay gathered for protection in William Pattle's stout log cabin (where The Woods Coffee now stands in Boulevard Park). They sent two men, Melville and Browne, out to the prominent glacial moraine to watch for the invaders. Unfortunately the men took a bottle of whiskey with them to bolster their courage. They drank the whiskey and fell asleep beside their fire. The Haida found them and soon had two more heads to take home as trophies. Thus the point had a new name, Deadman's Point.

Dan was an active man and entrepreneurial as well. He purchased the small schooner, *Phantom*, and took to transporting goods to and from Victoria and other ports on the inland waters of what is now called the Salish Sea. He was not known for his strict adherence to the laws of the territory and had a few scrapes with local law enforcement for bringing casks of liquid labeled "Honolulu Sugar" into the U.S. waters without paying the customs tax, and also for selling "spirituous liquor" to the Indians.

His enterprises were not limited to marine activities. In the fall of 1860 he worked in the mines of British Columbia. In 1875 he took a contract to build a three-mile-long road from Sehome to Lake Whatcom, and the story remains that he successfully built it single-handed. In another venture, he led a team of oxen deep into the Caribou country of British Columbia, up what was at that time a treacherous trail along the Fraser River Canyon. Dan was hard working and apparently hard playing, and he was not known for pristine personal habits. In time he began to be known as Dirty Dan, a name that has clung to him even to this day.

In January of 1883, joining the wave of excitement about rumors that the Northern Pacific Railroad would make Bellingham Bay their trans-continental terminus, Dan platted much of his land into a town which he named Fairhaven. He immediately began selling from his platted inventory of 680 town lots. In the first year he sold 238 lots and grossed a princely $22,000. Suddenly the rag tag Dan Harris had become a wealthy man. He treated himself to some new clothes and even began courting a 28-year-old Fairhaven gal, Bertha Wasmer. With his new found wealth Dan then built a hotel for his town calling it the Fairhaven Hotel. It was a simple three-story frame building at the NE corner of Harris Avenue and 4th Street. It was perfectly located to welcome the steamer passengers that were soon disembarking at the large deep-water dock that Dan also had constructed. Called Ocean Dock, it was an important adjunct to the town in an age when the only access to the towns of Bellingham Bay was by ship.

The *Whatcom Reveille*, the primary paper on the Bay, frequently mentioned Dan in its weekly news. Following are several gleanings from its 1883 and 1884 editions.

> Oct. 12, 1883; The Fairhaven Hotel under the management of Mr. James Weed is one of the best on the sound. Judge Gazley is putting up a two story building 16 by 20. D.J. Harris is building a 16 by 30.

> Nov. 9, 1883; It is rumored that Dan Harris of Fairhaven had $500 stolen from him last week. But that would not lower Dan's pile much. We are informed later that Mr. James Weed of the Fairhaven Hotel has sued Dan for $10,000 for saying that he stole the money.

5.2. Dan Harris's Fairhaven Hotel, circa 1905. This photo shows the old hotel vacant and in decay. It was demolished in 1906. Galen Biery Photographs #606, CPNWS.

Dec. 21, 1883; Every good citizen recognizes the need for a good cemetery somewhere on the bay. The people of the county feel justly indignant at the manner in which Dan Harris has appropriated the lands bought from him for graveyard purposes. Few men would do such a thing.

Dec. 21, 1883; Complaint comes to this office from Fairhaven that Dan Harris charges such outrageous prices for wharfage at Fairhaven that goods have to be unloaded at Bellingham wharf and taken by small boat to Fairhaven. Dan's disagreeable course of late has just about depopulated Fairhaven.

Jan. 11, 1884; Dan Harris is putting forth every effort to stop the Knox Mill at Fairhaven. Dan is a mossback of the genuine stripe and regrets to see his neighborhood peopled with civilized folks who wear clean clothes.

March 21, 1884; Dan Harris has bought a safe.

April 18, 1884; President Harris is grading around his hotel in our southern suburb sometimes called Fairhaven and says he has rented it to Mr. Foster of Yamhill, furnished. It will be open by the first of May.

May 2, 1884; Dan Harris will open his Fairhaven Hotel having obtained furniture and help from Seattle.

June 6, 1884; Dan Harris has furnished the hotel throughout in elegant style, curtains, walnut furniture, piano, carpets. The opening of this fine hotel in Fairhaven will give the beautiful cove in which it is located a more business like appearance.

Nov. 14, 1884; Dan Harris of Fairhaven has unfurled to the Cleveland breeze the largest flag on the Pacific Coast. It is 50 feet in length, properly proportioned, made of heavier material than usual. It weighs nearly 50 pounds and cost $116 in San Francisco. It is so large it will have to be suspended between two flag staffs at least 125 feet high in order to appear well, but Dan don't care for expenses. Dan says that the democrats have not had a chance to rejoice over presidential success for a quarter of a century, and now that Cleveland is elected he proposes to fly the largest flag on the Pacific Coast.

Dec. 5, 1884; Dan Harris of Fairhaven is again in trouble. This time a woman figured in the case. Dan is haunted with the idea that everybody is endeavoring to steal his property, and being of a suspicious turn of mind, accuses people right and left. On Monday he had Mrs. Kline of Bellingham arrested for stealing a few trifling articles. The case was tried before Justice Lindsay on Monday. Judge Roth appearing for the woman, and the case was dismissed at the cost of the cranky old bachelor.

Despite his increasingly truculent manner Dan apparently still had the capacity for romance. His courtship of Bertha Wasmer was successful. Dan and Bertha married. He was 48, 20 years her senior. It is presumed that his personal hygiene improved but it appears that his temperament did not.

The press of the day continued to feature Dan's escapades from time to time. One famous story, apparently true, is that Dan had a fancy piano in his hotel that he had paid $500 for. When he sold Fairhaven and the hotel to Nelson Bennett and C.X. Larrabee they did not want to pay for the piano. Knowing Dan would not be able to take the piano with him to California they apparently figured the piano would just stay with the hotel. The irritated Dan simply rolled the piano out the door, pushed it down to his Ocean Dock and into the bay.

After he sold Fairhaven to Bennett and Larrabee, his wife Bertha became ill. With his now considerable wealth, Dan and Bertha, hoping to improve her

5.3. Earliest Photo of Fairhaven, 1887, depicts Fairhaven as it must have looked when Dan Harris sold it to Nelson Bennett and C.X. Larrabee. Galen Biery Photographs #1606, CPNWS.

health, moved to Los Angeles for its healthy and dry climate. Perhaps Bertha had contracted tuberculosis as had so many others in our story. The climate of southern California did not help. Bertha died in 1888.

After her death Dan fell under the influence of a doctor and his wife, whom it is believed took advantage of him, perhaps even drugging him. Eventually they seemed in control of his affairs. Dan died in Los Angeles on August 18, 1890, at the age of 57. The press announced the value of his estate at $130,000.

Despite some of his unsavory personal traits Dan Harris had led a robust and productive life and had a profound influence on the town that he founded. His unique character and his pioneering life have made him a legendary figure in the history of Fairhaven. He is memorialized by a restaurant named after him, by the street and the bay that he named for himself, by community celebrations and by a beloved bronze statue placed in the Fairhaven Village Green where thousands each year sit beside him and have their photo taken. Daniel Jefferson Harris has achieved immortality.

Chapter 6

Coal and Gold

The pioneering settlers around the bay set to work to meet the conditions of the Donation Land Bill which required that before they would receive their patents on the land they must construct a dwelling and live in it while working the land. They each built crude cabins and moved in. The greater challenge was in eking a living from their property. It was a very difficult beginning.

Roeder and Peabody completed construction of their mill at Whatcom Creek, but the summer of 1853 was extremely dry and there was not enough water coming down the creek to power the mill. They had to wait for the fall rains before they could operate. They went into debt to survive.

South, along the eastern shore, Pattle and Morrison searched for coal on the partners' three claims. Morrison's claim apparently held the best prospects and a small mine was begun and the requisite 100 bags of coal were shipped off to San Francisco to be evaluated by the Syndicate. The evidence would indicate that the coal did not meet the requirements. Soon the record shows Pattle and Morrison selling portions of their coal rights to others.

Thomas reputedly began a cooperage making barrels from the local timber. It is presumed that Dan Harris helped Thomas in this endeavor.

The most promising economic development was Henry Roeder's find of a vein of quality coal on the shoreline east of the creek. He sold his mineral rights to San Francisco investors who soon developed the Sehome Mine which became the only truly viable economic activity in the early settlements.

Cash was a rare commodity on the bay. The population was very small, just a few workers at the mill and mine other than the original settlers on the 19 donation land claims that ringed the bay. Threats from the marauding northern Indians were a constant worry as were the unfriendly stirrings among the tribes east of the mountains and in lower Puget Sound.

In 1855-56, the Indian populations east of the mountains and in southern Puget Sound became restive, alarmed at the numbers of settlers who were swarming their land and changing their age-old way of life. Several skirmishes sounded the warning, and up and down the Salish Sea the male settlers formed into militia to protect their homes and families. The Lummi, Nooksack and Samish continued as friendly, or at least non-hostile neighbors.

To protect the settlers and perhaps to demonstrate to England the nation's intent to settle and stay in its new northern territory the United States Army was called upon. In the summer of 1856, Capt. George Pickett was sent to the bay with 60 men of Company H, United States Infantry. They came with orders to build a fort that would be called Fort Bellingham. They were expected to provide security for the fledgling settlements of the area. Pickett and his men would remain at Fort Bellingham until the July of 1859, when he was ordered to San Juan Island to participate in the famous 'Pig War' with England.

6.1. Northern Raiders, Edward Curtis photograph.

The greatest worry for the settlers of the Salish Sea was created by the warlike tribes from Canada that had raided in the area for countless past summers seeking slaves and other booty. They would come south in their great cedar war canoes; the Haida of the Islands north of Vancouver Island, the Tlinget from what is now south eastern Alaska, the Yul-kol-tots (as they are called in Roth's *History of Whatcom County*) from the area around the northern tip of Vancouver Island. These northern tribes frequently journeyed south to trade their furs at the Hudson's Bay Company at Fort Victoria, hoping to go back with new muskets, blankets and beads; and as they had for centuries, to pick up a few slaves to sell and trade to their northern tribesmen. These proud and warlike peoples had occasional clashes with white men in the Salish Sea.

The fearful and usually boring life on Bellingham Bay suddenly changed when in 1858 gold was discovered on the Fraser River in Canada. In the early summer of 1858, thousands of gold seekers came to Whatcom and Sehome, as they were the closest U.S. settlements to the gold fields. It was estimated that 10,000 gold-seekers descended on the tiny settlements. Tents blossomed on the beach above the tide flats. Ocean-going steamers arrived from San

6.2. The Town of Whatcom; circa 1858-1860. This very early photograph of Whatcom shows the T.G. Richards building. The first brick building north of San Francisco, now called the Territorial Courthouse. Note the dock extending out from what would become E Street. Galen Biery Photographs #3322, CPNWS.

Francisco bringing more gold hungry men, frame shacks were constructed anywhere and everywhere as the eager adventurers sought a way to get through the forest to the Fraser river. The settlers of 1853 who had thought their donation land grants almost worthless, now saw opportunity. Roeder and Peabody hired Alonzo Poe to plat a town. Their donation claims were promptly divided into building lots and the town officially named Whatcom. Surveyor Poe took his fee in ownership of city lots or in percentage ownership shares of city lots. Cash was short, the prices high. The first lots sold for $300 to $700. A newspaper was begun, *The Northern Light.*

The coal company gave its factor, E.C. Fitzhugh, the authority to plat and sell lots in Whatcom's neighbor to the east, Sehome, reserving their mineral rights and requiring that the lot or lots must be improved and occupied within six months.

Seeing a bright future, Richards, and Hyatt brought bricks in on the sailing ship *Anne Parry* and constructed the first brick building north of San Francisco. The building was to be a general store selling supplies to the thousands of gold miners heading toward the Fraser gold strike.[1]

The fragile pioneer settlements on Bellingham Bay had struggled since 1853 to make a living, always worried by the threat of the northern Indians and the sheer drudgery of pioneer life. Suddenly they were thrust into the wild excitement of gold fever. The population on Bellingham Bay soon exceeded that of the rest of the Territory.

---

1   That building still exists as the Territorial Court House on E Street in Bellingham.

The miners squatted on the beaches in a tent city. The newly platted towns resulted in sales of lots bringing much needed cash to the owners of those early donation land claims. Sehome was surveyed and platted on May 8, 1858, and Whatcom soon followed filing their plat on June 24. The clamor to purchase lots and erect wooden buildings created a lumber shortage. The local mill could not keep up and lumber had to be brought in by ship. The shallow tide flats were platted and thousands of pilings were driven into the soft mud, with buildings and streets built upon them. The now well-established encroachment onto the tidal waters of Bellingham Bay had begun.

Saloons and houses of ill repute opened in tents and crude frame structures. Early reports talk of Division Street (present day Prospect Street) being so crowded that "it would require half an hour's time to work your way through the vast multitude of people that thronged Division Street, from where the Terminus Hotel stood to the courthouse."[2]

The Gold Rushers were arriving at Whatcom and Sehome daily awaiting a license to cross the border into Canada and head up the Fraser River to find their fortunes—but they could go no farther, held up by two barriers. There was no trail through the almost impenetrable forests of Whatcom County, and the Canadians were not eager to issue permits to this rag-tag army of adventurers clamoring at their border.

Edward Eldridge and Henry Roeder organized a trail-building venture, planning to blaze a 30-mile trail to the Fraser River from Whatcom. While they were building trail, some impatient miners built crude boats and attempted to get to the Fraser from Bellingham Bay. Some went in canoes, rowboats, anything that would float. More than a few died in storms on the rough waters off Point Roberts and the treacherous sand dunes at the mouth of the Fraser. Whatcom and Sehome were classical gold rush towns replete with makeshift saloons, prostitutes, drunken Indians and prospectors, and fights in the streets.

Suddenly the excitement and opportunity for Whatcom and Sehome came to an end. James Douglas, Governor of British Columbia, proclaimed that no person could work in the gold mines of British Columbia without first obtaining a license to do so from the custom house in Victoria. You must present yourself at Victoria to buy a license. It quickly became obvious that if you had to go to Victoria for the license, it was easier to take a steamboat from there to the mouth of the Fraser than returning to Bellingham Bay and attempt to bushwhack through the almost impenetrable forest to the river. Douglas's action had exactly the result that he intended. The economic boom on Bellingham Bay immediately ended and shifted to Victoria, Douglas's capital city on Vancouver Island.

---

2   Roth, page 95.

Many of Whatcom's hastily built wooden buildings were taken down and transported to Victoria where they were re-constructed. The population that some estimated at 12,000 to 15,000 melted away in a mere ten days leaving only 150 people on the bay. Richards' and Hyatt's brick building remained, filled with prospecting supplies, but with no customers. Whatcom and Sehome lots that were selling for hundreds of dollars in 1858 couldn't be sold for taxes in 1860.

The Fraser River Gold Rush itself had a short life. While it was a disappointment, it did have some benefit for the towns on the bay. When it was over, thousands of prospectors had exhausted their resources and left British Columbia. Many of them returned to the towns of the Territory and settled to work the mines and begin to clear the forests. The Rush also brought this corner of the nation to the attention of the world, making it aware of this primitive land with its great potential. But times would be tough on Bellingham Bay in the coming two decades. The coming years would bring a succession of bad news.

The Roeder Peabody sawmill by the creek had never been a financial success. The soldiers had left for San Juan Island and the Pig War, and then the Civil War broke out. The nation's attention was diverted to its internal convulsions. There was little energy or money to be expended in western development.

The old saw mill at Whatcom Creek burned in 1873. The community suffered a major blow with the closing of the Sehome Coal Mine in 1878. By 1879-80, the population on the bay had dwindled to perhaps 20 families. The newspaper, *The Northern Light*, moved to LaConner. There was but one store on Bellingham Bay. Its residents, mainly the first land-holding families, settled into a long period of declining population and economic hardship.

Dan Harris, the cantankerous land holder on the south bay, hung on to his land and worked at various ventures trading with Victoria and the Hudson's Bay Company with his sailboat. He contracted to build the road from Sehome to Lake Whatcom, and being an entrepreneurial sort, it was said he was considering laying out a new town on his land on the south bay. He even proposed building a $50,000 saw mill when 100 lots of his envisioned city were sold. The project came to nothing. The years between 1858 and 1883 were dismal and discouraging in the extreme.

7.1. The Bellingham Hotel. The hotel was built in 1871 during the railroad excitement of that year. Considered the finest hostelry on the bay, it was built in the town of Bellingham which was later incorporated into Fairhaven. It was located on the northeast corner of 10th and Bennett near the Chrysalis Inn. Galen Biery Photographs #0605, CPNWS.

CHAPTER 7

Romance of The Railroads

There was nothing more important to the economic prospects of the Pacific Northwest's early settlers than the arrival of the trans-continental railroads. Every little settlement around the shores of the Salish Sea hoped and dreamed that one day a railroad would arrive, bringing with it prosperity, a connection to the markets of the populous eastern states, a way to market their lumber, coal and farm products and to make travel across the continent faster and safer compared to the rigors of the Oregon Trail, the Overland stage coach, or sailing around the Horn.

The struggling towns of Bellingham Bay were no exception. Their hopes and prospects of attracting the railroad seemed better than most. Their hopes lay with the method with which the United States Government subsidized and encouraged railroad expansion. The government granted to the railroads 20 sections[1] of land for each mile of track built across the western territories. The grants were reduced to a still generous ten sections of land per mile when the railroad was crossing state lands. The railroads were then able to sell those wilderness lands or use them as collateral to borrow the money to build the railroads. Those lands would rise in value as the track was extended and on them would be farmlands and cities, customers for the completed railroad.

These government land grants were a huge incentive calculated to attract the massive amounts of capital required to build and equip a railroad. To a government that possessed untold acres of unsettled land and sought to develop the West and unify the nation, the grants seemed a reasonable investment.

In 1864, Congress passed an act incorporating the Northern Pacific Railroad. The legislation was signed by Abraham Lincoln and authorized the new railroad to construct a line from Lake Superior to Puget Sound across the

---

1   In the United States and Canada, a section in land measure is one square mile, equal to 640 acres, or about 259 hectares or 2.59 square kilometers in Metric measures.

northern tier of states and territories. The Northern Pacific would receive the allotted 20 sections of land for each mile across the plains and mountains in addition to a 400-foot-wide right of way.

Much of the land in those sections would be seen as unmarketable and worthless, but a huge proportion of them contained rich land for farming or were along rivers suited for town sites. There were thousands of acres across heavily timbered mountain ranges which also contained rich mineral resources. The Northern Pacific ultimately *accepted* just under 40 million acres of land for their efforts. Their mileage built entitled them to almost 60 million acres, but much of it they determined they had no use for and rather than pay taxes on it later, they refused it.

The land was allotted in an alternating pattern on each side of the track, the railroad getting a one-square-mile section, the next section remaining with the government to be sold or given free to homesteaders. The result was a checkerboard map of ownership extending 20 miles on either side of the 400-foot right of way. The Northern Pacific either sold their sections or used them as collateral for loans from European investors. Much of their timberland sections in Washington Territory were sold to the Weyerhauser Company.

As early as 1853, investors planning the Northern Pacific had sent a survey expedition across the country to determine a workable route, and to find a likely terminus where the rail would meet the salt water of the Pacific Ocean. They concluded that the terminus should be either Seattle or Bellingham Bay.

The terms of the 1864 Northern Pacific franchise dictated that a branch of the railroad must extend south down the Columbia River to Portland, and that branch must leave the main line within 300 miles of the western terminus on Puget Sound. The intent was to build the line first to Puget Sound, then to build the Portland branch from wherever the main line crossed the Columbia River.

The railroad had spent five million dollars on surveys and preliminary work and then met with financier Jay Cooke seeking further funding. Cooke agreed to match the monies the railroad had already spent if he and his associates should have half of the stock, and that no further stock would be sold, but additional funds must be raised by the sale of bonds which could then be mortgaged. That arrangement required the consent of Congress, as the bonds were to be sold by the United States Government.

Politics quickly entered the picture. Oregon Territory wanted the line down the Columbia to Portland to be the main line, and a branch to Puget Sound to be secondary. Enough Congressional votes supporting Cooke's bond requirement could not be found without the votes of the Oregon delegation. In a compromise, the bond legislation was passed with the proviso that the Portland line would be built first. The triumphant Oregonians were confident that the line to Portland would become the main line and the expensive and difficult railroad branch across the rugged Cascade Mountains would never be built. Portland would thus become the great northern port on the Pacific Ocean.

At first the railroad refused to support the idea, but on further consideration they realized that by building the line to Portland—and then making Bellingham Bay the terminus and extending the line northward from Portland—they would receive land grants on thousands of additional sections of land from the Columbia River almost to the Canadian border.

When you consider that a section of land equals one square mile the railroad could claim every other mile of territorial land extending outward 20 miles from either side of the track. It is approximately 260 miles from Portland to Whatcom on Bellingham Bay. Were the railroad to receive 20 sections of land for every mile of track in that distance that would total 5,200 sections, 5,200 square miles of land. The potential future land values would be enormous.

Northern Pacific leaders decided the shorter route from Spokane Falls across the Cascades to the Sound could be delayed. The anticipated land sale profits from the Puget Sound sections should easily finance the expensive branch across the Cascades which could be built later. They decided to embrace the Oregon route.

In the spring of 1870 the railroad sent a new party of skilled engineers to examine the lands north of Seattle. They came to Bellingham Bay by canoe. The engineers met with a large group of eager landowners around the bay who volunteered to give the railroad half of their donation land grants if they would make Bellingham Bay the terminus. The expectation of a coming railroad was high and the excitement around the bay was palpable. Dan Harris, the owner of 188 acres adjoining the best deep water on the bay is thought to be among those who tendered half of their land to tempt the Northern Pacific. Powered by the expectation that the railroad would make Bellingham Bay their terminus, speculators rapidly began buying up the remaining Government land surrounding the original 1850 Oregon Land Act donation claims. The Government price was $1.25 per acre. Some of it changed hands at prices from $5 per acre to $50 per acre. A new name was now to be found on the County property roles, Erastus Bartlett.

A native of Maine, Bartlett had come west to California to participate in the 1849 gold rush. He owned and operated steamboats on the Sacramento River. He developed land in Portland. He bought thousands of acres in Whatcom County and in 1871, with Edward and Teresa Eldridge, he bought the Morrison and Pattle donation land claims in anticipation of the Northern Pacific arrival. Later the partners platted the new town of Bellingham (which

7.2. Erastus Bartlett, circa 1890. This is the only known photograph of Erastus Bartlett. Bartlett was a major investor in Whatcom County land, a partner with Edward Eldridge in Bellingham and the Eldridge and Bartlet sawmill at Pattle's Point (Boulevard Park). (Neelie Nelson found this photo by making contact with a great grandson.)

7.3. Arthur A. Denny was a Seattle Pioneer and real estate investor. Washington Pioneer Association archives.

filled the gap between Fairhaven and Sehome), and built the sawmill at Pattle's Point. Bartlett was to become a major player in Bellingham Bay development and a key player in Fairhaven history.

In the heady days of 1870, other eyes were watching the excited activity on Bellingham Bay. Seattle pioneers Arthur A. Denny and William N. Bell headed North seeking opportunity. They bought what remained of Alonzo Poe's donation claim from Poe's brother, Americus—260 acres along the waterfront comprising what is now Bellingham's most valuable residential land, Edgemoor. When Alonzo moved to Olympia in 1858 he had sold his Whatcom County interests to his brother Americus. Americus sold the Poe lands to the Seattle men, who each had extensive holdings in their hometown of Seattle, but were apparently hedging their bets on the location of the railroad terminus. Other prominent Seattle names found on the Bellingham Bay property roles were David Phillips and Dexter Horton. They shared 75 acres of Whatcom County land with A.A. Denny.

The prospects of the Northern Pacific terminating its track on Bellingham Bay were exceedingly bright. Extending the terminus 90 miles north of Seattle to Bellingham Bay would mean an additional 180 square miles of land grants, much of it in rich farm land, valuable waterfront and vast lowland forests. Cooke had completed negotiations with a syndicate of German bankers who would loan the 50 million dollars, which was considered enough to complete the financing. All arrangements were made for signing the papers. In 1871, construction began at both ends of the track—in St. Paul, Minnesota, and in Kalama, Washington Territory, where track laying began north toward Puget Sound and hopefully Bellingham Bay.

7.4. William N. Bell was a Seattle pioneer and developer for whom Belltown is named. Washington Pioneer Association archives.

Then the fates stepped in and the citizens of the Bellingham Bay towns suffered the first of what would prove to be many railroad disappointments. The Franco-Prussian War had broken out in July of 1870. By late 1871 the German investors determined to concentrate on their European concerns and pulled out of their commitment to Cooke. Their interest in American railroads was put aside for the duration of the war.

Political realities also acted to stifle the dream. The United States Secretary of the Interior, seeing the value of that shelf of land along the territorial inland sea, refused to grant Northern Pacific the right to make Bellingham Bay the terminus. Instead he dictated that it be Tacoma. Twenty sections of land per mile along Puget Sound north of Tacoma would have given too much of the usable land west of the Cascade Mountains to the Northern Pacific. Both Seattle and Bellingham Bay's hopes of being the Northern Pacific terminus were dashed. At least for the present. The transcontinental Northern Pacific was many years from completion and both cities retained a spark of hope.

By late 1873, the dream and the economic boom had come to an end. A national financial panic struck in that year, further dampening the hopes of the towns around the bay. A distinct pall fell over its little towns. The last general merchant in Whatcom failed, the only store left on Bellingham Bay was the Sehome Mine Store, which provided the sole opportunity for trade. It sold produce grown in the region, as well as necessary general goods brought in as ballast on the three sailing ships carrying coal in the employ of the mining company. Only the Sehome mine provided a payroll and a source of cash as it continued shipping its coal to San Francisco. The population on the bay again nosedived.

7.5. Chuckanut Quarry, approx. 1890. The sandstone quarry above Chuckanut Bay began operations in 1880 and continued until 1908. It was begun by Henry Burfiend & Casper Sidell and was eventually owned by Henry Roeder. Its stone was used for many buildings in Portland, Olympia, Seattle and the towns of Bellingham Bay. Galen Biery Photographs #3354, CPNWS.

Despite the collapse of the railroad dream, the enthusiasm of the short boom had made lasting changes on the bay. Before the boom faded, national attention had been focused on this heretofore unknown corner of the nation. It had attracted some wealthy and capable men who had invested heavily in the region. The seeds that would burst forth in a full fledged expansion boom in 1888 were sown in the year 1873.

Not everyone had given up hope. In 1874 it was reported that Dan Harris was considering laying out a town on his 188 acres at the south bay and that he promised to build a $50,000 sawmill after he had sold the first 100 lots. Some folks scoffed thinking Dan a blow-hard.

The year 1882 brought with it renewed optimism for the depressed citizens of Bellingham Bay. The Colony Mill was built on Whatcom Creek, replacing the old Roeder Mill that had burned in 1873. The Chuckanut Quarry was developing a reputation for excellent sandstone for building construction, much of it going to Seattle. Gold was found on Ruby Creek in the Nooksack river watershed, and now new rumors began circulating that the Northern Pacific might extend its track north from Tacoma, making Whatcom its northern terminus after all. The NP was finally getting very close to completing its transcontinental line and the Canadian Pacific Railroad was building its rail across the Canadian plains and planning to descend the Fraser River Canyon to salt water at New Westminster, now Vancouver.

The Canadian Pacific opportunity was of major importance if the Canadians could be persuaded to connect with U.S. rails at the border. Capitalist interests on the south side of the border were quick to react.

Railroad titan Henry Villard organized the Seattle Lakeshore and Eastern Railroad, a project intended to connect Seattle with the Canadian Pacific at the border town of Sumas in northern Whatcom County. The Seattle interests would run their railroad from Seattle to Woolley (now Sedro-Woolley), and north up the south fork of the Nooksack River far to the east of Bellingham Bay.

Their track ran up the valley which now hosts Highway 9. Seattle was wary of Bellingham Bay towns as competitors and purposely avoided bringing rail by the salt water route. Their goal was to connect with the Canadian Pacific, completely bypassing Whatcom and Sehome.

The forthcoming arrival of the Canadian Pacific also caught the attention of Pierre Cornwall and his wealthy San Francisco friends, owners of the Bellingham Bay Coal Company, the Sehome Mine, and thousands of acres of land surrounding Whatcom and Sehome.

A third bid for the connection with the Canadian Pacific was a newcomer to the scene, Eugene Canfield from Illinois. He proposed a line from Fairhaven to the international border following the Telegraph Road to Sumas. He later changed the plan to connect at Blaine and New Westminster along the waterfront. He also proposed to build in a southerly direction to connect his line with Seattle. Canfield had been a lawyer and state senator in Illinois. With other investors he had purchased large tracts of land in Whatcom County, including even Eliza Island in Bellingham Bay. *The Whatcom Reveille* of July 6, 1883, reported that he owned 15,000 or 20,000 acres in the county. He arrived in July of 1883 to promote his railroad dream. Lottie Roth described him as a man with a vision "larger than his resources." Nonetheless Canfield incorporated his company as the Bellingham Bay Railway and Navigation Company on July 19, 1883, with capital stock of $1,000,000.

Not to be outdone, Pierre Cornwall announced that the Bellingham Bay Coal Company was forming two new corporations, the Bellingham Bay Improvement Company (BBIC) and the Bellingham Bay and British Columbia Railroad. The railroad would be built to connect the Sehome Wharf to the City of Sumas and the transcontinental traffic of the Canadian Pacific.

The BBIC would concentrate on developing the many acres owned by the coal company. They also would build a sawmill and would concentrate on land sales and civic improvement. Cornwall published a preliminary plat in July 1883 showing Whatcom and Sehome, and soon followed it with the map of New Whatcom on August 31, 1883. Cornwall had extended his original plat of Sehome showing it now surrounding the old town of Whatcom. He called the now combined and enlarged towns, New Whatcom.

1883 had dawned as a pivotal year on the bay. It began in January when Dan Harris, sensing the change in the economic pulse powered by Canfield, Cornwall and Villard's railroad visions, laid out his town on the 188 acres that he had owned for almost 30 years. He filed the plat for his new town with the County Auditor on January 2, 1883, and he called his town Fairhaven. He also bestowed his name on the protected deep water cove adjoining the town and on one of its central streets. His plat map boldly labels the cove Harris Bay. Harris also announced that he had sold the mill site on his waterfront and that a large saw mill would be constructed on it by that summer.

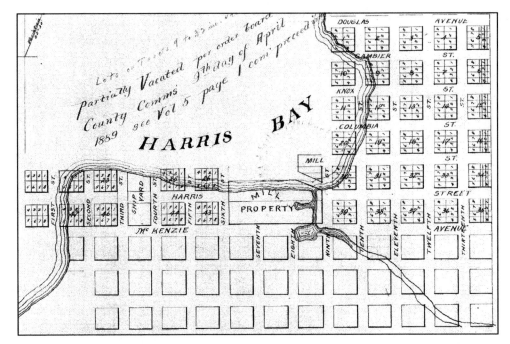

7.6. Plat of Fairhaven; Dan Harris, 1873. This copy of the original plat of Fairhaven was provided by Shirley Forslof, former County Auditor. Whatcom County Courthouse records.

Harris's plat was quickly followed by that of Edward and Teresa Eldridge and their wealthy partner Erastus Bartlett. They owned the Morrison and Pattle lands just north of Fairhaven. On April 24, they filed a plat on those old donation land grants, and they called their new town Bellingham. They announced that they would be building a large saw mill on their waterfront at Pattle's Point. Now there were four towns on Bellingham Bay.

Adding to the excitement of the year, a newspaper was born, *The Whatcom Reveille*, publishing its first edition on June 15, 1883. Their front-page lead article was an excellent recap of the history of Bellingham Bay written by none other than Edward Eldridge, the pioneer who had arrived on the bay at the very beginning in 1853.

The Eldridge history offers such a succinct and authoritative portrait of the community's beginnings that I have included it in the Anecdotes and Recollections section.

The *Reveille* added fuel to the growing boom by reporting that the new developments had filled the hotels of Whatcom, Bellingham and Fairhaven. Gold seekers returned to the bay reminding old timers of the rush of 1858. Speculators flocked in to buy lots and assess the opportunities of the awakening bay towns. As the boom progressed, two boats per week from Seattle were not adequate to handle the eager crowds.

The newspaper revealed that Robert Knox from Abilene, Kansas, had bought the Mill property in Fairhaven from Dan Harris and would have his Knox and Musser sawmill operating soon. He was moving from Kansas and would bring a colony of Kansans with him.

Just weeks after filing his Fairhaven plat, Dan began selling lots. In that first year of 1883 he sold 238 of his 680 lots and grossed $22,000. Suddenly Dan Harris was a wealthy man. As the money began to pile up he quickly re-invested some of it. He built a three-story wooden-frame hotel at the corner of 4th and Harris Street on his waterfront, and beside it began construction of a large wharf that would extend from 4th Street out into Harris Bay to deep water. He called his hotel 'The Fairhaven Hotel' and his wharf 'Ocean Dock.'

The surge of good news in 1883 electrified the towns around the bay, and the *Whatcom Reveille* joyfully reported it. Some of the articles are typical booster euphemisms that seemed so prevalent in those days, some reported actual fact.

Following are selected items gleaned from the *Reveille* of that year that reflect the tenor and the excitement of the times.

> June 15, 1883; There is a rumor that an unnamed railroad is considering building a track from New Orleans to Denver and then to Whatcom.

> June 15, 1883; High quality oil has been reported seeping from the ground near a local stream.

> June 22, 1883; Eldridge and Bartlett's mill; the excavation has begun for their steam sawmill.

> June 22, 1883; Dan Harris announced that the sawmill machinery had been bought and shipped and would arrive any day. There will soon be three mills operating on the Bay.

> July 13, 1883; A general desire is expressed to have a road cut through from Whatcom to Bellingham and Fairhaven.

> July 13, 1883; There is a good suggestion made to have Whatcom, Sehome, Bellingham and Fairhaven incorporate under one name as soon as possible.

> July 13, 1883; Fairhaven; 15 lots sold last week. Mr. Harris is building at his new wharf; timber about to be cut for the new mill. A new bridge is to be built leading to Fairhaven. Judge Gazeley is erecting two houses on his block.

> July 20, 1883; 27 lots were sold by the Whatcom Town Co. last week.

Aug. 3, 1883; Dan Harris has almost completed his wharf to the landing at Fairhaven. Dan is a worker.

Aug. 3, 1883; Eldridge and Bartlett are building a new wharf at Bellingham near the mill site, a full force of workmen are engaged in the work of excavating and preparing the ground and framework for the mill machinery which is to arrive from San Francisco the latter part of next month. Several new buildings are underway. The hotel is crowded to its utmost capacity.

Aug. 17, 1883; Robert Knox says their portable sawmill will be in operation at Fairhaven in less than 30 days.

Aug. 31, 1883; Whatcom has made good progress for a single summer. Lots have doubled since May. A wharf has started from deep water, probably two hundred buildings have been erected, a paper started, several stores opened, and Whatcom will soon be a reality of two thousand people. Bellingham has built a hotel, run out a wharf, and sold one half of its lots. Fairhaven boasts its peculiar sheltered position and deep water. The whole country is in full tide.

Sept. 7, 1883; A new schoolhouse is being built between Bellingham and Fairhaven. (I believe this is the first mention of the 14th Street school, which preceded Lowell School on 14th Street between Douglas and Taylor Avenues.)

Sept. 28, 1883; Knox mill sawed its first log yesterday, large mill to follow. Knox was to bring a large group from Kansans to see Bellingham Bay. He came with a group of 17 including the editor of the Abilene newspaper.

Sept. 1883; The New Whatcom Town Company (Bellingham Bay Improvement Company) has 107 men on their payroll grading, slashing, building wharf and sidewalk.

Oct. 5, 1883; Bellingham now has two saloons.

Oct. 12, 1883; Bellingham, Thos. Monahan has recently opened up a neat bar on Front Street. The mill, an immense structure, over 300 feet in length is being pushed rapidly.

Oct. 12, 1883; Fairhaven; The Fairhaven Hotel under the management of Mr. James Weed is one of the best on the sound. Several new buildings are going up. Judge Gazley is putting up a two-story building, 16 by 20; D.J. Harris is building a 16 by 30. Chas Schering has his two-story restaurant nearly completed, it is one of the best buildings on the townsite. Knox and Musser's portable saw mill is now running and active operations will be commenced on the large saw mill as soon as material can be got out.

The great enthusiasms of 1883 were based on some solid geographic and economic realities which were well illustrated in the following San Francisco newspaper column, captioned "San Francisco's Northern Rival." San Francisco had long been seen as the "Queen of the Western Seas," the city without rival as the port to the vast opportunities for trade with Japan, China, Australia and the other ports of the Pacific. But faced with the construction of three transcontinental railroads that would soon reach salt water at the Salish Sea the news article says the following;

> "That Puget Sound will produce such a rival is a thing already in sight. Portland on the Willamette, is not to remain the commercial metropolis of the north. It is too far inland—120 miles from the sea, and the navigation by far too uncertain. The Columbia River bar is the terror to seamen. At least it is not good for more than 18-feet of water at mean tide and that damns it. It is not susceptible for permanent improvement. The sands dredged out in the summer, the winter storms restore again and again and forever. Villard of the Northern Pacific for this and other reasons, will not suspend operations on the NP till he gets a road straight over the Cascade Mountains to deep water on the Sound; and there will be laid the foundation of a city for the future, which is to enter into sharp competition with San Francisco for the commerce of the ocean. It may be Tacoma, Olympia, Seattle, Ship Harbor, Whatcom, or some new point at present un-thought of. But it will be. And it may be that the two great railway companies will agree upon a common terminus for both, say somewhere on Bellingham Bay."

The article continued at some length citing the economic reasons for the future of a northern port.

The article was reprinted in the *Whatcom Reveille* on June 22, 1883, and nicely portrayed the reasons that the hopes and plans of the promoters of Bellingham Bay were more than wishful thinking.

The year 1883 had achieved a great leap forward for Bellingham Bay, but the good times were not to last. Another period of depression and disappointment lay ahead. The new Bellingham Mill at Pattle's Point operated for a while and then was leased to an association—which in some sort of a strategic marketing move, closed the mill for the remaining term of the lease. In Fairhaven Dan Harris turned rather truculent, quarreling with mill owner Robert Knox and with Whatcom County over the small graveyard that they maintained on Poe's Point, and his truculence seemed to drive business and people from

Fairhaven. The Sehome Coal Mine remained closed. The Bellingham Bay and British Columbia Railroad was making little progress in building its rail through the heavily timbered county towards Sumas, and after building two miles of track suspended further track laying. Eugene Canfield's railroad was mired in financial and legal delays. The gold find on Ruby Creek was a disappointment. Of most importance, the Northern Pacific had completed their rail-building across the continent with a grand *Last Spike* ceremony at Gold Creek, Montana. Their line was now complete to Portland, and it did not seem likely that they would build the branch across the Cascades to the sound. Tacoma would be their terminus, not Whatcom. The population waned once again as the communities on the bay entered another period of economic repose, awaiting the next period of wild optimism.

By 1887 the Seattle investors of 1870 and '71 had died. Their sons David Denny and Austin Bell, as executors of their fathers' estates, divided their considerable real estate holdings among the relatives. The next generation's owners of the Bell properties were his children, Laura K. Coffman, Austin Bell, Olive J. Stewart, and Mary Hall. Laura Coffman may have received title to the Fairhaven properties. They too awaited the next uptick in Bellingham Bay fortunes and the news of the railroad.

They did not have to wait for long.

CHAPTER 8

Bennett's Vision

L
ate in 1883, the officers of the Northern Pacific (NP) made a decision that surprised and disappointed the Oregon interests. The NP decided to begin construction of their Cascade Division. They would build their rail directly across the Cascade Mountains to Tacoma, thereby cutting many miles from the trip to Puget Sound via Portland. They determined to barge trains across the Columbia River from Ainsworth, at the confluence of the Snake and the Columbia rivers, to the little town of Pasco. From there they would build north through Prosser and Yakima; up the Yakima river gorge to Ellensburg, and then over the mountains at Stampede Pass. The arduous route over the mountains included the need for a two-mile tunnel at the crest of the pass that would be the world's longest tunnel.

The NP's decision also disappointed the folks on Bellngham Bay, for it seemed to emphasize the NP's satisfaction with Tacoma as their salt water terminus. The hopes for the Northern Pacific building to the bay appeared dim. While the Cascade decision may have deflated hopes for train service to the towns of the bay, the decision did throw together two men who would have a profound influence on the future of Fairhaven and the other towns on the bay.

8.1. Nelson Bennett. This photo appeared in the Dec. 29, 1890, holiday edition of the *Fairhaven Herald*, Bennett was the prime mover of the Fairhaven boom. A wealthy railroad contractor, he made his home in Tacoma. Donovan Family Papers #1734, CPNWS.

The major contractor on the entire Cascade Division project was Nelson Bennett. Bennett had earned his experience in the rough and tumble West, first as

8.2. John Joseph (J.J.) Donovan became arguably the most important man in Bellingham history. He died in 1936 after providing leadership in almost every facet of community life. Gordon Tweit collection.

a teamster driving mule teams and hauling goods on wagon trains. He had been an Indian fighter. He became a rail building contractor for the NP in Montana. He and his brother, a hardened Civil War officer were a tough combination. They were the kind of men who could push others to work in the deep snows of winter and the hot dry days of summer.

While working for the NP on several Montana contracts, Bennett had met a young Northern Pacific civil engineer who was surveying, planning and supervising construction. His name was John Joseph Donovan. Only two years out of engineering school in Massachusetts, Donovan had quickly developed a reputation for competence and reliability. The men would meet again on the Cascade Division. Donovan was placed in charge of much of the route selection and engineering for the entire project, while Bennett bid on and won contracts for the entire project from Pasco to Tacoma. Bennett and Donovan would work together for the next four years.

By the spring of 1887 the Cascade Division project was completed. Bennett had won his daring gamble with his low bid to build the Stampede Tunnel, meeting the contractual time requirements and gaining fame and financial reward. He would now consider his next challenge. Donovan had solidified his reputation as an engineer of great competence and reliability. His job finally completed, he headed back to New Hampshire to marry his fiancé Clara Nichols, while considering a number of job offers both domestic and foreign.

Nelson Bennett had developed a vision. His position as a leading contractor for the expanding national railroads had placed him in a position of friendship and association with the powerful railroad czars of the late 1800s. Among those leaders of the development of the West was J.J. Hill, the incredibly wealthy president and major stockholder of the Great Northern Railway. It is likely and probable that Hill had told Bennett of his plans to bring his Great Northern track to Spokane Falls, and then across the Cascade Mountains to salt water at Puget Sound. It is also likely that Hill had indicated that Sauk Pass and the headwaters of the Skagit River were the probable course for his rail. Bennett saw in this information a great opportunity.

He knew that the little town of Woolley, where the Skagit left the mountains and flowed out onto its flat delta, would be the point from which the Great Northern would build its track to salt water. Its salt water terminus would likely be determined by the closest protected deep water available. That terminus was destined to become an important port city and a major gateway to the Pacific Ocean and the world beyond.

For more than a decade railroad men had been hinting at Bellingham Bay as a likely terminus for a railroad. The Northern Pacific had seen its virtues; proximity to the Strait of Juan de Fuca, the entrance to the open ocean, deep water, good anchorage, open to the trade potential of British Columbia, situated in the midst of some of the world's best timber resources, an area rich in coal and minerals.

8.3. Edward Merton Wilson became Vice President of the Fairhaven Land Co., an officer in many Fairhaven corporations, Mayor of Fairhaven and a key figure in the Fairhaven boom. Donovan Family Papers, CPNWS.

Bennett's resourceful and ambitious nature led him to the conclusion that an unparalleled opportunity lay in helping the Great Northern find its western terminus, and in fact, in owning and developing that terminus. He determined to locate the best deep-water port near Woolley, and to connect it to the Great Northern line with a railroad that he would build and eventually sell to the Great Northern.

Realizing the immensity of the project, he knew that he would need to enlist both additional capital and proven management skills. Quite naturally, he looked to his long and successful railroad contracting experience for the management assistance he would need for his plan. Bennett had employed two younger men as managers of major sections of his recent Cascade Division project. Both men had extensive background in business, and both men were wealthy in their own right. Edward M. Wilson had been an independent contractor building sections of the Northern Pacific in Montana before Bennett had hired him for the Cascade project.

Edgar Lea Cowgill was an accomplished financial man who had managed parts of the Cascade project. Both men had gained Bennett's confidence. It was to them that he entrusted the first reconnoiter of potential sites. In 1887 he sent them to the little village of Fairhaven. It had been recently platted in the pretty cove just south of the towns of Whatcom and Sehome, and immediately adjoined to the north by the fledgling town of Bellingham with its hotel and lumber mill. He sent both men to assess its possibilities and availability.

Wilson and Cowgill found that Fairhaven was the least developed of the four towns around the bay, but that it had the greatest potential for Bennett's vision of a railroad terminus on saltwater. It had a three-story frame hotel and a handful of rudimentary buildings and dwellings and a population of only 140 souls. Its chief asset was an excellent harbor protected by a high point of land and a large wharf to deep water. It also had a great deal of undeveloped and potentially available land surrounding the platted town. The town itself had 680 platted lots, of which 440 were still owned by Dan Harris, who had platted it. The key would be Harris's willingness to sell.

Harris was found willing to negotiate. Edward Eldridge and Erastus Bartlett, the owners of the unsold property of Bellingham to the north, were speculative businessmen and also willing to talk. There were hundreds of additional surrounding acres that might be added by purchase to the tiny village on the waterfront. The economic situation around the bay had not been flourishing and it would likely be an advantageous time to buy land. Wilson and Cowgill reported that Fairhaven was a favorable place for Bennett's vision to flourish.

Bennett decided to act. He would build a modern city on Bellingham Bay and connect it to Woolley with his own railroad. His plan would require massive capital investment if all of the infrastructure of a modern city were to be built. He would need the capital to purchase the platted towns of Fairhaven and Bellingham, and much of the lands around them. He would need to construct the connecting railroad, construct city streets and sidewalks, water and sewer systems, electricity for lights and power, gas for lights and cooking, a staggering list of challenges to bring a village of several muddy streets to the shining "Imperial City" of his dreams.

Bennett knew where to find the needed capital. Years before in Montana he had met the Larrabee brothers. Charles X. Larrabee, who had made a fortune in the copper mines of Butte, and another fortune in land development in Portland; and his brother Samuel E. Larabie,[1] a banker and rancher now living in Deer Lodge, Montana, who was wealthy in his own right. Bennett had partnered with C.X. Larrabee in a land development project in Portland. He knew that the Larrabees had money and he shared his vision with them. C.X. Larrabee was convinced and he enlisted his brother Samuel to join the project.

Needing their management skills and business acumen, Bennett also shared his vision and opportunity with Wilson and Cowgill, and they became co-investors and Bennett's operatives on the scene. The men built their fledgling empire carefully and thoroughly. First they located a promising coal vein

---

1   S.E. Larabie changed his name after he left home. His reasons are unknown.

8.4. The Cokedale Coal Mine. The mine was developed in 1887 to provide coal for the development of Fairhaven. Its coal was shipped from Woolley via the Fairhaven & Southern Railroad. Galen Biery Photographs #0620, CPNWS.

near Woolley and in 1887 purchased its mineral rights and land. Railroads ran on coal, city light and power facilities ran on coal power, gas for street lights and home heating and cooking was made from coal. Coal was a basic and efficient energy source. On October 22, 1888, the three men incorporated the Skagit Coal and Transportation Company. The mine was located just northeast of Woolley, near where the Northern State Mental Hospital would one day be located.

Together Bennett and Larrabee convinced Dan Harris to sell and Dan Harris became a wealthier man. He received $75,000 for his townsite, retaining just a few lots for his future activities. Now the investors had a townsite and a coal mine. On November 27, 1888, they incorporated the central corporation of the coming Fairhaven Boom. The called it the Fairhaven Land Company. Its owners and trustees were Nelson Bennett, Edward M. Wilson, Edgar Lea Cowgill, all listed as residents of Tacoma. Samuel E. Larabie and Charles X Larrabee, residents of Montana. Wilson, Cowgill and Larrabee would soon become residents of Fairhaven, as the resident directors of operations. They would shortly be joined by other men eager to participate in Bennett's rapidly growing dream.

Bennett and Larrabee had purchased Fairhaven as individuals prior to the formation of the land company in 1887. They paid Harris $75,000 for his town. Now the partners sold their purchase to the newly formed Fairhaven

Land Company for the increased amount of $205,000, a quick paper profit of $130,000. Perhaps the five initial owners of the land company felt the amount paid to Harris was a great bargain and wanted to reward the initial partners by paying the higher price. Perhaps Bennett and Larrabee got their purchase money back and being the major investors drove a hard bargain. Only the minutes of the Fairhaven Land Company could tell us. Unfortunately those minutes are lost to history.

Now the work of building a city began in earnest. The tasks were numerous. They needed to get the railroad built between Woolley and their new city. They also needed to develop the coal mine they had recently bought near Woolley. Bennett knew just the man for both jobs, John Joseph Donovan, the young civil engineer that he had first met in 1882, and worked with during the four intense years of building the Northern Pacific rail across the Cascades.

J.J. Donovan was on his honeymoon when he received a letter from Bennett that would be of lasting importance to the history of the towns on Bellingham Bay. The letter offered Donovan a job mentioning that "the probability is it will be the on the Sound." Donovan accepted, and would become perhaps the most important citizen in the history of the eventually consolidated city of Bellingham.

8.5. The Cokedale Coal Mine. Jim Wardner sits at the left in this photo of the mine entrance. Coal from the mine fueled the railroad, the electric company, the gas plant and any other endeavor needing coal energy in early Fairhaven. Galen Biery Photographs #0678, CPNWS.

8.6. The Henry Bailey. The steamboat Henry Bailey carried passengers and freight from Seattle to the towns along the Skagit River. Whatcom Museum.

In the summer of 1888, Donovan and his bride Clara Nichols, moved to a rented room in Tacoma, and J.J. began his work developing the coal mine in Woolley and planning the railroad to Fairhaven. Taking a steamer from Tacoma to Utsalady at the north end of Camano Island, he and an assistant boarded the paddle-wheeler *Henry Bailey*, to ascend the Skagit River to the now non-existent town of Sterling on the north bank of the river, just down stream from Sedro and Woolley. It was July 21, 1888, and the small party with a hired Indian guide headed north through the tangle of swamps, under-brush and fallen timber, seeking the best route for Bennett's railroad north to Fairhaven. Four days later J.J. Donovan arrived in Fairhaven, as he used to say in later years "with a pack on my back."

Bennett assembled a powerful team of men that possessed great business skill, entrepreneurial energy and great wealth. They all shared his vision of a great city rising from the mud and stumps of Dan Harris's village. Together they began an incredible flurry of activity that would fuel what would for-ever be known as the Fairhaven Boom.

In rapid succession their energy and management efforts resulted in the following actions and organizations to create their envisioned city.

1888   The Fairhaven Land Company incorporated.

1888   Fairhaven and Southern Railroad incorporated.

1888   Skagit Coal and Transportation Company incorporated.

1889   Fairhaven electric Light, Power and Motor Company
        incorporated.

1889   Fairhaven Water & Power Company incorporated.

1889   Purchase of Canfield's Railroad, Bellingham Bay Railway &
        Navigation Company.

1890   City of Fairhaven incorporated.

1890   Bellingham Bay Gas Company incorporated.

1890   Fairhaven Publishing Company incorporated.

1890   Fairhaven Sandstone Company incorporated

1890   Fairhaven Electric Street Railway Company incorporated.

1890   The Fairhaven Hotel at 12th and Harris completed and
        opened.

By the summer of 1890, Bennett's vision was well on the way to becoming
a reality.

CHAPTER 9

A City Is Built

Building a modern city, even to 1888 standards, from what was a recently logged landscape of mud and stumps was a monumental challenge. A new arrival from New Hampshire wrote in his diary in April of 1889, "the city before me is not at all like the precise lithographs. Instead, only crude raw beginnings, the primeval forest of giant firs and cedars barely pushed back to the hillsides, mud streets gouged out, raw with jumbled piles of burning stumps, flames and smoke obscuring the sky. On the beach, tents flap in the breeze and a few unpainted wooden structures suggest civilization is to come."

Undaunted, Nelson Bennett announced that the Fairhaven Land Company would be building a magnificent hotel at 12th and Harris that would rival Tacoma's pride, the majestic Tacoma Hotel. The word on the street was that he had ordered one million bricks from Whittaker and Johns, the new brick makers in Happy Valley. Frantic activity was everywhere.

The previous summer of 1888—as J.J. Donovan was slogging through the swamps and forests surveying the route for the railroad—Bennett, Cowgill, Wilson and Larrabee were busily buying more land.

First they negotiated with Edward Eldridge and Erastus Bartlett, the platters of the town of Bellingham and its sawmill on Pattle's Point (now Boulevard Park). Their negotiations resulted in the six men forming a new corporation, the Bellingham Land Company. It was incorporated on Nov. 28, 1888. The Bellingham saw mill was not included in the deal for the time being. Corporate trustees were Eldridge, Bartlett, Bennett and Larrabee. Within months Eldridge and Bartlett were bought out for a reported $1,000,000, a truly immense sum for the day. The new corporation was soon folded into the Fairhaven Land Company. That meant that Bellingham had now become a part of Fairhaven.

9.1. The Eldridge & Bartlett Sawmill circa 1895. The mill was sold to the E.K. Wood Company. St. Josephs Hospital can be seen high on the hill surrounded by its white picket fence. The mill burned in 1925 and is now the site of Boulevard Park. Galen Biery Photographs #744, CPNWS.

The city builders also purchased land from Maurice O'Conner bordering Fairhaven on the east, and from the Lysle family in the valley between the two hills. Soon the Fairhaven Land Company could direct its civil engineer, Donovan, to prepare a re-plat of a now larger Fairhaven, which added not only the former Bellingham, but four blocks to the south border of the city and extending to the eastern border all the way to 21st Street. The new plat filed in August of 1889, included street names honoring its new owners—Cowgill Avenue, Wilson Avenue, Larrabee Avenue—and the young civil engineer with Irish pride was able to include his own family name, Donovan Avenue. The true founder, Nelson Bennett had his name attached to the street Dan Harris had called 4th Street, down by Ocean Dock. The usually meticulous Donovan made an untypical error on the plat map, misspelling his employer's name as Benntt.

When Donovan got to the last street on the southern border of the new Fairhaven, he acted with familial affection and took the opportunity to memorialize his mother and many other women in his family by naming the street Julia Avenue. Julia O'Sullivan Donovan was his mother's name and there were several Julias in every generation of his family. Donovan was already leaving his mark on Fairhaven, and on the town that would become Bellingham.

Among the busiest of men, Donovan was also supervising the development of the coal mine near Woolley and the construction of the railroad that when completed would be called the Fairhaven and Southern Railway. Its general manager was E.M. Wilson, J.J. Donovan was its superintendent and chief engineer.

9.2. Building the streets of South Hill, 1889. One by one, with horse and manpower the streets of Fairhaven were carved from the mud and stumps. This picture looks up the slope of South Hill. Galen Biery Photographs #2623, CPNWS.

Over time Larrabee would continue his land acquisitions, including the shoreline and Chuckanut Mountains to the south, and land in the northern parts of the county.

On May 16, 1890, he bought the remaining 270 acres of Alonzo Poe's claim, which is now Bellingham's exclusive residential area called Edgemoor. The purchase was made from the heirs of A.A. Denny and William Bell, Seattle pioneers. Larrabee paid them $108,437. Twenty years earlier Denny and Bell had purchased the land from Americus Poe for $325. Larrabee bought the land as an individual. It would be another five months before he transferred the land to the Fairhaven Land Company, which he now owned outright. The eventual sum total acreage of his holdings is not known, but he had enough that his heirs were able to gift 20 acres to the State in the year after his death to create Larrabee Park, the first park in the State's park system.

1889 and 1890 were years of almost frantic activity and development by Bennett and his growing cadre of investors and doers. By 1889 the magnificent Fairhaven Hotel was being constructed at 12th and Harris, corporations were being formed right and left to provide the utilities and services that a city would require. Incorporation as a city required a petition to Whatcom County, civic elections and the formation of a city government. The petition was made, elections were held and leaders chosen. A newly elected mayor

9.3. The Trolley Barn & Power House. After the merger, the trolleys bore the name, Fairhaven & New Whatcom. Galen Biery Photographs #1602, CPNWS.

and city council were soon busily enacting the ordinances and protocols required for a city government.

This frenzied rush to build a city was led by those men who had conceived the vision and had invested in it; consequently most of the basic corporations formed were started by principals of the Fairhaven Land Company.

On October 15, 1889, Pierce Evans, George A. Black and James F. Wardner incorporated the Fairhaven Electric Light & Motor Company. Black was the land agent for the Fairhaven Land Company; Pierce Evans, was an attorney for and a stockholder in the company. Wardner, fresh from the mines of Idaho, was a major investor in the new community and the president of the Fairhaven National Bank, whose principal stockholders were Larrabee and Bennett.

High on the list of needs for the city builders was a water supply. Lake Padden was perfectly located on the high land just east of Fairhaven. To tap its clear waters a new corporation was formed. On October 19, 1889, the Fairhaven City Water and Power Company was formed. Its trustees were Cowgill, Wilson, Wardner, and Black.

Even before the appearance of electricity in the new town, eager business people were proposing a transportation system that would be powered by electricity. On February 4, 1889, the Bellingham Bay Street Railway Company was created with stated plans to build a rail/trolley system from McKenzie

Avenue in Fairhaven, north on 11th Street through Bellingham; through Sehome on Elk Street (now State Street) to Indiana, and then west to Broadway and back through Whatcom to Elk. The line was to have a branch to the shores of Lake Whatcom. Its promoters were D.K. Huntoon, P.D. McKeller and Thomas Gise. These were Whatcom and Sehome people. The idea apparently failed to take root or perhaps it stirred the competitive hearts of Fairhaven's powerful, as four months later in January of the next year, Nelson Bennett, C.X. Larrabee, Pierce Evans, J.F. Wardner, H.Y. Thompson, George A. Black, and E.M. Wilson incorporated the Fairhaven Electric Railway Company. The Fairhaven Land Company was showing its muscle.

9.4. Trolley Ticket. Five cents would get you across town. This is a Stone & Webster ticket dating after 1902. Collection of the author.

This was perhaps an early indication of the growing competition and rivalry between the older towns at the north shore of the bay and the upstart town to the south that was enjoying such explosive growth and enthusiasm. This rivalry would grow and exist in many forms and even survive the consolidation of the rival towns into the City of Bellingham in 1904.

9.5. The Trolley rails. The old electric street trolley rails are still visible as they curve down into 11th Street toward the Terminal Building stop. Photo by the author.

The street railway battles continued. The Whatcom/Sehome interests launched another strong bid on July 7, 1890, when they incorporated the Bellingham Bay Street Railway Company. Its shareholders were Eugene Canfield, P.D. McKellar (who had backed the earlier effort), Pierre B. Cornwall, Jameson L. Perkins, H.B. Williams, J.W. Morgan and J.H. Stenger—all important names from the north.

The competition heightened the creation of two separate electric street railroads. The Whatcom interests formed their trolley system; the powerful Fairhaven group built their trolley system. The two rails met at the border between the towns where State Street comes down the hill and the Boulevard

9.6. 12th and Douglas, 1892. The photo appears to have been taken from the newly graded 12th Street at the yet-to-be-built Douglas Avenue intersection. The two prominent houses still stand there. The Gamwell house at 16th and Douglas, and the Riedel house at 1005 14th. Galen Biery Photographs #2973, CPNWS.

begins. A passenger going from one city to the other would have to disembark from the trolley, walk across the border, and board the trolley car of his destination city.

This ludicrous situation continued until 1892 when the trolley companies finally merged to become the Fairhaven and New Whatcom Railway. The decision to call the consolidated company either Fairhaven and New Whatcom, or New Whatcom and Fairhaven was not an easy one. It was decided by that voice of reason J.J. Donovan tossing a coin. The new company ran their five cars from the Ocean Dock in Fairhaven to the Whatcom County Courthouse.

It left 11th Street and Harris Avenue every 15 minutes and a ticket cost five cents and ten cents for the spur line to Lake Whatcom.

The trolley system was sold to the Stone and Webster Corporation of Boston in 1902 and re-organized as the Whatcom County Railway and Light Company. The tracks of the old trolley can still be seen in the street where 11th Street veers off from State Street at the Finnegan Way junction.

Not all of Fairhaven's development came directly from the Fairhaven Land Company. Fairhaven had attracted nationwide attention as the next great opportunity in the development of the West. C.W. Waldron, a banker, came to start a bank and built a large brick building that still stands on the corner of 12th and McKenzie Avenue.

Roland Gamwell arrived with his New England wealth and culture to be a major investor in a number of businesses and to build his magnificent mansion at 16th and Douglas. Civil War veteran Henry Bateman, with family money, built his home at 15th and Knox Avenue, catty-corner from James Wardner, and started a home savings and loan business.

A few of the folks that flocked to the Fairhaven Boom came from just a short distance. Thomas E. Monahan had been operating his Board of Trade saloon at the corner of Front and Mill across the street from the Bellingham Hotel since 1871. Now realizing that he was out of the center of activity, he bought a lot near the corner of 11th and Harris and built his New Board of Trade saloon. He moved his family into its upstairs and became a prominent citizen of the booming town. He served on its city council for many terms. The building still stands there, now the home of Fairhaven Runners, a popular shoe store. If you look to the center of its cornice you will see 'MONAHAN BUILDING 1890'.

9.7. Henry B. Bateman was a lieutenant in the Union Army during the Civil War. This photo of him was purchased at an estate sale at his 15th Street house after his daughter Elena's death. The photo, a promotion paper, his saber and Colt Revolver were gifted to the Whatcom Museum by the author.

Allen Mason of Tacoma purchased land on 12th Street, directly across Harris Avenue from the Fairhaven Hotel, and constructed his huge brick office and commercial building called the Mason Block. The Mason Block still stands on that key corner of Fairhaven, providing the community with restaurants, retail stores and office space. Its historic dignity only slightly marred by its being re-named "Sycamore Square" by its present owners.

Highlighting the astonishing progress made during that year in the growing Fairhaven was the completion of the massive and ornate Fairhaven Hotel. It stood at its high spot at the corner of 12th and Harris, its four stories and ornate tower visible from the approaching steamers filled with excited immigrants. The immigrants were pouring into Fairhaven, the phenomenon of the Sound, the city called the "Focal City" by its boosters, "The Imperial City" by J.J. Hill in an early speech. The magnificent and luxurious Fairhaven Hotel was evidence and proof positive of the splendid future of this new city and for all who would come to settle here. The Fairhaven Hotel opened on the night of September 15, 1890 to a huge celebratory dinner.

The population of Fairhaven had leapt from the 140 souls that J.J. Donovan reported to his bride upon arriving in 1888, to a population of 8,000 claimed by the December 29, 1890, holiday edition of the *Fairhaven Herald*. People came from all parts of the country rushing to get in on the opportunity to buy land,

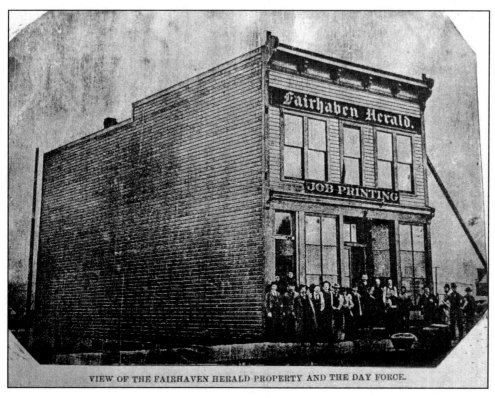

VIEW OF THE FAIRHAVEN HERALD PROPERTY AND THE DAY FORCE.

9.8. Picture of Herald Building showing a wind prop on the right hand side. Whatcom Museum.

to start businesses, to experience a new beginning and to start a new life in the extravagantly promoted boom town of Fairhaven.

One of the requirements of booming a city was effective publicity, and for that purpose the Fairhaven Land Company needed a newspaper. On January 23, 1890, the Fairhaven Publishing Company was incorporated by E.M. Wilson, George A. Black and E.L Cowgill. They hired a swashbuckling editor named Will F. Visscher and the *Fairhaven Herald* was born. Its first edition, a tri-weekly, was published on March 11, 1890.

It was not to be the only Fairhaven newspaper, for in October of that same year, Horace Brown and the Culver brothers, Otis and Fred, incorporated the World Publishing Company to print the *Weekly World*. There was also the *Fairhaven Plaindealer*, put out by the Plaindealer Publishing Company.

The *Fairhaven Herald* was the Fairhaven Land Company's creation and its mouthpiece. The *Herald's* voice was strident and extreme in its rhetoric selling the wonders of Fairhaven. Editor Visscher was a master at *Boom-speak*, the hyper-excited language that extolled the virtues of emerging towns all over the west. It was commonly in use during the western expansion, but there are no better examples of *Boom-speak* than found in the *First Holiday Edition of the Fairhaven Herald*.

9.9. First holiday edition of the *Fairhaven Herald*, 1890. Collection of the author.

The *Herald* normally printed an eight-page paper, but the Holiday Edition was celebrating the city's first holiday season since incorporation. This special 24-page edition was printed and distributed as a publicity piece by the Fairhaven Land Company. It provides a priceless look at Fairhaven as it approached the peak of its famous boom period.

The massive edition was published on December 29, 1890. In the editor's notes in its mast head, Visscher reports that 30,000 copies were being printed, each copy expected to be read by ten persons—clearly a substantial advertising thrust by the Fairhaven Land Company. Visscher goes on to credit and thank "Robert E. Strahorn of the Fairhaven Land Company" for providing much of the information and much of the writing for what must have been a huge undertaking for a pioneer newspaper.

The front page features the lithographic image of "The Fairhaven," which had opened just three months previously and had become the iconic symbol of this new city. The edition is filled with photographs and drawings depicting Fairhaven's recently built mansions, its prominent citizens, its churches and commercial buildings. It proclaims its economic realities and, of course, its magnificent and certain future.

An ad for the Fairhaven Land Company on the second page states:

> "Fairhaven needs no booming. A place that has grown from a population of 500 January 1, 1890, to nearly 8,000 January 1, 1891, speaks for itself.

> "The shrewd capitalist or business man and the thoughtful home-seeker or laborer must conclude that Fairhaven is invincible in location, unequaled for harbor facilities and all the resources that create great cities, and is not only alive with the spirit of success but has the backing to command it."

Orchestrating all of this growth and promotion were the leaders of the Fairhaven Land Company whose names can be found on all of the corporations that formed the foundation of this aborning city.

Chapter 10

City Government Begins

D an Harris's Fairhaven named and platted in 1883 was simply a town subject to the laws and ordinances of the county, but now in 1890 the Fairhaven Land Company wanted to incorporate a true city. A citizen's petition to the County Council for incorporation was begun and not surprisingly its first signatory was E.M. Wilson, Vice President of the Fairhaven Land Company.

Entitled "Petition for the incorporation of the city of Fairhaven," it described the boundaries of the town which was to commence at "the northwest corner of the W.R. Pattle Donation Claim marked by the letter "P" cut into solid rock on the shores of Bellingham Bay."[1] This description brought the former town of Bellingham into Fairhaven city limits.

It declares that as "nearly as can be determined there are 2000 people living within the bounds of the city. And they pray that the said city of Fairhaven be incorporated."

Petitions signed by hundreds of prominent names were filed with Hugh Eldridge, Whatcom County Auditor on April 1, 1890.

In a display of the animosity between the rival cities on the bay, the town of New Whatcom countered with an attempt to prevent Bellingham from being joined to Fairhaven.

New Whatcom boosters sponsored a petition asking the County Council to annex Bellingham onto New Whatcom's southern border instead. Their counter measure resulted in even more petitions from residents of Bellingham asking to be included in Fairhaven. The following petition was filed on April 17, 1890:

"The undersigned respectfully represent that they are residents and property owners within the limits of the territory known and

---

1   The author has searched in vain for the "P" incised into the rock by William Pattle. Sadly, it has long been covered or removed by railroad track construction.

designated as the town of Bellingham and that for personal and business reasons we earnestly protest against being incorporated in the proposed new town of New Whatcom and we respectfully ask the Commissioners to so determine the boundaries of the City of Fairhaven as to include within its limits our property and the town of Bellingham."

An election was held on May 6, 1890. The resulting act was dated May 12, describing the boundaries and announcing the votes which favored incorporation of Fairhaven including Bellingham and electing its mayor and councilmen. There were 1407 votes for incorporation and 1406 votes to elect Edward Turner mayor. There were also over 1400 votes spread among six councilmen.

The act was signed by C.F. Keesling, Chairman of the Board of County Commissioners.

On May 14, 1890, the newly elected Mayor and City Council met to begin the tedious process of establishing a new city's government. The preamble of the minutes of that first meeting read:

"Be it remembered that the first city council of the
City of Fairhaven, county of Whatcom, State of Washington
met in the DeFries Hall on Wednesday evening, May 14, 1890."

The oath of office was administered by George Mc SoRelle, a local realtor and notary public, and the new government began its deliberations.

Chairing that first meeting was Fairhaven's first mayor, Edward A. Turner. Turner was also a realtor who operated from an office between 11th and 12th streets on Harris Avenue. Councilmen elected were:

Edgar Lea Cowgill, the secretary of the Fairhaven Land Company;

J.J. Donovan, chief engineer of the Fairhaven & Southern RR, and
   civil engineer for the Fairhaven Land Company;

James M. Miller, realtor, George Mc SoRelle's partner whose office
   was at the corner of 14th and McKenzie;

Malcolm McKechnie, a carpenter;

James F. Wardner, president of the Bank of Fairhaven (owned by
   Fairhaven Land Company principals);

Wellington A. Woodin, owner of Curry & Co., Woodin Brothers,
   and Fairhaven Lumber and Planing Mills.

The Council's first order of business was the selection of the major city positions.

W.S. Parker was elected City Marshall, John D. DeFries Street Commissioner, and G.A. Kellogg City Attorney. Alfred Riedel, elected City Clerk wrote and signed the first minutes.

The next day the council met again. They learned that attorney Kellogg had declined his position citing ill health, and so they elected former Utah Governor and Land Agent for the Fairhaven Land Company, George A. Black as City Attorney.

They established staggered terms for the council positions and decided who would serve one year or two-year terms by drawing names out of a hat. Three would serve one-year terms, three would serve two-year terms. Cowgill, McKechnie and Miller drew one-year cards, Wardner, Woodin and Donovan would serve two years.

They decided that the police force should consist of the Town Marshal, two night policemen and two day policemen.

The council decided that City Hall would temporarily be at DeFries Hall, the upper room over the DeFries Store on Larrabee Avenue. They agreed to rent the space for six months at $75 per month. The rent included daily janitorial care of the room, and DeFries agreed to install railings dividing the room into six compartments. Apparently each councilman was to have his own compartment.

Next they addressed building construction codes, controlling spirituous liquors, horses, mules and teams left untended in the streets, taxing and killing of dogs, the working of city prisoners, suppressing gambling, suppressing houses of ill fame, blasting within the city limits. They defined vagrancy and prescribed the punishment for same.

Ordinance #2 established the requirement of a $1,000 faithful performance bond for the City Marshall. Within six months this ordinance would be found woefully inadequate in amount.

Ordinance #4 proscribed a fire code for buildings built within the blocks between 9th and 14th streets and Mill and Larrabee avenues. It required that all buildings of any kind or description be built of stone, brick, or terracotta with metal roofs.

Many of the adopted ordinances are amusing now when viewed through modern eyes. However they provide an interesting insight into the Fairhaven society of 1890.

Ord. #7 defines disorderly persons and describes the penalties for being disorderly. Examples include the fast or immoderate driving of horses, mules or other animals in any of the streets. A later ordinance defined speeding as being "in excess of six miles per hour."

10.1. The Terminal building which now houses Tony's Coffee and the Harris Ave. Café is a wood frame building, covered with brick veneer. It was built in 1889 and narrowly escaped the frame construction ban. Whatcom Museum.

Ord. #24 to suppress gambling. Gambling was declared illegal and subject to a fine of $20 to $100, or ten to 30 days in jail.

Ord. #25 to suppress *Houses of Ill Fame.* "Every person who keeps, or who assists In keeping, or who is an inmate of, or who is employed in, in any capacity whatever, or who solicits or invites any person or persons to enter, visit or frequent, or who frequents any house of ill fame, or any house resorted to for the purpose of prostitution, within the City of Fairhaven; and every person leasing or permitting either as agent or owner, any building or premises, or owner of any ground on which said building as mentioned in said City to be used as a house of ill fame or house of prostitution, shall upon conviction thereof before any police justice of the City, be fined in a sum not less than ten nor more than one hundred dollars, or be imprisoned in the City Jail not less than ten nor more than thirty days.

Ord. #119 prohibited the running at large of horses, mules, cattle, sheep, swine, goats, or domestic fowls within an area carefully defined. The restricted area ran from 16th street to 9th, and from the Fairhaven and Southern Railway right of way on the south to Lenora Avenue and Douglas on the north.

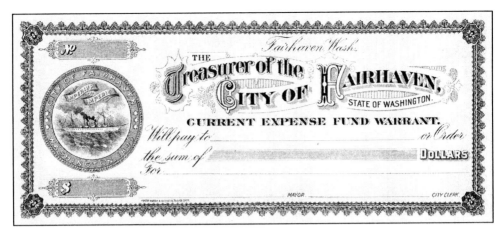

10.2. City Of Fairhaven Promise To Pay. Fairhaven's cash flow, dependent upon paid taxes was slim. The city issued these warrants for necessary goods and services, a promise to pay in the future. Collection of the author.

The new city government was extremely busy contracting for street construction, sidewalk building, sewers, franchise issues for water, electric and street trolley companies. They established separate funds for each street improvement project, assessing the property owners along the new streets.

The administrative person responsible for collecting late and unpaid street assessments was the City Marshall W.S. Parker. Parker also collected fines and license fees.[2]

The newly elected government worked long and diligently to establish the framework of city government and to address the challenges of building a modern city where just a year or two before there had been only forest and swamp. Many of the streets west of Padden Creek in lower Fairhaven were platted across swampy lowlands and had to be elevated, most of the streets were simply graded dirt streets which became terribly muddy in the long rainy season. Streets planked with heavy timbers of fir were gradually built and were partnered with planked sidewalks on the central streets.

The inaugural year 1890 was a heady time of excitement and growth as the Fairhaven Boom grew to a crescendo.

---

2   Six months after taking office Marshall Parker disappeared. Read "Town Marshall, Winfield Scott Parker" in Part Two.

"THE FAIRHAVEN"

FAIRHAVEN. WASHINGTON.

11.1. Fairhaven Hotel Lithograph. This lithograph was drawn in 1891 by G.W. Pierce, the same artist who had produced the Fairhaven Birdseye. Both lithographs were commissioned by the Fairhaven Land Company as advertisements. The light-colored building on the extreme right never existed, it is believed to be the artist's effort to balance his drawing. While hundreds were printed, only three originals are known to exist. Collection of the author.

CHAPTER 11

The Boom

BOOM! A most descriptive word, and it was a well-worn word in the latter part of the 19th century as the railroads penetrated the vastness of the west and town after town along the track was boomed. The wild optimism of this period of post Civil War expansion—coupled with a national fascination with and desire to achieve sudden wealth—caused scores of opportunities to boom a new town. It was a technique of hyper salesmanship, frequently slipping into the realm of fraud and lies.

The technique was to buy acreage and to plat a town in a likely spot along the coming RR line, then advertise it as the next great metropolis. Publicity minded promoters would acclaim the area's economic promise, extolling its myriad virtues and opportunities and the certainty of its great and prosperous future. A land office would be set up to sell lots and business sites. Usually there would be a start-up newspaper to provide fuel to the fire. Eager realtors would come to the location like vultures to carrion and add to the excitement with their sales efforts. Soon a *Gold Rush* fervor would develop.

Booms attracted both the good and the bad. Earnest investors were eager to make their way in a new land. Store owners came from the established East seeking the adventure and opportunity of the West. Young people with little opportunity in the East saw a chance to get a start in a new land. Immigrants from Europe were looking for their chance. Booms also attracted the worst—crooks and shysters of every stripe, prostitutes, ne'er–do–wells, and a few criminals avoiding the law in their home country seeking a place where their reputations had not reached.

Populations soared, land sales and prices rose to amazing heights and then (just *before* the fervor died down), the boom promoters would often move out of town to the next opportunity.

Fueling the boom psychology was the fact that there were plenty of examples of legitimate booms where a town had indeed exploded in growth,

11.2. James Wardner was a larger than life, wealthy miner/banker with a legendary sense of humor. His mansion, built at the corner of 15th Street and Knox Avenue, has been called "Wardner's Castle" since it was built in 1890. Galen Biery Photographs #2429, CPNWS.

energy and prosperity. San Francisco after the 1849 Gold Rush was a classic example, and so the reality and the hope were ever present. At its best the term *boom* was a positive one—a rapid expansion of population wealth and opportunity as a new town grew. At its worst *boom* came to mean the manipulation for a profit—of the expectation of the growth of a community, even when such expectations were unlikely to occur.

The Fairhaven experience was surely a boom of magnificent proportions. It contained in large measure all of the good and the bad previously mentioned; however, the author would submit that it was an honest boom. There was every reason to believe that rapid growth would come, that the railroad would terminate in Fairhaven, and that when that happened the grand expectations would become reality. The legitimacy of the Fairhaven Boom is evidenced by the fact that Bennett and Larrabee and the other principals of the Fairhaven Land Company invested huge amounts of capital into their planned city. They invested personal funds to develop the necessary infrastructure of a major city. They attracted serious and accomplished businessmen from across the country who believed in Fairhaven's future and invested their own treasure. Men like Roland Gamwell, James F. Wardner, and Henry Batemen, whose palatial homes still grace Fairhaven, give testimony to the authenticity of the Fairhaven dream.

It cannot be denied that the Land Company did a great deal of promoting and that they were profiting from land sales. In fact, they did a very skilled and professional job of it, and the influx of capital and immigrants from around the nation was ample evidence of the success of their sales efforts. In its defense it must be said that there were plenty of reasons to think that the Company's hyperbole would come true.

The Fairhaven Boom was founded on Nelson Bennett's belief that the Great Northern would cross the mountains at Sedro and choose Fairhaven as its Pacific terminus. Bennett expected the Great Northern to descend from

11.3. Charles Xavier Larrabee. This image of his grandfather was provided by C.X. Larrabee II. Collection of the author.

the Cascade Mountains onto the Skagit flats. He was confident he had chosen the best and only logical place for its terminus on salt water.

The Boom began with the purchase of the land from Daniel Harris in 1887, and the announcement that Bennett and Larrabee would build a railroad from the Skagit River to Fairhaven. Development began almost immediately. 1888 saw the completion of the Terminal Building, still standing at the corner of Harris and 11th, soon followed by construction starts on major buildings such as the Mason Block, The Knights of Pythias Building, the Monohan Building, the Waldron Building, and of course, the iconic Fairhaven Hotel.

As homes were being built on the slope east of 13th Street, wood-frame stores, hotels and saloons, rooming houses and houses of ill repute were hurriedly erected in the central business district, mostly facing Harris and McKenzie Avenues. A red light district developed on McKenzie below 11th. The Thistle Opera House, a small theater, was built on the corner of 11th and Mill, north of the Village Books store of today. Lumber mills dotted the shoreline, a brick-making business opened in Happy Valley beside the planned track of the Fairhaven and Southern Railway. Fairhaven's rapid growth was considered the wonder of the Pacific Northwest. It appeared that nothing would prevent the new city from matching Seattle and Tacoma in growth and opportunity.

People came from all over the country to invest in Fairhaven real estate, and many lots were sold sight-unseen to Eastern investors who wanted in on the action. By the fall of 1891, 9,000 people had flocked to the new city. The population had exploded from the 140 souls that J.J. Donovan had reported in a letter to his bride in 1887. Houses and commercial buildings were still going up everywhere. Mansions had been built on the hill overlooking its harbor, some of which still add distinction to the hillside such as Wardner's *Castle* at the southeast corner of 15th and Knox, and Henry Bateman's home on the northwest corner. Roland Gamwell's classic Victorian at the corner of 16th and Douglas was under construction and showed promise of being the best of them all.

1890 may have been the high point of the great Fairhaven Boom with the completion of the Fairhaven Hotel. You could buy a city lot for $1,500 in the morning and sell it for $2,500 in the afternoon. The Great Northern was progressing with its construction across the prairies toward Puget Sound and expectations were sky high. The Fairhaven Boom entirely depended on that railroad selecting Fairhaven as its terminus.

The great hotel had opened on September 15, 1890, with a sumptuous celebration of the finest wines and cuisine. Steamers were arriving at the Ocean Dock daily, bringing even more excited immigrants with money and talent and energy to invest. Thousands of men were at work building the infrastructure of the new city. The great railroad tycoon himself, J.J. Hill, had come to speak at the behest of the newly formed Chamber of Commerce, and he had said to a packed audience under the rotunda of the sparkling new Fairhaven Hotel, "There is no reason in the world Gentlemen, why you cannot have here, not only a large city but an Imperial City." His words struck off a community spark and launched a new theme for the surging city. No longer Fairhaven the Focal City, now it was Fairhaven the Imperial City.

But there were dark clouds on the horizon. An astute *Herald* reporter noticed what perhaps his enthusiastic audience had not. Hill had not actually said that the Great Northern was coming to Fairhaven. He wrote, "Hill is a master of mis-direction and he appeared to be playing his coy game with every city along the sound." Was it possible that Bennett and Larrabee had been misled by the canny Hill?

Another dark cloud had appeared on the horizon in September of 1890. It had been noted by the *Fairhaven Herald* reporter covering the grand opening of the hotel that two notable citizens of Fairhaven had not attended the opening: "Daniel J. Harris who had passed to his reward in Los Angeles, August 19, and Nelson Bennett, expected here on such an auspicious occasion." The article went on to say, "On excellent authority, the rumors of September 3rd are true; Mr. Bennett will henceforth have his entire interests in Tacoma and Butte Montana. It is said that some dissension of a serious nature within the company is the supposed cause of Mr. Bennett's withdrawal."

Four days later, on September 19, the *Herald* reported. "Mr. C.X. Larrabee has taken the place of Mr. Nelson Bennett in all Fairhaven companies, so the *Bellingham Bay Reveille* reports today. It seems that Mr. Bennett became too Napoleonic in his methods and procured his own dislike. This resulted in selling out to Mr. Larrabee."

Could Bennett's decision to withdraw from his Fairhaven investments, the Fairhaven of his vision and his creation, have been entirely from internal disagreements with his partners, or did he have some private knowledge of the Great Northern's plans.

11.4. Sidewalks of Wood, 1890s. The streets were built up above the mud with four-inch-thick planks of wood. The sidewalks were only two inches thick. Galen Biery Photographs #3412, CPNWS.

History has failed to record just what caused Nelson Bennett's abandonment of Fairhaven. It is known that he sold the hotel and his shares in the Fairhaven Land Company to Larrabee, but that he did retain his stock ownership in several Fairhaven corporations. We have sure knowledge of his majority ownership in the Fairhaven City Water and Power Company, the corporate minutes of which we possess. He owned 390,000 shares of its stock and was its corporate President at least up to March of 1893. He continued as a director of the Fairhaven 1st National Bank and several other corporations, so he did remain involved in Fairhaven's fortunes but in a much reduced fashion.

Bennett and Larrabee might well have been at loggerheads. They were certainly men cut from different cloth.

Bennett was a tough character. He had to be tough, as an Indian fighter, a muleskinner, a man who with determination and grit had driven a tunnel two miles through the crest of the Cascades, ignoring the bitter cold and snows of the mountains to meet the demanding terms of his contract. A man accustomed to command and perhaps a man dictatorial in manner. The corporate records of the Fairhaven City Water and Power Company give evidence of his roughshod self-serving handling of a bond-selling effort by that company, in which Bennett's actions bordered on the illegal. The Board of Directors was so unhappy with him that they chose to write a complete summary of the dispute and include it in the corporate minutes. Bennett might have been an overbearing and difficult partner.

C.X. Larrabee, on the other hand, was a very private man with a reputation for absolute honesty and probity. His longtime friend and attorney Evan McCord, in a letter to son Charles Larrabee after Larrabee's death in 1914, had described C.X. as, "Absolutely the best man he had ever known, always completely fair and honest in every dealing with others. His moral convictions were unshakable." He was obviously ambitious and shrewd but a generous man with unquestioned ethics. He had a lifelong abhorrence of alcohol, which resulted in the following article.

The October 4, 1890, *Weekly World* reported, "The Hotel Fairhaven has experienced a radical change this past week. Its bar has been discontinued and Mr. Presbrey, its manager has resigned. Presbrey is expected to be appointed manager of Nelson Bennett's big hotel in Tacoma. The management changes at The Fairhaven may stem from Mr. Larrabee's strictures on the serving of alcohol."

Immediately upon buying The Fairhaven, Larrabee had closed the bar and banned alcohol from his hotel. His moral convictions overrode what must have been an obviously unwise move from an economic point of view in that hard drinking age. In a later article, the *Reveille* wrote, "It is his inviolable policy that no alcohol be served in his hotel, a policy derived from observation, first hand of the effects of alcohol in the mining camps of Montana. Mr. Larrabee is the last person in the world to question how others live, but he doesn't approve of liquor and as he owns the hotel, he is ready to put his money where his mouth is and so forbids alcohol at The Fairhaven."

In August of 1891, Larrabee wrote a check to Bennett drawn on the First National Bank of Portland in the amount of $495,954.50.[1] It is believed that check paid for The Fairhaven Hotel and Bennett's interest in the Fairhaven Land Company.

By the time that Larrabee wrote his check, the Fairhaven Boom was beginning to show signs of weakening. An international money crisis was causing a world-wide depression. The Great Northern track construction across the west was halted or slowed because of the monetary crisis. The negative psychology usual to recessions began to stifle investment in new ventures across the nation, and Fairhaven as a new venture began to suffer.

---

1   This figure was revealed to me by C.X. Larrabee II, the grandson. He declared that he had seen the cancelled check.

11.5. A city among the stumps, 1890. Fairhaven was logged in 1889-90. Stumps and wet were everywhere. Note the tents and the bare hills. Galen Biery Photographs #3412, CPNWS.

Community leaders put on an optimistic face, but doubts about the future had entered the picture. In October, the *Weekly World* asked, "What shall be the future of Fairhaven? ... It is very clear from President Hill's memorable speech here that the GN does not propose, as some have vainly hoped, to build a town here and make everyone that is here or has acquired property here wealthy."

Nelson Bennett was quoted by the press as urging a railroad to be laid out along the waterfront. He sees better times for Fairhaven "when the clouds shall have rolled away."

Despite the economic slow down, Fairhaven continued to progress. Streets were being graded and extended. Many of the streets had been planked with 4" x 4" timbers. Soon some of the wooden streets had to be rebuilt to provide for the rails of the new Electric Street Railway. Buildings continued to be built, now of brick or fireproof material, because of the fire code adopted by the first City Council in the early months of 1890. To keep up appearances many of the older wood frame buildings, such as the Terminal building built in 1888, received an exterior shell of masonry. C.W. Waldron, still optimistic of Fairhaven's future, added a fourth floor to his bank and office building at 12th and McKenzie.

1891 closed with this dreary commentary in the December 14 *Fairhaven Independent*.

> "These are not particularly cheering days in Fairhaven. The days are gloomy and the minds of many are the same. We are passing through a trying time—a period of depression is upon the entire Sound country and we in common with our brethren of other places feel it too—perhaps for some potent reasons more intensely than others. We believe in the future of our young city and though the sun is not shining extremely bright upon her just now, soon the clouds will break away and she will make rapid strides which will in truth make her both a beautiful and an 'Imperial City'. There has been quite an exodus of Fairhavenites to Port Gardner, to take in the 'boom' temporarily."

1892 saw a further slowdown in Fairhaven's activity, and then the bomb hit. The Great Northern announced it had chosen Steven's Pass to cross the Cascades and Seattle would become its terminus.

The great Fairhaven Boom was over!

CHAPTER 12

The Bust

Perhaps the *Whatcom Reveille* described it best with this wry verse in their April 7, 1893 edition.

> Sweet smiling village; loveliest of the Sound,
> How busy once, now hardly to be found;
>
> Only one master grasps the whole domain
> And CXL alone is in the game
>
> He faces the land to hastening ills a prey,
> Where wealth accumulates and men decay.
>
> Closed is the boast and pride, of all the country round,
> Thy great hotel is now alas! Fast crumbling to the ground;
> Where oft the thirsty traveler for something cooling eager,
> Was much to his amazement told to go to the Bodega.
>
> Vain transitory boom town could not all
> Your advertisements save you from this fall?
> Obscure you sink, nor can aught now impart
> The rustle that must give you a fresh start.
>
> Days, months and years pass by and still
> You sit and fold your hands and wait for Hill
> Downward you'll move, a melancholy band
> And gather clams by moonlight on the strand;
> At last to all outside world a mark for pity
> You'll seek consolation with this City.

12.1. Empty streets. The dark days of the recession of 1893 and the collapse of the Fairhaven Boom are portrayed in this photograph. Galen Biery Photographs #2727, CPNWS.

The citizens of the now consolidated towns of Whatcom and Sehome had watched with a sense of jealousy the meteoric growth of the tiny village to their south during the previous five years of boom. Now their newspaper was perhaps expressing their satisfaction at Fairhaven's humbling. They were surely accurate in their final sentence as a mere ten years later, the citizens of Fairhaven voted to consolidate their city with Whatcom to become Bellingham.

In the meantime, the boom had surely turned to bust. By the end of 1893 the population of Fairhaven had plummeted to a mere 3,000. Whatcom, its neighbor to the north, boasted 7,500 residents. The three-year-old *Fairhaven Herald*, a daily paper, the creation of the Fairhaven Land Company, was forced to merge with the *Weekly World,* changing its name to the *Weekly World-Herald.* It would now be a weekly.

The folks in Whatcom and New Whatcom had their own concerns. The national depression and the Panic of '93 effected everyone. By the summer of 1893 Whatcom banks were failing. On June 22, the First National Bank of New Whatcom was closed. The next day Whatcom's Columbia National Bank closed its doors. Two weeks later the Puget Sound Loan, Trust and Banking Co. of New Whatcom fell, and on the first of August the Bellingham Bay National Bank closed. Across the nation bank failures and runs on banks were daily news. Strangely, the bank panic of 1893 did not close any Fairhaven banks. In fact, Fairhaven was the only city on the Sound that did not have a bank failure in '93.

The capitalists representing the two cities of Bellingham Bay did not give up their efforts, nor did they let the community rivalry that had grown over the years distract them from sharing an opportunity that would eventually improve their communities beyond their wildest dreams. Whatcom County had been chosen to be the location of a new State Normal School, a college to train teachers.

In the fall of 1893, Governor John McGraw was chairman of a commission to choose a location for the Normal School, which had met in The Fairhaven Hotel reading room. Despite a strong bid by supporters of a Lynden site, McGraw and his commission chose the ten acres on Sehome Hill that had been offered jointly by the Bellingham Bay Improvement Company and the Fairhaven Land Company. The acreage in the valley between the hills was partially in New Whatcom and partly in Fairhaven. The two companies each gave a part of the acreage. That site, now considerably expanded, is the modern day site of Western Washington University with its 15,000 students and its massive economic and cultural influence on Bellingham and Whatcom County.

12.2. Pacific Clothing Store Sign. Incredibly, the sporty gent painted on the bricks of the Mason Block is still there, a lingering reminder of the bankrupt store of 1893. Photo by the author.

National economics were in a terrible state. The Northern Pacific Railroad fell into receivership. The Great Northern RR was reported to be reducing salaries 15-30%. The Pacific Clothing Store in Fairhaven's Mason Block declared itself bankrupt and moved out of town, leaving only the dapper gentleman painted on the bricks of the building for Fairhavenites to remember it by.

Despite the bitter economic times and the great civic disappointment in Fairhaven's fall from glory, from time to time there were hints of a better day to come. The choosing of Sehome Hill as the Normal School site was a bright spot, then in September of 1893, a newspaper article hinted at a development that would have immense importance for the struggling city. "Get ready! An important industry is aborning! We hear from Point Roberts, most admirably located for the catching of salmon, of devices called fishtraps. These traps, 50-feet deep and 40-feet square, fished once a day, catch 5,000 fish at a time.

Some report 23,000 fish caught per day." This news augured well for a possible canning industry.

But bad news seemed to rule. On January 24, 1894, The Waldron Building burned. It was occupied by the bank of Fairhaven and the Cissna's Fair Store. C.W. Waldron had just finished adding the 4th floor to his building, and still a believer in Fairhaven, he vowed to rebuild. Charles Cissna however, had had enough and moved his store north to Whatcom.

The Fairhaven City Council, in a cost-saving move, reduced the number of electric street lights from 52 to 38. Each light cost them $10.50 per month to keep lit. Superintendent Gillette of the Electric Company, said the company will keep them lit even though the cost for electricity resulted in a loss to the Company. By the end of 1895, the lights would only be left on until 1:00 AM, and the Council would be considering whether they could afford to keep them on at all.

The *Whatcom Reveille* reported, "On every street corner we see distress. Some say that Fairhaven is over-run by hobos. Opposite the hotel they congregate asking alms of passerbys." In a heavy blow to the spirits around the bay, on April 9, 1895, a disastrous explosion occurred at the Blue Canyon Mine on Lake Whatcom. Twenty-three men were killed in what is still the worst industrial accident in Whatcom County history.

Despite all of the bad news, faint glimmerings of hope remained. J.J. Hill and his Great Northern tease continued to ignite the dreams of optimists. He and C.X. Larrabee apparently had joint business interests, and they met from time to time to deliberate. It was the popular notion that Hill had made massive investments in Whatcom County real estate and that Larrabee was his silent partner holding the property in his name, shielding Hill's interest via a partnership agreement. On several occasions the papers reported that C.X. Larrabee had traveled back east to confer with Hill. Then it was reported that Hill would be visiting Larrabee in Fairhaven on June 19, 1895.

The community was ablaze with excitement. Perhaps this would be the long-awaited announcement of Fairhaven as the Great Northern terminus. Precisely at two and nine-tenths minutes past six o'clock, the train with Hill's luxurious private car, *Manitoba*, arrived at the Fairhaven station "at a smart dog-trot and—hades—it never stopped but rolled on through at its dog trot pace and went up to Westminster." Hopes dashed once more, Fairhaven was livid. Larrabee said nothing.

The city was outraged. Once again Hill had teased, built up hopes and then dashed them.

August 14, 1895, "Mark Twain is coming!" was the talk of the town. Smoke from forest fires filled the air. The fires had begun in a heat wave that hot

12.3. Lighthouse Building, built of Chuckanut sandstone, stood on the southeast corner of Holly and Cornwall until 1959, when it was demolished to make way for the Seattle 1st National Bank Bldg. Its top floor held a 700-seat theater/opera house. It received its name from its builder, Col. John C. Lighthouse of Rochester, New York. Galen Biery Photographs #2456, CPNWS.

summer which had seen the thermometer hit 87. The community was worried. Twain's opinion of Fairhaven was considered important to its future and citizens were told to treat him as a distinguished guest. He should "receive the attention of the Board of Trade and the Cascade Club."[1]

He would speak at the 700-seat Lighthouse Theater above the bank in Whatcom. He was put up in Fairhaven's best accommodations, the third floor bridal chamber at the Fairhaven—a suite of rooms in the corner turret, with a private bath (one of only two in the hotel), and a veranda available to his room complete with rocking chair.

The day before Twain's arrival, August 13, 1895, Frances Payne Larrabee gave birth to the Larrabees' first child, Charles Francis Larrabee. The infant was born in the Larrabee's suite on the third floor of the Fairhaven.

Twain's performance was a great success, and he was escorted back to Fairhaven by Roland Gamwell, entertained at the Cascade Club and sent to bed at the Fairhaven across the street. Smoke from the forest fires had concealed his view of Mt. Baker and most else, and seemed to create Twain's major impression of Bellingham Bay's cities.

---

1   The Board of Trade was Monahan's tavern, and the Cascade Club was the gentlemen's club and bar on the third floor of the Mason Block.

1896 saw Fairhaven's economic status sinking further and further as the national recession continued. There were few tourists at The Fairhaven Hotel, the Fairhaven National Bank closed, while paying its debts with "100 cents on the dollar." The Bennett National Bank of Whatcom, that had begun as the First National Bank in Fairhaven, also closed. Only C.X. Larrabee's Citizen's Bank survived. Businesses were closing or moving out of town. W.A. Woodin, in business in Fairhaven since 1882, went into receivership. John Cissna, no longer hopeful of business in Fairhaven, announced he would move his stock of groceries to Whatcom where he would build a large store at Champion and Grand. P.J. Lair moved his factory to New Whatcom.

One bright spot was the Fairhaven Pharmacy. D. Alverson, proprietor, moved into new quarters in the Mason Block.

Hopes were stirred again in November when it was learned that Sam Hill (son-in-law of J.J. Hill) was conferring with Larrabee. The rumor was they were talking about a Japanese steamship line docking at Fairhaven. The community hoped for a good result, and its remaining optimistic leaders continued working toward civic improvement.

In April of 1896, Mayor Eli Wilkins proclaimed Arbor Day in Fairhaven. He appointed an Arbor Commission chaired by J.J. Donovan. The Commission raised $167 by popular subscription and planted 417 shade trees along the streets of Fairhaven. Of particular significance were the 119 smooth-leafed elms, planted 25 feet apart along 3,000 feet of Front Street (now State Street), to the border with New Whatcom. Thirty-five of those trees still stand there at the date of publication in 2015.

The stated purpose of this ambitious project was to hide the unsightly cedar stumps left from the clearing of the Fairhaven town-site only eight years previously.

The spring of 1897 began to see a flicker of revived hope. "Lord" Newton built his salmon cannery in Chuckanut Bay, just south of the productive Chuckanut Quarry. The quarry had been cutting stone for building construction from the cliffs beside the bay for many years. In Fairhaven, the first salmon cannery was being built. The Puget Sound Sawmill and Shingle Company was working on its waterfront. The W.A. Woodin mill was operating again. And perhaps the greatest news of all was that gold had been discovered in the Klondike. The Alaska Gold Rush began, and the ever enthusiastic boosters of Fairhaven predicted that an Alaskan steamship company would be making Fairhaven its southern terminus. Once again, that honor went to Seattle and it would be almost 100 years before passenger travel from Bellingham Bay to Alaska would be realized.

12.4. A Smoky Fairhaven. The numerous sawmills, smokestacks and forest fires created an unhealthy atmosphere in early Fairhaven much to Mark Twain's dismay. Galen Biery Photographs #1186, CPNWS.

Times were still bad. George A. Black, who had been a stalwart of the Fairhaven Land Company, moved to greener pastures in Idaho. In September of 1897, perhaps the darkest news of all, it was announced that the iconic Fairhaven Hotel would be closing its doors.

The landmark hotel would now simply be the residence of the growing Larrabee family and a monthly rental residence for several others. As if to put an exclamation on the announcement, the Larrabees were able to announce the birth of Edward Payne Larrabee who was born that August in the Larrabee's suite.

Fairhaven would remain in its depressed state until early in 1898 when it was saved by the salmon.

Fairhaven in 1897

The Sanborn Fire Insurance Maps provide a reliable and accurate depiction of the buildings of the Fairhaven of 1897. We show here the eight key blocks of the cities business district. This image depicts the buildings in those blocks at the height of the boom in 1890. It also shows the economic deprivation seven years later as Fairhaven's boom turned to bust.

The Sanborn Company conveniently showed the result of that economic decline by indicating vacancies. To emphasize the dilemma facing the now depressed city we have indicated the vacant buildings with a large 'VAC'.

Most of these buildings were small wood frame structures hurriedly constructed during the boom years of 1889 and '90. Many of them were so lightly built that they were braced on the north side to prevent swaying in the prevailing southerly windstorms.

As Fairhaven's economic woes continued many of the wooden buildings decayed to the point that demolition became necessary. A few of them burned. The resulting vacant lots stood empty for many years.

We have indicated important structures relevant to todays' reader with large numerals.

1. The Fairhaven Hotel
2. Mason Block
3. Waldron Block
4. Terminal Building
5. Knights of Pythias Building
6. Morgan Block
7. Monahan Building

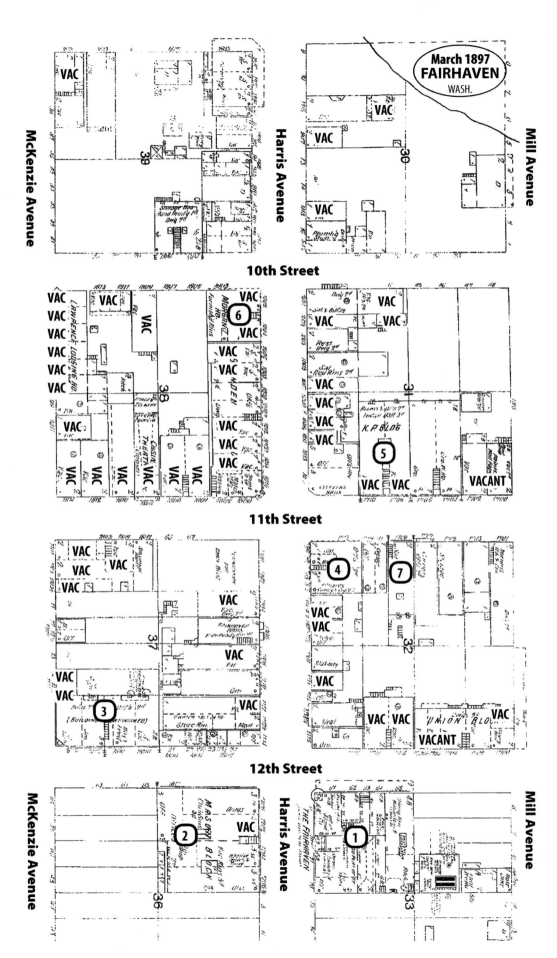

McKenzie Avenue

Harris Avenue

Mill Avenue

March 1897
FAIRHAVEN
WASH.

VAC

VAC

VAC

VAC

Plumb'g Shop

10th Street

VAC
VAC
VAC
VAC
VAC
VAC

VAC

VAC

L'AWRENCE LODGING HO.

VAC
VAC

VAC

VAC

VAC

VAC

VAC
VAC
VAC

VAC

VAC
VAC

6

VAC

VAC

VAC
VAC
VAC
VAC
VAC

K. P. BLDG

VACANT

VAC
VAC

5

11th Street

VAC
VAC
VAC

VAC

VAC

VAC

VAC
VAC

3

4

7

VAC
VAC

VAC

VAC
VAC

VACANT

UNION BLO

VAC

12th Street

McKenzie Avenue

Harris Avenue

Mill Avenue

MASONIC
BLOCK

VAC

2

THE FAIRHAVEN

1

13.1. Ocean Dock and the cannery site, 1891. This photo was taken from the top of Poe's Point showing a fully functioning Ocean Dock served by the Fairhaven & Southern RR, and several steamships. The cannery would grow in the foreground. The tide flats east of the RR trestle would eventually be filled and used for industrial land but the RR track would remain on that same right of way to this day. Galen Biery Photographs #1598, CPNWS.

CHAPTER 13

Saved By The Salmon

In February of 1898 the depression finally ended for Fairhaven. The *Fairhaven Herald* announced in that month that a tin can factory would be built at the foot of Broadway (now 10th St.), and operating by that April. "The factory would be making 125,000 cans per day for the new Fairhaven salmon cannery to be built at the foot of Harris street, Ben Seborg of Ilwaco had purchased the cannery site and will be investing $40,000."

The announcement proved to be accurate. The Pacific Sheet Metal Company soon built a large red brick building on their site, just north of the present Chrysalis Inn. The site is now a city park. The foundation and cement floor of the old building can still be seen at the railroad track level.

Further help for the depressed economy came when the Fairhaven Foundry and Machine Company was established at the foot of Harris Avenue to make machinery for canneries. Then the newspaper announced, "The Franco-American Packing company will build at Fairhaven at a favorable site chosen by Mr. Larrabee on the waterfront."

By June of 1898, *The World Herald* was able to report,

> "Fairhaven is canning 1,200 cases daily. Aberdeen packing 2,500 cases salmon daily, Franco-American 12,000 cases salmon daily, Bellingham Bay at Chuckanut 2,000 cases daily. Thompson Fish since July 1897, 100,000 salmon pickled, Seaborg-ready June 25."

The salmon canning business had exploded onto the scene bringing relief to Fairhaven's struggling economy and hope for its future. Soon the newspapers had more good news to report,

> "The Fairhaven Land Company is repairing Ocean Dock, and The Fairhaven Hotel will be reopened on March 1st."

13.2. Salmon Trap. A salmon trap is being installed with a pile-driving construction scow. Note the lead from the shore guiding salmon into the trap, and the watchman's shack where a man was stationed to ward off fish pirates. Salmon traps were outlawed in Washington in 1934 by Initiative 77. 64.17% of voters favored closing the traps. Galen Biery Photographs #3321, CPNWS.

By January of 1899, the papers were able to boast "Fairhaven is Booming", and the next month, "A Gigantic Fish Deal", "Pacific American Fisheries Capitalized." The newly formed PAF would soon buy Eliza Island for their shipyard and purchase a large number of fish traps, injecting a significant amount of money into the economy. They purchased the bankrupt Franco-American Cannery, and on its site began construction of the largest roofed structure in the state of Washington. They packed 30,000 salmon in August of 1899 and that summer over 1,000 people were employed on the Fairhaven waterfront.

As if to add seasoning to the stew, the Normal School opened that September and C.X. Larrabee opined of the new teachers college, "It is as good a business addition for us as a factory employing 75 men." (If he could only know how right he was and how much he had under-estimated its eventual impact.)

In August of 1899, surveyors for the Great Northern began locating a waterfront track along the coastline to Skagit County. They were calling it the Chuckanut Cutoff. Population began to return to Fairhaven. The newspapers announced there were now 3,500 residents.

1900 also brought changes for the Fairhaven Land Company. C.X. Larrabee retired from its management, and A.L. Black assumed control. In dividing its assets, Larrabee retained the 260 acres of the old Poe Claim, which his heirs would eventually develop into the Edgemoor residential district. He also kept four lots on Harris Avenue, 50 lots in the second addition, 15 outside acres, and The Fairhaven Hotel. To manage his large real estate holdings he incorporated a new company, Pacific Realty. He and his wife Frances were the president and vice president. Other stockholders were Cyrus Gates, Bert Huntoon, and lawyer E.S. McCord.

In May of 1900, the newspapers were able to report a new building that would grace the corner of Harris and 11th. "Architect Cox was supervising the construction of the P.J. Nelson Block." It was to be the home of Citizens' Bank, reorganized under S.M. Bruce, president. Its construction was a direct result of the Pacific American Fisheries purchase of the salmon traps. P.J. Nelson had sold his traps to Onffroy, the organizer of PAF, and was now re-investing some of his proceeds.

The salmon canning industry had rescued Fairhaven from its financial destitution and would sustain its economy for the next 66 years.

•••

Two radically different new developments of the 19th century had ushered the salmon canning industry into early Fairhaven. The coming of the railroads to the Pacific Northwest and the invention of the lowly can opener.

The canning of foodstuffs had its beginnings in the prior century when Napoleon Bonaparte, seeking a way to feed his massive and mobile army, offered a lucrative prize for anyone who could invent a way to preserve and transport the necessary foodstuffs. A Frenchman, Nicolas Appert, discovered a way to preserve food in bottles in 1809 and claimed the prize. Eventually an Englishman, Peter Durand in 1810, developed the first method of preserving food in metal cans. By 1817, the fledgling canning business had a promising start, however packing of meats in the early hand-made cans was extremely expensive. In the beginning a can maker could only turn out three of the labor intensive cans each day.

The sale of canned foods was largely limited to governments purchasing canned meat to feed their military forces. The rudimentary cans were not easily used. Soldiers were forced to open their cans with bayonets. The naval forces used hammers and chisels. Finally in 1840 the can opener was invented. Production of readily opened cans by automatic machines was developed, and the canning industry blossomed.

The first salmon cannery was built on California's Sacramento River shortly after the Civil War. Its success and the resultant overfishing of the

Sacramento began a gradual movement up the coast and caused canners' attention to focus on the seemingly inexhaustible salmon runs in the Columbia River. By the latter decade of the 19th century, the runs on the Columbia began to diminish and salmon packers again focused their attention northward—to the significant salmon runs in the inland sea behind Vancouver Island. These prodigious runs were created by the dozens of rivers flowing to the sea from the surrounding Olympic and Cascade mountains, and the mighty Fraser River which drained almost the entire area of British Columbia.

•••

The industry had a slow start on the Salish Sea. The first cannery was started in Mukilteo in 1877 by George T. Meyers. The first cannery in the northern area of the Sea was begun in 1892 on the Semiahmoo spit across the bay from Blaine, Washington. The next year that cannery was sold to the newly formed Alaska Packers Association of San Francisco (APA), and operated on the spit for many years, both as a cannery and as the stateside staging area for its Alaskan operations.

The abundant salmon runs and the obvious economic opportunities were attracting speculators to many sites in the region. Just a few weeks after the Fairhaven Canning Company opened in 1897, a cannery opened in Chuckanut Bay. Henry "Lord" Newton and John Baines formed the Bellingham Bay Canning Company. Their cannery was built on the eastern shoreline in sheltered Chuckanut Bay, about three miles south of Fairhaven. Newton, an Englishman, was nicknamed "Lord" Newton because of his British accent and his dignified ways. He optimistically built a very large house at the top of Knox avenue at 19th Street, that would in later years become O'Cain's Nursing Home; then in 1977, the site for (SPIE) The Society of Photo-Optical Instrumentation Engineers' handsome modern structure. Newton's company was short-lived, but the cannery was not. The Corporation went bankrupt after its first season. The cannery was bought by Dan Campbell and the Astoria and Puget Sound Canning Company, which operated it successfully until after the Second World War.

Fairhaven had entered the salmon processing industry in 1885, when an opportunist named Oswald Steele opened a fresh fish operation and shipped salmon to the East Coast by rail. His idea was to freeze individual salmon in blocks of ice, pack the salmon-bearing blocks in sawdust in a box car, and send them on their way to the waiting Easterners. With good luck the trip took five days and the salmon arrived still surrounded in ice. With bad luck the trains were late and the salmon was inedible. His fresh fish business was short-lived, but in 1897 he leased a tidelands lot adjacent to the Hill-Welbon Dock (Taylor Avenue Dock), and with $10,000 of capital built the first Fairhaven

13.3. Bellingham Canning Company. The white buildings in the foreground are the Bellingham Canning Company. Owned by the Welsh family, it was located between PAF's cannery and its shipyard. Galen Biery Photographs #480.1, CPNWS.

cannery. Steele employed Chinese workers, introducing a labor practice that would become standard for Fairhaven packers.

1897 was the year of a big Sockeye salmon run. Steele's Fairhaven Canning Company did reasonably well. Well enough to show its promise and to be re-capitalized in 1898. It continued to operate for two more years and then in 1901 Steele sold to the Pacific Packing and Navigation Company.

1898 saw the opening of two other canneries in Fairhaven, one was the Franco-American North Pacific Canning Company, which eventually became Pacific American Fisheries. The other was the Aberdeen Canning Company, a Columbia River packer. It would become the Bellingham Canning Company in 1905 when Robert Welsh and the Loggie brothers, Bellingham shingle mill owners, purchased it and renamed it. These two canneries would be neighbors on the Harris Bay beach adjoining Dan Harris's old Ocean Dock until the 1930s. The Bellingham Canning Company eventually sold its Fairhaven cannery to PAF, but continued operating several canneries in Alaska until the mid-1960s.

The canneries were both situated on land provided by C.X. Larrabee. Larrabee was eager to encourage economic development in Fairhaven where he had invested so much of his treasure and his enthusiasm. The collapse of the Boom in 1893 had left him eager to support new economic activity for the city's depressed economy.

13.4. Roland Onffroy. Whatcom Museum.

He is thought to have offered very reasonable lease rates on the cannery land. It is probable that part of his arrangement was accepting stock in those risky ventures. It is likely that his son Charles Larrabee's long-time presence on the PAF Board of Directors was a result of that initial stock ownership.

Franco-American North Pacific Canning Company was created by the promotion of a legendary pitchman, Roland Onffroy.

Onffroy had been born in France of a French father and an American mother. He was educated at St. Cyr, the French military academy. He served in the Franco-Prussian War of 1870-1871. He came to the United States in 1880 and soon gained his U.S. citizenship. Onffroy arrived in Fairhaven in early 1898, determined to make his fortune in the salmon canning industry. As was his usual modus, he came with little money, but with the sales skills to sell his dreams to those with money. He was a consummate promoter.

He succeeded in convincing C.X. Larrabee to provide the cannery site under favorable lease terms. It is believed that Larrabee invested $2,500 as well. Onffroy was associated with the French Consul in Seattle, and the rumor quickly spread that the capital for the business was provided by wealthy French investors. (Franco-American had been capitalized at $25,000.) In reality Onffroy had neither the capital, the management skills, nor the knowledge of salmon canning techniques necessary to make the business prosper.

The cannery was constructed largely on credit, and the business promptly failed. Franco-American filed for bankruptcy in November of 1898 when it could not pay its gas bill of $341. In addition, the cannery owed money to Morse Hardware, Quong Tuck a labor contractor, Puget Sound Saw Mill & Shingle, the Sunset Telephone Company, and Deming & Gould.

Deming and Gould were Chicago food brokers representing canneries and packing houses, selling their goods to wholesale grocers across the country. They were the marketing agency for Onffroy's salmon. Their connections to Chicago wealth were the key to Onffroy's next promotion.

Realizing that one of the reasons for Franco-American's failure had been the inability to buy adequate supplies of salmon at affordable prices, Onffroy secured options on 25 prime fish trap sites around the Salish Sea at outlandish prices. He then borrowed money for rail fare and expenses, and boarded the train for Chicago to sell his dream, Pacific American Fisheries.

With Deming and Gould in the vanguard, the proposition was made to the financial barons of Chicago. Food brokers, railroad men, lawyers and financiers agreed to invest and Roland Onffroy's dream was realized. In February of 1899, Pacific American Fisheries was incorporated in the state of New Jersey and capitalized at $5,000,000. The stock was divided into 50,000 shares at $100 par value. 10,000 of those were preferred shares. The officers of the corporation were H.B. Steele, a Chicago wholesale grocer, President; John Cudahy, a Chicago meat packer, Vice President; T.A. Moran, a prominent Chicago attorney; and major Chicago financiers, Charles Councilman, John Harris, Samuel Scotten, and Joseph Snydacker.

The Fairhaven community was ecstatic at the news. A $5,000,000 canning company was replacing the failed $25,000 cannery. The fish trap owners had reaped a bountiful harvest, and the approximate $600,000 paid for their traps added immensely to the wealth of the community. The expected annual payrolls for the community were projected at $250,000. Perhaps most important, these seasoned and competent Chicago businessmen would build a lasting business based on sound and proven business judgment.

In short order, PAF purchased the bankrupt Franco-American cannery for a mere $11,000 and began enlarging it. They purchased the Island Packing Company at Friday Harbor on San Juan Island, and they would soon purchase Eliza Island in Bellingham Bay to be used as their shipyard and fish trap storage area.

By the first week of August 1899, the cannery was in operation canning the flood-tide of Sockeye and Pink salmon that ran in that year. At times the cannery was overwhelmed with the fish being delivered from the traps. The first year for the new company was a huge success. The newspapers reported a first year profit of $500,000. In addition, more than 900 men, women and children had found employment; along with 100 Chinese workers and another 400 men employed on the fish traps or outside the cannery. Pacific American Fisheries had arrived to make its lasting contribution to the economy and culture of Fairhaven.

Roland Onffroy's future was less rosy. He was on the Board of Directors of the company. He had served as cannery manager in that first exciting and successful year, but soon rumors began to circulate that the Chicago owners did not want him running the company. His lack of management skills and his record of promotion may have counted against him with the solid (and perhaps stolid) business folks who had invested so heavily in the enterprise.

In mid-February 1900, Onffroy traveled to Chicago to present to the Board of Directors his proposal for a slate of new projects: a fertilizer plant,

13.5. Inside the warehouse. When first built this was the largest roofed building in the state. Galen Biery Photographs #0482, CPNWS,

an expansion of the cannery, new docks and a shipyard. The directors were not prepared to move that fast, they were not comfortable with Onffroy the promoter. He was forced to tender his resignation. The word of his resignation sent shock waves through the Fairhaven community.

The directors chose Onffroy's successor wisely. Everett B. Deming—the younger of the Deming brothers of the Deming and Gould brokerage firm—moved to Fairhaven in 1900 to assume the presidency and management of Pacific American Fisheries. He would lead it to growth and profitability for the rest of his life. He would become an important leader in the Bellingham business community until his death in 1934. His contributions to Bellingham's growth and culture were many and of major importance.

Pacific American Fisheries' role in the economic health of the greater Bellingham was immense, but its importance to the viability of the Fairhaven district cannot be overstated. The huge corporation which grew to have 13 canneries in Alaska and became the largest salmon packer in the world, was supported by surrounding suppliers—all providing employment and vital help for the Fairhaven economy. Their large Fairhaven operation was the world's largest individual salmon cannery.

13.6. Pacific American Fisheries officers, (L to R) E.B. Deming, president; Bert Huntoon, engineer; Thad McGlinn, sec. treas.; Arthur Deming, gen. mgr.; and M. Brousseau, auditor. Galen Biery Photographs #1141.1, CPNWS.

Burpee and Letson, which made canning equipment, was located on Harris Avenue across from PAF. Reid Boiler Works, which built boilers and canning retorts, also was located on Harris originally, moving to their new location at 10th and Douglas in 1912. The PAF shipyard, which moved from Eliza Island to the Fairhaven site in 1918, was a major industry in its own right.

PAF was simply the glue that held the economic fabric of Fairhaven together. Generations of young people in Fairhaven learned the value of work in the PAF warehouse or their summer jobs in its Alaska canneries. Hundreds of Fairhaven households owed their survival to its year-round payrolls. The large Croatian community depended on the canneries for much of their livelihood. The men were fishermen and mill workers. Many of the Croatian women worked in the cannery in season.

Pacific American Fisheries provided its economic support to Fairhaven until 1966. The world-wide market for canned salmon had waned. The salmon runs in the Salish Sea had dwindled drastically. The business had struggled each successive year since the end of World War II. Finally, the directors of the company (which had physical assets worth $30 a share), realized that by selling they would make a large profit for the share-holders, most of whom had paid $10 a share. The directors chose to sell.

13.7. Purse Seining. After salmon traps were outlawed in 1935, purse seining became the primary way of catching salmon for the canneries. Galen Biery Photographs #0481, CPNWS.

The Friday Harbor cannery was sold to George Jeffers, who reopened it as a pea cannery. The majority of the Alaska canneries were sold to a consortium led by Peter Pan Seafoods for $2.4 million.

The Bellingham land and buildings were all sold to the Port of Bellingham for a mere $598,000, in a deal that then-Port manager Tom Glenn said (in an oral history interview) was the best business deal of his long career as Port manager. The remaining Alaska canneries were sold or simply closed, and the storied history of the world's largest salmon packer came to an end.

Fairhaven entered another bust period.

CHAPTER 14

Terminus At Last

Becoming the terminus of a transcontinental railroad had been the dream of the towns of Bellingham Bay since just after the Civil War. The very real possibility of the Northern Pacific ending its line at the bay had caused the excitement of 1871. Nelson Bennett's belief that the Great Northern would build its terminus on the bay had fired the great Fairhaven Boom of 1888-1892. Now, perhaps too late, in 1902 it all came to pass. Both of the great railroads were to terminate on Bellingham Bay, perhaps facilitated by a court decision in the Whatcom County Superior Court.

The Great Northern Railroad, using its subsidiary, Seattle and Montana Railway Company, purchased the Fairhaven Land Company's Fairhaven & Southern Railway in 1902, giving it rail from Seattle, through Sedro, to Fairhaven and Blaine.

The Northern Pacific had made a purchase agreement in 1902 with the Bellingham Bay & Eastern Railway, the line built by Donovan and the Blue Canyon Mine owners, from the Blue Canyon mine on Lake Whatcom to the coal bunkers on Bellingham Bay. The BB&E, encouraging a deal, quickly extended its line from Blue Canyon up to Wickersham where they connected with the Northern Pacific.

Knowing that the NP wanted to service the prosperous Fairhaven canneries, Donovan negotiated with Fred Wood of the E.K. Wood Company for a right of way through the mill site (now Boulevard Park). Donovan's 1901 diary notes, "Went to visit Fred Wood, offered him three options." A few weeks later his diary mentions him visiting with Earles of Puget Sound Lumber and Shingle for the same purpose. He succeeded with Woods and with Earles and was able get permission to extend the BB&E rail south to the foot of Harris over a wooden trestle above the tide flats.

The BB&E had optioned a small piece of land at the foot of McKenzie and Harris from the Fairhaven Land Company in 1901, on which they wanted to build a passenger depot They still needed to cross a small strip of Great Northern and PAF land to get to the depot site. In January, the papers announced that J.J. Donovan would send a "force of men" to begin excavating at Deadman's Point for a terminal building site.

Apparently Donovan's vaunted skills as a negotiator did not succeed with the Great Northern or the salmon packing company, and so suit was brought petitioning the court to condemn the right of way to the depot site under the Washington State laws of Eminent Domain.

Now the plot thickened as it was made evident that the Great Northern also wanted the site for a depot, and wanted to stop the Northern Pacific advance. On Jan. 31, 1902, the Seattle & Montana sued to condemn the depot site that both companies desired. The land in dispute was only 0.55 of an acre at the foot of Harris and McKenzie.

On March 21, 1902, Superior Court Judge Jeremiah Neterer found for the Bellingham Bay and Eastern Railway Company in its petition to condemn a 28-foot right of way to the depot site.

One of the arguments used in the lawsuit was that the Bellingham and Eastern had reached accord with the Northern Pacific to sell their line to the transcontinental giant, conditioned upon laying their track up from Lake Whatcom to Wickersham and to connect there to the Northern Pacific line. They had also agreed with the NP to extend the BB&E rail from the coal bunkers just north of what is now Boulevard Park, to the foot of Harris Avenue in Fairhaven to property they had optioned in 1901 from the Fairhaven Land Company. On that parcel they would build a passenger depot for the Northern Pacific. This would then make Fairhaven the salt-water terminus of the Northern Pacific upon completion of the sale. The Judge considered this result would be in the public interest and ruled for the condemnation to proceed.

With the condemnation of tide flats and land now approved, the BB&E was able to construct their rail line across the Great Northern track at the E.K. Wood Mill, across the mill property paralleling the Great Northern track (which ran along the shoreline). Then, with the use of trestles, across the tide-flats and open water, curving their line to just touch at the Taylor Avenue industries (the can factory and warehouse buildings); and across Harris Bay to the foot of Harris Avenue on dry land. The Northern Pacific had thus completed its westward journey at last.

It is an interesting side note to mention that J.J. Donovan had helped them much of the way. First in Montana in 1882 and 1883 as a fledgling civil engineer. Then on their Cascade Division project building across and through the Cascade Mountains in 1884 thru 1887, and now on Bellingham Bay in 1902. Donovan's diary mentions that the BB&E was sold to the NP for $570,000.

14.1. Cutting through Poe's Point. The track had to be cut through the great mound of glacial till and a trestle built across the face of the southern beach. The Great Northern Depot at Harris and 4th can be seen through the gap. Galen Biery Photographs #0446, CPNWS.

Although Donovan had engineered and negotiated the sale he was a very minor shareholder in the BB&E and would have profited little from the sale.

Donovan's role in community history was further assured when the Fairhaven and Southern Railway (that Donovan had engineered from Sedro to Fairhaven and then on to Blaine as an employee of the Fairhaven Land Company), was sold to that other great hope for a transcontinental line, James Hill's Great Northern Railway.

Shortly after their purchase in 1902, the Great Northern began their Chuckanut Cutoff, first penetrating the great glacial moraine of Deadman's Point and later negotiating with the Northern Pacific to purchase the contested depot site and build their Fairhaven passenger depot. The Great Northern paid $66,000 for the depot site, and by December of 1902 were excavating Deadman's Point for their track and the beginning of the 23-mile line along the Chuckanut shore southward. The completed cutoff was reported to have cost two million dollars.

The Northern Pacific settled for a small freight and passenger depot built on piling alongside their trestle just a few feet south of its connection with the Taylor Avenue Dock.

Fairhaven and Whatcom found themselves finally serviced by three transcontinental railroads, if one includes the Canadian Pacific and the Bellingham Bay & British Columbia railroad connections over the international border at

14.2. The Chuckanut Cutoff. A steam engine runs along the new Great Northern track built in 1902. Galen Biery Photographs #0022, CPNWS.

both Sumas and Blaine. These three railroads were to provide vital transportation for the economies of the soon-to-be consolidated City of Bellingham, transporting the timber products, coal, and canned salmon upon which the economy was based.

The railroads arrived too late to make Fairhaven the Imperial City, or Whatcom the *Empress of the North*. Those plaudits had already been handed to Seattle and Tacoma and Vancouver BC—each developing the port facilities to service marine transportation to the Pacific Ocean and the Orient. But they did arrive in time to sustain the industry that had settled on Bellingham Bay allowing the community to prosper and grow.

CHAPTER 15

Consolidation

T he growth of four small towns around the shores of Bellingham Bay was a historical anomaly. Whatcom and Sehome were created side by side by their separate owners at about the same time. Fairhaven, owned entirely by the somewhat cantankerous and independent Dirty Dan, developed just a mile or two down the bay. Finally, filling the gap between them, the coal mining village of Unionville grew around its coal mine, and existed briefly until it completely burned in a forest fire that swept the land. The charred land was later purchased and platted as Bellingham by speculators. Now there was a continuous strip of towns joined border to border around the bay. Their separateness made little sense from the start and there was talk of consolidation from the very beginning of settlement.

Consolidation was a gradual process retarded by personal interests, factional jealousies and typical human resistance to change. Whatcom and Sehome made the first move in 1891, when the efforts of Pierre Cornwall caused Whatcom and Sehome to become one city and be renamed New Whatcom. That rather awkward name was changed in 1901 to just Whatcom. Bennett and Larrabee, in 1888, bought Bellingham from Eldridge and Bartlett, and merged it with Fairhaven. Now there were only two cities to consider consolidation. It took seven more years for the leaders of both cities to gather enough support to put consolidation to a vote.

On July 22, 1895, a petition signed by more than 20% of the qualified electors of each of the cities of New Whatcom and Fairhaven—"praying that the cities of New Whatcom and Fairhaven be consolidated"—was presented to the City Councils of the two cities

The minutes of the Fairhaven City Council tell the story. Ordinance number 198 of the City of Fairhaven called for a "special election to consolidate Whatcom and Fairhaven into one municipal corporation under the name of The City of Bellingham." It sets the date of the election, Sept. 21, 1895. A similar ordinance was passed in the New Whatcom council and the election was held.

The *Whatcom Reveille* reported the results.

> "Only 25% of Fairhaven voters favored consolidation. In Whatcom 75% were in favor. Perhaps Fairhaven fears being swallowed up by her more commercially significant neighbor. Perhaps she still awaits the miracle named J.J. Hill and still harbours dreams of commercial affluence within Hill's empire."

Discouraged but undaunted, the business leadership continued its efforts. The *Herald* reported in 1897.

> "There is a new thrust for consolidation with Whatcom. Larrabee favors it, Donovan favors it, Fairhaven still feels Whatcom will steal what business they have left. Lawyer Kerr argued in a consolidation meeting urging Fairhaven to combine forces with Whatcom to work together. 'Not drive away manufacturing enterprises by each.' A vote was taken at the meeting, it was 70% to 11% against consolidation."

Once again, in 1902, the consolidation question came to a head. C.X. Larrabee declares he is for it and has always been for it. J.J. Donovan wrote a letter to the papers favoring it. Those Fairhaven interests opposing it distributed a flyer listing the dire consequences consolidation would bring to Fairhaven.

The question was taken to the voters on October 28, 1903. This time the result was different. Fairhaven voted 580 for consolidation and 339 against. Whatcom voted 1583 for and 252 against.

J.J. Donovan declared in a letter to the papers "My Fellow Citizens, you have done the best days work that has ever been done for the benefit of this community."

The new city of Bellingham would have a population of 25,000 according to the Polk city directory. It would be the fourth largest city in the state behind Seattle, Tacoma, and Spokane.

The consolidation became official in July of 1904.

A FEW CONSOLIDATED FACTS
on CONSOLIDATION

PLAIN QUESTIONS TO PLAIN PEOPLE!

Consolidation Will Consolidate Business Centers.

Do the property owners of Fairhaven who purchased lots from the Fairhaven Land Company on the assurance that the center of business would be about the corner of Twelfth and Harris, desire that business center removed two and one-half miles to the north?

Would this removal of the business center enhance the value of Fairhaven property?

Consolidation Will Consolidate Post Offices.

Do the people of Fairhaven who get their mail at the general delivery of the postoffice; those who purchase stamps and money orders; send and receive registered letters and parcels, wish to go to Whatcom to transact this business?

Consolidation Will Consolidate Insurance Offices.

Is it the desire of our people to drive out every Insurance Agency in the city, and by that means lose a number of our best business citizens?

Consolidation Will Consolidate the Railroad Depots on the Bay.

Do the people of Fairhaven desire to release Mr. James J. Hill from the written contract by which he is now bound to maintain and support *in the City of Fairhaven*, as good a depot as anywhere on the line?

Consolidation Will Consolidate Telephone Offices.

Do people who send and receive long distance telephone messages, desire to have our Telephone Office removed to Whatcom?

Consolidation Will Consolidate Express Offices.

Do the citizens of Fairhaven who send and receive express matter want to be compelled to go to Whatcom to do so?

Consolidation Will Consolidate Telegraph Offices.

Do the citizens of Fairhaven who send telegraph messages want to go to Whatcom to transact that business?

Consolidation Will Consolidate School Districts.

Such School District will be entitled to but one High School. It will necessitate the construction of an expensive building. Such building will be located in Whatcom, where there is a majority of High School Scholars. Do the citizens of Fairhaven desire to compel their children to go to Whatcom to attend High School?

Consolidation Will Consolidate Fire Departments.

Do our Fire Boys desire that their Chief and our Fire Engine, shall be transferred to Whatcom?

Consolidation Will Consolidate Population.

Do business men and property owners desire that the population of Fairhaven be decreased twenty-five per cent. within 60 days after consolidation?

Do the people of Fairhaven desire to release the Street Car Company from all obligations by which they are now bound, so that in future, they can make all improvements at the Whatcom end of the Bay?

Do the people of Fairhaven want to be placed under the rule and dominion of the "Cornwall Company;" a corporation that never pays a tax; never fulfills a promise, and never does anything to advance and develop the industrial interests of the Bay?

Consolidation will place the City Government in the hands of the Whatcom Council. Can Fairhaven laborers and contractors expect recognition and employment at their hands?

All Electors, should give these and other questions, deliberate consideration before casting their vote.

15.1. Anti-Consolidation Flyer. This flyer listing the dire results for Fairhaven should consolidation be approved by the voters was found among the J.J. Donovan papers. Donovan supported consolidation, but must have wanted to study the opposition's arguments. All of their dire predictions came to pass after consolidation. Donovan Family Papers, CPNWS.

16.1. Fairhaven High School before the fire. Galen Biery Photographs #2960. CPNWS.

16.2. The ruins of Fairhaven High School after the fire, 1935 (looking north). Galen Biery Photographs #640, CPNWS.

CHAPTER 16

After Consolidation

Fairhaven ceased to exist as a city in July of 1904, when the new charter of the consolidated City of Bellingham went into effect. For now and forever Fairhaven would be just a neighborhood, a location, an Urban Village, and a memory. The name Fairhaven would live on however. The village was sometimes called South Bellingham, or The Southside, but the name Fairhaven would never leave the vernacular of the people living on Bellingham Bay.

The consolidation of the two cities was not without challenges. Not the least of those was the forging of a sense of community among a populace that had formerly been active rivals. The two high schools, Whatcom and Fairhaven, had a long and well-established rivalry, which slowed the ability of the community to come together. The two high schools were now to be governed by the consolidated Bellingham Board of Education. Initially there was an effort by the Board to ignore the old school names and just call them North High School and South High School. For several years a joint graduation ceremony was held in a neutral location. Beck's Theater on Cornwall Avenue was the venue for several of the early combined ceremonies.

Despite the school board's best efforts the old school names persisted on local tongues. Whatcom High School and Fairhaven High School continued their heated rivalry until halted by fire. On January 1, 1935, Fairhaven High School burned in a catastrophic fire. Sad as the loss of the old school was, the fire might have had a beneficial effect on Bellingham's emotional divisions. The School Board determined to build a new, modern consolidated high school. In September of 1937, a sparkling new Bellingham High School opened its doors on Cornwall Avenue to the great excitement and pride of the entire community. The surviving Whatcom High School was changed to a junior high school, the role it plays to this day. At last all of the teenagers in Bellingham were attending high school under the same roof. They soon forgot their sectional differences and were joined in a common loyalty to their school and to their community. Consolidation was complete.

The opponents of consolidation back in 1903 had predicted dire effects on the Fairhaven business community should consolidation be approved. Their predictions proved to be correct. Rather quickly business activity shifted north to Holly Street. That was where new stores were built, that is where the national chains saw the best opportunity. The former Whatcom was where the theaters were built. Kress, Newberry, JC Penney, and Sears built their stores "downtown" where, served by the electric trolley line, south-side residents could shop just as efficiently as the larger population that lived north of Holly Street.

The governmental center was in former Whatcom. The 1892 New Whatcom City Hall became the Bellingham City Hall, and was just a few blocks from the County Courthouse. It made sense that former Fairhaven lawyers would move their offices north. The post office, the major library, the doctors' offices were all in Whatcom.

Fairhaven, while not the business hub of the community, still prospered modestly because it hosted the rapidly expanding salmon packing industry and those businesses that supported it. Pacific American Fisheries and the Welsh family's Bellingham Canning Company provided hundreds of steady year-round jobs, and thousands of seasonal jobs during the fishing season. The two canneries sat side-by-side on the south shore of Harris Bay, the present location of the Alaska Ferry, the Shipyard and Fairhaven Marine.

Fairhaven also retained a number of local retailers, Fairhaven Pharmacy, Brown and Cole Grocers, and a block north on 11th, the grocery store owned by the big Croatian, Andro Mardesich, serving the large Croatian community that had developed in Fairhaven over the years.

There was a hardware store in the old Knights of Pythias building, and a few small merchants up and down Harris Avenue. Fairhaven settled into a stable neighborhood economy, always retaining its own sense of identity, but now as an integral part of the City of Bellingham.

Perhaps the best way to describe what was happening in the Fairhaven of those years just after the consolidation is to list stories from the local newspapers.

The *Fairhaven Herald* continued to report the news of the day:

> Sept. 16, 1904. The 60-foot-tall Deadman's Point is to be removed at a cost of $50,000.[1]

> 1904 also brought the news that the Larrabee-owned Fairhaven Hotel was for sale. Contact Cyrus Gates at Pacific Realty.

---

1   This would not be completed until 1935.

April 22, 1905. *The Herald* announced that Dan Harris's old hotel on 4th Street would be demolished to make way for a railroad track. The track construction would also require that the historic Fairhaven Land Company Store building, across the street from the hotel would have to go. The Fairhaven Land Company Store was the only general store in town in 1888-9. It was twice moved to new locations and finally landed at 4th and Harris across the street from Dan Harris's hotel and adjacent to Ocean dock.

By July of 1905 the population of Bellingham had increased by 5,000 people and prospects looked good.

Feb. 25, 1906. The Larrabee family still lived in the Fairhaven Hotel, and on this day, their second son, Benjamin Howard Larrabee was born in the hotel.

June 23, 1906. The Nelson Block, the bank building on the corner of 11th and Harris got a new tenant when the Northwestern State Bank moved from their corner location in the Fairhaven Hotel.

1906. The Fairhaven Land Company store building at 4th and Harris was demolished.

June of 1906. The *Herald* reported a rumor that Cyrus Gates and his brother would be buying the Fairhaven Hotel from Larrabee, along with his other Fairhaven interests. Larrabee's worth was estimated to be $8,000,000. "C.X. Larrabee and J.J. Hill have had a dispute for a long time. If Larrabee would dispose of his interests in Fairhaven, the Great Northern would invest."

February 1907. Charles E. Lind bought the old Bellingham Hotel site on Bennett and 11th for $5,000, planning to build bunkers to hold gravel. Lind was a paving contractor and the owner of Lind Gravel Company.

June 1907. Polk says Bellingham population is now 35,736.

July 7, 1907. Larrabee is to spend $250,000 improving a large tract of land, 196 acres, as sites for fine homes.

December 5, 1908. City population is now 40,000.

On September 17, 1914, *The Herald* reported perhaps the greatest change of all, the death of C.X. Larrabee. One of the major figures in Fairhaven's growth and development, the principal businessman of Fairhaven—and perhaps the wealthiest man in Bellingham—Larrabee "collapsed at the Harris Street entrance to his hotel home. He died of a heart attack on the steps of the Hotel. He was seventy-one years of age."

17.1. Earles-Cleary Sawmill. This large mill on the filled tide flats was a major employer for southside workers. "Rocky" Hansen, Joe's father, worked here. Galen Biery Photographs #3065, CPNWS.

Chapter 17

The Prince and The Pauper

It was mid February, 2008, on a cold wintry day that Steve the mailman delivered to my mailbox a distinctive yellow envelope. My attention was immediately riveted to its return address: C.X. Larrabee, Durham, North Carolina. My curiosity aflame, I tore open the envelope to find, typewritten on what I was to learn was his signature yellow paper, a letter from C.X. Larrabee II, the grandson of the C.X. Larrabee of historic Fairhaven fame. That letter was to initiate a fascinating round-robin of correspondence between three devotees of Fairhaven history that would continue until Larrabee's death in 2014 at the age of ninety-two.

The letter, written in his unique style, complimented me on my book, *Boulevard Park,* and explained how he had come upon it with this paragraph:

> "My copy of your excellent work has come courtesy of Joe Hansen, formerly of Donovan Avenue, who has been founder, CEO, recruiter, fund-raiser, editor, utility infielder and Honorary-Chairman-into perpetuity of the Fairhaven High School Alumni Association. My genuine thanks to Joe."

I had been told a bit about C.X. by his childhood friend Bob Miller. X, or Xie, as he was called from childhood was reported to be exceedingly bright and witty. Our subsequent years of correspondence surely confirmed that. I was to learn that he had written for a San Francisco newspaper, and retired on the East Coast after a career as editor and communications executive for a prestigious scientific organization headquartered in Durham. I was excited to make his acquaintance, as he was surely a prime source of information about Fairhaven and his prominent family. Xie did not disappoint.

His charming letter put me in touch with an additional source of Fairhaven history, Joe Hansen, who I was to learn was equally committed to preserving the Fairhaven story and could tell it from a far different perspective.

I found myself in a three-way correspondence with these two gentlemen.

17.2. The prince, C.X. Larrabee II. Young C.X. by his grandmother's pond in 1931-32. Collection of the author.

17.3. The paupers. Joe Hansen (left) and his brother, Doug, with their expedition leader Rocky. The Chuckanut sandstone quarry can be seen in the background. C.X. Larrabee II collection.

We wrote shared letters that gave great pleasure to each of us. Each letter written was copied to all parties. We wrote almost weekly in the beginning years as we sought to share and learn Fairhaven history. This profusion of frequently lengthy letters resulted in two three-inch-thick binders absolutely filled with the correspondence. It was a perfect partnership. I would fire them questions about growing up in Fairhaven in the 1920s. They would eagerly respond with reminiscences that leapt from their minds, stimulated by my searching and sometimes impudent questions. The letters are filled with good humor, the joy of remembrance and the excitement of discovery. Their pages reveal a fascinating look at growing up in the Fairhaven of the 1920s and '30s, and are filled with historically important information.

At some point in our correspondence Joe Hansen described the two of them as *the prince and the pauper.* I thought it the perfect way to describe the vast economic and social distance between Larrabee and Hansen in their youth. Joe was the *pauper,* having grown up on lower Donovan Avenue. His father Rocky, every day walked to work at the Earles-Cleary Lumber Mill.

C.X. was the *prince* in Joe's analogy, having lived with his wealthy and influential parents in the lovely home they had built at #2 Hawthorn Road, just across the street from the home of his widowed grandmother Frances Payne Larrabee. Frances lived in her mansion at the Edgemoor hilltop (now called Lairmont Manor). The Larrabees were surely the wealthiest family on Bellingham Bay. Xie indeed lived a princely childhood.

17.4. The Charles Larrabee family moved to their magnificent new home at #2 Hawthorn Road, seen in the background of this snowy photo. Lairmont is pictured to the right. C.X. Larrabee II collection.

A brief biographical sketch of these two notable Fairhaven residents is entirely in order in a book of Fairhaven history. Not only did they play a role in that history, but they grew up in the 1920s and '30s in Fairhaven, and offer their individual memories of that period of the village story.

C.X. LARRABEE II

X was born in 1922 to Charles F. and Mary Brownlee Larrabee. His grandfather and namesake had died in 1914, and his grandmother had moved out of the Fairhaven Hotel two years later, into her new home in what is now called Edgemoor. Her eldest son Charles was her assistant in running the family businesses. Their real estate holdings were managed under the name Pacific Realty. They owned a coal mine in Roslyn, Washington. Their offices were in the old hotel building. Charles and his family lived across the street, at 1304 Harris Avenue, in a house that still stands on the southeast corner of Harris and 13th as of this writing.

In 1928, the Charles Larrabee family moved to their magnificent new home at #2 Hawthorn Road, and there young Xie grew up with his two sisters, Frana and Jean. He roamed the fields and woods of the family estate with his dog Murphy, reveling in the wildness of what is now Edgemoor and Dry-dock Point (commonly called Clark's Point). He attended the Campus School at the Bellingham Normal School, the teachers college that has morphed into the present Western Washington University.

He was a freshman at Fairhaven High School in the class that would have graduated in 1939, and he was in awe of its Student Body President, star halfback on the football team and champion sprinter, Joe Hansen.

On New Year's Eve, 1935, Fairhaven High School burned to the ground. X was sent off to a prep school in the East the next year and didn't make contact with his high school hero again until they were old men. He married Margaret Dwelle, Bellingham High School class of 1940. His career at Dartmouth College was interrupted by World War II, and like most men of his generation he went off to war. He served in the U.S. Marine Corps in the South Pacific.

17.5. C.X. Larrabee II in 1992. Collection of the author.

Upon his return he worked for a time at the *San Francisco Chronicle*, then the Stanford Research Institute, then a brief stint as an editor for *Colliers Magazine*. He finally settled in as manager for information services, public relations and publications for the Research Triangle Institute—owned jointly by the University of North Carolina and Duke University. The Research Institute works in many disciplines, under contract to clients in business and in government. He retired after 26 years at Durham and lived there for the remaining years of his life. He and his wife had seven children.

17.6. Garland's Lagoon and Marsh. Taken with Sandison's cirkut camera this photo shows: (L to R) Fairhaven High School on the hill; the ice skating pond in the marsh; the Chinese Garden with the long shelter where the Chinese raised pigs; PAF shipyard mast-making skids and work area on the beach; the Larrabee mansion high on the bare expanse of the moor; Sailor Jack's shack on the beach; Cap Garland's shipyard and home on piles at the extreme south end of the lagoon. Sandison, 1918, Gordon Tweit Collection, Whatcom Museum.

JOE HANSEN

Joe was born in 1919. He was raised in a modest home that still stands at 614 Donovan Avenue in lower Fairhaven. His father Roy "Rocky" Hansen, worked in the Earles-Cleary Lumber Mill, just a short walk from their Donovan Avenue home. Joe and his brother Doug remember a boyhood of freedom wandering the beaches of Fairhaven, climbing the stile to enter the undeveloped Larrabee lands to the south, swimming in the lagoon behind 1st trestle in the summer, and ice skating on the "rubber ice" of the lagoon in the winter.

17.7. Joe & Barbara Hansen. Joe and Barbara at their retirement home in the Sawtooth Mountains of Idaho. Courtesy of Sherrie Hansen.

The brothers were star athletes. When they reached high school age their prowess on the playfields resulted in treasured memories for Xie, who idolized them. Joe would later go on to play sports at the Normal School, until he too was drafted into war service.

Joe became a U.S. Navy pilot and spent most of his war years ferrying personnel to and from the Pacific Theater in hundreds of flights across the ocean. After the war, Joe earned an engineering degree and spent his working years in the pulp and paper industry. He retired to Anacortes with his wife Barbara, where they lived for many years as Joe enjoyed his passion for sailing. After years of cruising the San Juan Islands on their boat, Joe and Barbara moved to the Sawtooth Mountains of Idaho, where they owned a

mountain cabin. Joe still lives in the small town of Grangeville, Idaho, where his son and grandchildren live.

The *prince* and the *pauper* provided me with much of my knowledge of Fairhaven of the 1920s and '30s. You will find nuggets of their insights and memories throughout this history. One day, the hundreds of letters that passed between us will be gifted to the Center for Pacific Northwest Studies at the Washington State Regional Archive in Bellingham, to be included with their historical papers. Researchers in future years will find much of historical interest in them and will find them amusing reading as well.

I have selected just a few of the interesting stories told me by these grand gentlemen to illustrate what life was like in Fairhaven in the 1920s and '30s. In many cases I have quoted directly from their letters.

Joe Hansen may have had the better childhood. He grew up in lower Fairhaven just a couple of blocks from the canneries and shipyard, and only a few blocks from Garland's Lagoon. He could watch the Chinese cannery workers with their hair in queues,[1] tending their vegetable garden and pig farm on the slope behind the marsh, where Bellingham now processes its sewage. He recalls them walking back and forth between the China House and the cannery and their garden plot, with baskets of vegetables suspended from each end of a pole carried over the shoulder.

He has vivid memories of Saturday challenge football games, in which the lower Fairhaven kids would play the Happy Valley or the South Hill kids in a rough and tumble game—played with the only football they could afford, a tin can wrapped with layer after layer of tape until it looked like a real football. He remembers the kindly neighbor woman, who reputedly had worked at the brothel on lower Harris run by "Black Mammy." She invited the neighborhood kids in for cookies to his mother's dismay.

My frequent letters asking for information and locations prompted Joe, in his neat engineers style to draw a map from his memory. I have included the map and Joe's detailed explanations. I think the reader will find them as interesting and informative as I did. There is much to be learned from his drawing. Note that he marks off those streets that are "filled streets," meaning that they were buttressed with wood posts and filled with gravel to raise them above the swampy land. Look the map over closely. Joe has located places and structures now long gone and mostly forgotten. Find the X-marks delineating the fence around the Larrabee property. Then note the two stiles that the Larrabees installed to allow folks to cross the fence and enter their property. The Larrabees never meant to keep people from their vast acreage with the fence, they just wanted to contain their cattle.

His other memories follow the map key, shown on the next two pages.

---

1 Archaic, a braid of hair worn at the back.

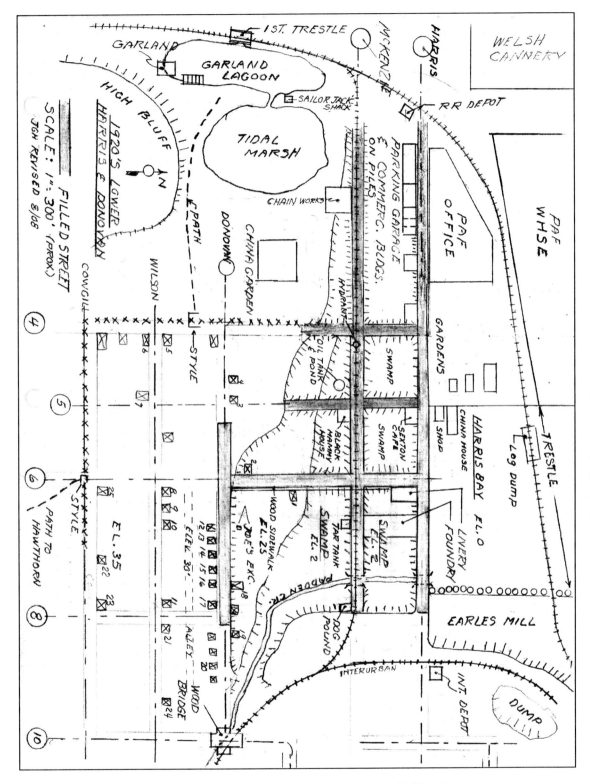

17.8. Joe Hansen's memory map, 2013. Joe drew this to illustrate his stories of childhood. Collection of the author.

Houses shown on the Hansen Map, identified by number, described with Joe's words.

1. John Johnson, longshoreman. John's wife was the lady believed to have worked in some role for the "black mammy" and was very kind to the neighborhood kids.

2. Sigfusson family of five girls and two boys. Later occupied by the Brandt family. The two-story house was supported on posts to provide entrance at street level. Turk Brandt, one of four sons and two sisters raised in this house, built a 30-foot gill-net boat beside the house. The keel was about six feet below street level. This was just before WW II. I never knew how he got it to a launch site.

3. McNealy home. Not much recall of McNealy other than he had the first home-built radio in the neighborhood and a huge antenna in the yard.

4. Bowen Family; little recall.

5. Bloxham family of three girls who enjoyed the swimming at first trestle, and joined the boys for after dark beach bonfires. Garland provided a dressing room for the girls in one of his boat sheds, the boys dressed in the bushes.

6. Hazen family home. Virgil Hazen was a four-year letterman in all sports at Fairhaven High in the early 1930s.

7. Chevalier home. Dad was a machinist for PAF and was observed rolling a small pedal car up 6th Street a few days before Christmas—built for his two small sons.

8. Leroy Harshman home. Leroy was our Ward Councilman. Mrs. Harshman was perhaps the only female in the neighborhood with an education beyond high school. She taught my mother shorthand and other secretarial skills.

9. Blondheim home. Earl Blondheim and I strung an overhead telegraph line between our homes. Source of the fine copper wire for this came from dismantling a Model T Ford spark coil.

10. Dahlstorm family. Vic Dahlstrom was the engineer on the steam tugboat that Richard Holyoke operated for Puget Sound Tug and Barge.

11. Mr. Small had a very large vegetable garden. Mother would give a boy 25 cents and say, "please go to Mr. Small's and bring home a dozen ears of corn."

12. My boyhood home at 614 Donovan. This modest bungalow was built by my uncle Dave Dana, from lumber scraps carried home from the sawmill on his bicycle. I did a bit of remodeling over the years while visiting, and found pieces as short as 16-inches spanning wall studs. Tons of nails. I suspect a few other neighborhood homes may have been built in this fashion. This home and others had what was called a wood-shed fronting on the alley. These structures were built like a small barn, with an attic and overhanging roof ridge with hook or steel ring for hoisting heavy objects (hay bales?) from the alley to attic storage. At ground level, a sliding barn door permitting entrance of a car or a wagon. There were no cars in the neighborhood in the period of my early youth (1920-30). Stacked firewood, a small workshop, and a wire enclosure for a few chickens occupied the floor space in our woodshed, until the arrival of Dad's first car, a six-cylinder Model B Ford.

    Across Donovan from #s 12, 13, 14, and adjacent to #18, was our grassy baseball diamond. After supper on a warm summer evening, a dozen or more kids and parents would play softball. A long fly ball might end up rolling into the swamp.

13. Brooks/Marko Gazija home. In the 1920s this house was occupied by a Mrs. Brooks and two very pretty daughters, Mary Ida and Dorcus. Marko Gazija, a purse seine owner, and his family bought this house in the early 1930s, and were still living there when I left in 1942.

14. Rousch/Sourney Thiel house. Ben Rousch and family occupied this home in the early 1920s. Ben was a Washington State Highway Patrolman, and a favorite of the kids because of his powerful motorcycle. The family had the first factory-built radio in the neighborhood. The rest of us had crystal sets or home-builts. Neighbors were invited in to hear *Amos and Andy* and other favorites of the times, all from KVOS.

   Ben's only son, Ben Jr., was an early World War II casualty. The next occupant was the Thiel family. Sourney Thiel had a firewood business and owned stands of timber near the Old Samish Highway. He would cut and deliver firewood for a price, or a homeowner could arrange to buy firewood logs laid on the ground. The homeowner would cut and split the firewood. My brothers and I earned money for school with this arrangement. Mrs. Thiel played her banjo at high volume with the doors open on a warm summer evening.

15. Henry Green house. Henry worked in the Earles-Cleary Lumber Mill until it burned. If memory serves me correctly, he was rescued from the conveyor to the waste burner, after an accident in the mill.

16. Brandt/Weirach home. The large Brandt family occupied this house before re-locating to 6th and Donovan, I have little recall of the Weirach family.

17. Joe Donnelly home. Joe was the Superintendent of the Bellingham Water Department. The kindly Mrs. Donnelly allowed the neighborhood kids to come to her home on Sundays to read the *Seattle P.I.*'s colored funny papers. Few homes in that period could afford a newspaper.

18. Plancich home. This house was unique for its large size and appearance. It was built on the grade below Donovan Avenue. It was supported on posts. Much garlic was raised in a large garden, and I recall the fragrance from the long strings hung to dry from the floor joists under the house. I believe the family were purse seiners. One entered the house by walking across an elevated walkway from Donovan Avenue.

19. Costello family house. I believe the Costello family to have been one of the few fishing families of Fairhaven of Italian descent.[2]

20. Hoag family house. Mr. Hoag was in an early day mechanical refrigeration business. His son, Gail, had a talent for building interesting steam- and chemical-powered devices in his woodshed workshop—all this while attending Lowell Grade School. I well remember his rocket-powered boat models, which burned the fuel underwater.

21. Battenfield house. Bill Battenfield was an unfortunate young man with a mental problem that required infrequent commitments to the mental hospital in Sedro-Woolley. Insensitive kids of that day were very cruel and teased Bill a lot.

22. Rowland house. I remember little of the Rowland family, except that son Leonard was a very large and handsome Fairhaven High Schooler and a powerful athlete. For all that size and formidable appearance, Leonard was a marshmallow.

23. Briscoe house. Little is remembered about the family, but daughter Ethel and her big white horse are unforgettable. The horse had the build of a draft horse and she rode him bareback. With so many open fields to ride, Ethel was seen at any time and in any part of the neighborhood. With long hair down her back, I often thought of Ethel as our clothed Lady Godiva.

24. There was an un-named young man raised in this house and he seemed destined for a future in prison, and so it turned out.

---

2   In this case Joe was wrong. The Costellos were Croatians who changed their name from Kostolonivich.

17.9. Cap Garland's shipyard and home on piles, 1918. Excerpt from Sandison cirkut photo.

GARLAND'S LAGOON: The lagoon between the railroad track and the present City of Bellingham sewage treatment plant was once called Garland's Lagoon, so named for the Captain "Cap" Garland, whose houseboat and shipyard once occupied the southern end of the lagoon. Garland had lost an arm in some earlier and unknown catastrophe, but despite his handicap he built exquisite cedar "clinker-built" lap-strake rowing boats and yacht tenders. His boats were about 10 feet in length and sold for the princely sum of $35. Joe remembers Garland very skillfully sculling his boats, with a transom-mounted oarlock, down the lagoon and into the bay with his one arm. His house was built upon large cedar logs more than capable of floating it, but somehow he had managed to get the whole thing built atop pilings driven into the bottom of the lagoon. The piling held his home above all but the highest of tides. Garland had a talking parrot.

The lagoon was connected by a floodable passage to the tidal marsh behind it. At high tide the salt water would flow into the marsh and mix with the residual freshwater, coming from the surrounding high lands and the frequent rains. In freezing winter weather, the brackish salt-infused water would freeze into what Joe Hansen described as "rubbery" ice, creating fun skating and sliding opportunities for the kids of the neighborhood.

SAILOR JACK: In a shack on the beach at the north end of Garland's Lagoon lived Sailor Jack. Jack had a large aggressive black dog, which kept strangers and curious young boys away and allowed Jack to live the solitary life that he apparently desired.

WOODCUTTERS IN THE LAGOON: The beach on the east side of the lagoon near Sailor Jack's was the location of a wood-cutting operation. There, men with a large drag-saw would saw logs too large for the head rigs of the various local saw mills. The logs would be floated to the lagoon to be reduced to firewood, sold to local residents for $5–$10 a cord. The drag-saw was a reciprocating saw with an 8-foot blade. It was powered by a gasoline engine attached to a wooden frame. The blade and engine were connected by a trombone-like slide arrangement, leaned up against a large log, and secured to it by "dogs" driven into the bark. Laying on the ground, some of these logs were taller than a man. Some of the logs were so large they were split with a partial stick of dynamite.

CHINA GARDEN: The slope and hillside behind the salt marsh contained the China Garden and a pole-supported galvanized, corrugated-roof building where the Chinese workers at PAF raised their vegetables and kept pigs. The building was about 50-feet wide

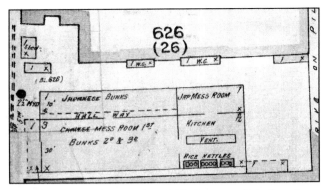

17.10. China House. Shown on the 1906 Sanborn map. Note the water closets on dock over the water. Harris Avenue at 6th.

and 100-feet long. The entire area covered about three acres. The Chinese workers at the PAF salmon cannery lived in the China House, a rough-hewn building on piling over the water. It too was a pole structure with galvanized, corrugated-steel roofing. Hansen does not ever remember seeing a Chinese worker in the upper Harris business area.

BLACK MAMMY'S: This was a house of ill repute on the corner of McKenzie and 5th Street. Joe recalled the all-hours taxi traffic. A neighbor woman who was reputed to have worked for Black Mammy in some capacity would invite the kids into her home to read the Sunday funnies and enjoy cookies and graham crackers. Joe's mother was alarmed. Joe said, "I do not remember when black Mammy's house ceased operations. It had to have been somewhere in the period of my high school years (1932-1936)."

I asked Joe if the homes in lower Fairhaven had outhouses or sewers. "The sanitary system for that neighborhood was anything but sanitary. Indoor plumbing was in most houses. I don't recall ever seeing an outhouse. I suspect that was because the slope of the land allowed for the use of the open ditches which carried away the effluent from cesspools (a dug pit with a concrete cover and a clay tile pipe leading the liquid overflow to the nearest ditch. If the soil was sufficiently porous much of the liquid waste never got to the ditch). The ditch on Donovan emptied into the swamp between Larrabee and McKenzie. Cesspools were never pumped as in a modern septic tank system. If it filled with solid waste a new pit was dug."

Young C.X., the *prince*, had quite different memories of his childhood and I suspect had less fun than the *pauper*. His letters reported playing with his sisters at their grandmother's home, climbing the water tower on the crest behind the house, and rowing the rowboat in the small lake his grandmother had built on the property. He confirmed that the vast acreage of Edgemoor was made available to the locals. He even told about the "Hooverville" encampment that developed behind 2nd trestle during the Great Depression.

18.1. Hooverville in Edgemoor, This was part of the Hooverville on Larrabee property at "second trestle" there were more habitations on the beach below. Galen Biery Photographs #1710, CPNWS.

18.2. Hooverville site in 2015. The site is verified by triangulation of Orcas, Lummi and Pt. Francis in the background. This is now 422 Bayside Road in the Edgemoor district. Photo by the author.

CHAPTER 18

The Thirties and Forties

THE GREAT DEPRESSION

The great depression slammed Fairhaven as hard as it did the entire nation. The giant Earles-Cleary Lumber Mill that had provided employment on the Fairhaven waterfront since 1904, was forced into bankruptcy in 1929 shortly after the stock market crashed. All businesses were severely stressed, but the salmon still ran every fall, and people still had to eat. Canned salmon remained a food staple, so perhaps Fairhaven fared better than many areas of the country. Pacific American Fisheries and the Bellingham Canning Company, Bellingham Chain and Forge, Reid Boiler Works, the can factory at Taylor Dock, the Croatian fishermen and their purse-seine boats all kept working. Life in Fairhaven continued quite normally, and in fact, at least for some folks, Fairhaven was a haven of employment.

HOOVERVILLE IN EDGEMOOR

The vast Larrabee acreage that would later be developed into the Edgemoor residential district extended west to the saltwater and to the Great Northern railroad track. Where the Larrabee land met the water of the bay behind "second trestle" was a pleasant beach and a natural camping spot. The location was too ideal to be missed by the "knights of the road", those wandering men made homeless by the Depression and riding the rails looking for work and a warm meal. The beach was adjacent to the railroad. It was within walking distance of Fairhaven and was shielded from the disapproving glances of those citizens who still had roofs over their heads. All over the nation the homeless were seeking shelter in temporary small encampments that came to be called *Hoovervilles*, a slam at President Herbert Hoover who had the misfortune of being elected just before the Depression struck.

Frances Larrabee was not one of those who disapproved of these unfortunate people. Rather, she sympathized with them, and as long as they did no damage or harm, she allowed them to set up their camps on her property. In fact, she installed an iron pipe which brought fresh water from a spring on her property to the beach. The Larrabee family with its great wealth never lost sight of the needs of their community nor those less fortunate than themselves.

18.3. Charles Francis Larrabee, 1895-1950. Charlie Larrabee, the son of C.X. and Frances Larrabee was a prominent and much respected businessman and community leader. Galen Biery Photographs, #3492, CPNWS.

THE OKIES

In 1934, as the twin devils of the Depression and the Dustbowl pounded the now impoverished state of Oklahoma, entire families fled to the west. Among them was the Bowman family. Three generations of Bowmans boarded their Model T Ford trucks in Oklahoma and headed west for Fairhaven. There was little cash in their pockets. When their meager cash reserves ran out, they would stop in farm country and seek work in the fields to earn the gas money to continue. The youngest member of the family was little Jack. He had been born in 1932. It is from him that I have learned this story, and it is because of him that I include it.

The Bowman's finally arrived in Fairhaven after their cross-country exodus. Jack's father, Lonnie "Jack" Bowman, immediately found a job in the Pacific American Fisheries warehouse. It was the best paying job that he had ever had. The family was ecstatic. Times were hard, but they were grateful for work and an income. Young Jack recalls that they ate a lot of *dents*. A dent was a can of salmon that had somehow been dented in the cannery operation and, as damaged goods, was not saleable in the marketplace. The dents were sold to the employees at a very reasonable price. Jack reports that he likes canned salmon to this day.

18.4. Bowman Home, 2015.

Eventually the family was able to buy a house on 21st Street. Jack attended the southside schools, Larrabee and Fairhaven Jr. High, and then graduated with the author, from Bellingham High School in the class of 1950.

What is truly special about this story is that this refugee from and sur-
vivor of the Dust Bowl went on to achieve great success in the business world.
After high school, Jack attended Western Washington State College, gradu-
ating with a teaching degree. He soon left teaching and took a job with a
pharmaceutical company as a sales representative. He rose through the ranks
in the drug business to the position of Company Group Chairman, in charge
of the pharmaceutical operations of Johnson & Johnson, one of the world's
largest drug companies. Jack retired in 1994, but remained on their Board of
Directors until 2004. Jack and Joanne returned to Bellingham upon retirement, where their philanthropy and community spirit have advanced the
cultural life of Bellingham in great measure. His life is a classic American
rags-to-riches story.

18.5. Finnegan's Shopping Tower, 2015. The concrete building was built in 1929 to house Finnegan's Fairhaven
Pharmacy and two rentals. The Pharmacy occupied the corner until 2015. The combined rental spaces have
been the home of Dos Padres restaurant since 1973.

FINNEGAN'S TOWER

George Finnegan was the owner of the Fairhaven Pharmacy, which had
been located for many years in the corner of the Mason Block, and later in the
Monahan Building. In 1929 Finnegan built the Fairhaven Pharmacy building
at the corner of 12th and Harris Avenue where the drugstore, through several
owners operated until its closing in 2015. The skinny Irish druggist possessed
a prodigious sense of humor and natural Irish wit. He boasted that his shopping *Tower* was as wide as it was tall and if it ever blew over in a windstorm
it would still be straight up.

He added that he would be putting into a time capsule in the cornerstone
of the building an "original Aztec horned toad" whose "heart beat only once
ever five minutes and which ate every fifty years." Finnegan was delighted
when the Humane Society took the bait and scolded him publicly for his inhu-
mane treatment of a toad. Finnegan relented and announced that he would

OUR CANDYDATE

Hon. Geo. Finnegan

18.6. George Finnegan. This delightful caricature of Fairhaven's great humorist was drawn by Harold Wahl of the Wahl's Department Store family. Gordon Tweit collection.

be placing the toad on the roof where it would enjoy a "better view of beautiful Bellingham Bay."

Finnegan's timing was far less successful than his humor. The building was no sooner completed than the great Depression struck. Finnegan was soon in financial trouble. The word on the street was that the beloved pharmacist was about to lose his building.

One day Charlie Larrabee walked into the drugstore and sought out his friend. "George, I would like to buy your building and rent it back to you at a favorable rate." The friends made the deal, Finnegan remained in business until his death in 1939 at the age of 56. Years later, when better times returned, Larrabee sold the building back to Finnegan's successor Rene LeCasse, again at a favorable price.

Finnegan was a fixture in Fairhaven and in the larger community. Known and loved for his levity, good humor and generosity.

In 1952 an earnest young lad was hired by Rene LaCasse to deliver prescription drugs from the Fairhaven Pharmacy. Gordon Tweit began his epic career as the delivery boy for Fairhaven Pharmacy. He would eventually own the building and the business and establish his own legacy as friend, pharmacist and historian for generations of Fairhaven families. Gordie's eclectic collection in the basement of the pharmacy ranks as one of Bellingham's historic treasure troves. In 1991 Gordie sold the business to Robb Johanson who had been his delivery boy. Robb carried on the historic business until its closing in 2015. An era had ended.

FINNEGAN WAY

In the summer of 1935, only a year after the Bowmans arrived in Fairhaven, the City Planning Commission and a Chamber of Commerce committee came forward with a plan to change the route of the Pacific Highway as it entered Bellingham.

Until the opening of Chuckanut Drive in 1916 and its paving in 1921, the only way to get to the City of Bellingham had been by boat or train or on foot

18.7. The Pacific Highway was squeezed down into the 25-foot-wide 12th Street until Finnegan Way was constructed.

through the forest trails. In the 64 years since Dan Harris had landed on the beach at what would become Fairhaven, there had been no road access to the towns of Bellingham Bay.

When Chuckanut Drive was completed and became a part of the Pacific Highway, vehicular travel to Bellingham was finally possible. The new international highway came off of the scenic cliffs of Chuckanut and right through the heart of Fairhaven. It crossed Padden Creek on the 12th Street bridge in front of Fairhaven High School, passed the Mason Block, the Fairhaven Hotel and leaving the 50-foot-wide commercial streets of Fairhaven, headed straight up the much narrower 12th Street in front of the Carnegie Library. 12th Street had been platted as a residential street and was only 25-feet wide.

When 12th Street was designated the Pacific Highway, the enterprising Gilmore Oil Company built a gas station at the large curve in the street at Douglas Avenue. Douglas had been the borderline between early Fairhaven and the old town of Bellingham. The early towns had both been platted in 1883, but by different owners and different civil engineers. They had failed to make their streets connect, and consequently when Fairhaven and Bellingham were joined in 1890, the jog in 12th Street became necessary. With the arrival of the Pacific Highway the awkward curve made a perfect location for a gas station.

18.8. There is no known photo of the Gilmore gas station at 12th and Douglas. This photo shows the location at the jog in the street. Photo by the author.

Gilmore Oil Company had recently built their tank farm and fuel dock beside the Taylor Avenue Dock. A dwelling now stands at 929 12th street where the Gilmore gas station was located.

Farther north, where 12th Street descends to State Street, a motel was constructed to serve the travelers on the highway. The log-sided motel buildings can still be seen there. They are now rental residences.

An international highway running through a narrow residential street was clearly not an ideal situation. Civic leaders sought a solution, and that solution was to build a *cut-off* from where 12th Street narrowed to the much wider 11th Street. 11th was the former Front Street of the old town of Bellingham, and was platted to be twice as wide as 12th Street. It also contained the rails of the municipal trolley line up its center, and still had room on either side of the rails for a lane of traffic and a lane of parking.

The proposed cut-off would begin its deviation from 12th at Mill Avenue, and would continue two blocks, flowing into 11th and eventually State Street. It was the obvious solution to a serious transportation problem.

Because it was the international highway, Federal funds were found to be available and both state and local politicians got behind the plan. The cost was estimated at $30,000, most of which was for the purchase of private land, as the cut-off would cut through two city blocks filled with buildings.

Negotiations to purchase the land were begun. Much of the land was assembled by H.M. Petterson, the realtor for the Larrabee family's Pacific Realty Company. Petterson was a canny and capable realtor known for his negotiating skills, but he apparently met his match with Frances F. Waldron, the widow of C.H. Waldron. Waldron, the banker, businessman and participant in the great Fairhaven Boom had died in 1929.

Among the many properties that Waldron bequeathed to his wife was a strip of land necessary to the cutoff. Frances Waldron set an outlandish price on it and refused to budge. It appeared that she alone might end the project. Her hold out was pushing the project deadline perilously close to the date that the Federal funding opportunity would disappear.

Once again it was Charlie Larrabee to the rescue. This liberal and generous businessman advanced $6,000 that would purchase the Waldron property. The Federal financing was preserved and the project was able to proceed.

The most notable of the buildings in the cut-off footprint was the venerable Kulshan Club. The Kulshan Club had its beginnings as the Cascade Club at the height of the Fairhaven Boom in 1889. It was a prestigious gentlemen's club first located on the third floor of the Mason Block. It was to the

18.9. The Kulshan Club, The building, now an apartment house, still stands on Finnegan Way. Galen Biery Photographs # 2350, CPNWS.

Cascade Club that Roland Gamwell had delivered Mark Twain, thirsty for a whiskey or two after his 1895 address in downtown Whatcom. The Cascade Club boasted a membership of about 150 men, the prominent and notable men of South Bellingham. They were forced to change their name in 1904 when they attempted to incorporate. A name search revealed that Everett already had an incorporated Cascade Club. The Bellingham club changed its name to Kulshan, the Native American name for Mount Baker, and completed their incorporation. Now they could build their club building on 12th Street. Its grand opening was on September 2, 1909.

In 1935 the Kulshan Club found itself in the way of the cutoff. They either had to move their building or see it demolished. Their solution was to simply move the building westward to a lot purchased on 11th Street, directly behind the original location. Now it had its eastern entrance on the new cut-off and a western entrance on 11th Street. The building still stands in that location today, now rental apartments.

There were several residences in the way of the new roadway. Most of them were demolished, but the new residence of grocery-man Andro Mardesich was simply moved up hill half a block, where it sits today across from the Carnegie Library, the first house up-hill from the Flag Plaza at 1101 12th Street.

The cut off was completed in 1935. It was named Finnegan Way to honor the beloved pharmacist George Finnegan, who had played such an important role in the Fairhaven community and was so admired for his humor and wit.

FAIRHAVEN HIGH SCHOOL BURNS

In the early morning hours of January 1, 1935, fire broke out at Fairhaven High School and the school burned to the ground. The School Board took the fire as an opportunity to consolidate the community's high schools and began the planning for a new Bellingham High School. During its planning and construction years, the high school students from both sides of town were crowded into Whatcom High School.

A sparkling new Bellingham High school opened in September of 1937 and Whatcom High was converted into a junior high school. A new building at the charred high school site in Fairhaven became Fairhaven Junior High. Community pride in the modern new high school, and the assimilation of students from both sides of town did much to erode the ancient rivalries between Bellingham's northside and southside.

18.10. The Fairhaven Boathaven. Port of Bellingham Records, Whatcom Museum.

THE FAIRHAVEN BOATHAVEN

In 1937 the Port of Bellingham, responding to the need for protected moorage for the growing fleet of salmon seine boats and a modest fleet of pleasure craft, financed a *boathaven* on the Fairhaven waterfront. Douglas fir piling was driven into the sea bottom in front of the old Earles-Cleary mill site. The individual piles were cabled together making a strong stockade-like barrier providing protection for the commercial salmon fishing fleet and the very few pleasure boats owned by local residents of the day. The new "Boathaven" was especially convenient for the Croatian fishermen, most of whom lived nearby on 11th 12th and 13th Streets of the South Hill.

A NEW INDUSTRY:
BELLINGHAM PLYWOOD CORPORATION 1941–1953

Eleven months prior to the U.S. entry into World War II, a group of Bellingham business leaders found a new use for the lumber mill land previously occupied by the Earles-Cleary mill.

Cecil Morse – President of Morse Hardware Company, Charles F. Larrabee – scion of the Larrabee fortune and prominent businessman, Lewis "Lew" Wallace – the Bellingham Chevrolet and Buick dealer, Dan Campbell – salmon canner, Henry P. Jukes – Bellingham National Bank, Percy Browne – lumber retailer, and two Seattle men joined forces and incorporated The Bellingham Plywood Corporation.

With $628,000 of invested capital they built a large plywood plant on the Fairhaven industrial area below the bluff. Their 100,000-sq.-ft. frame building was built on piling to hold it above the filled tideflats. The Company was incorporated on Jan. 7, 1941. Morse was President, Larrabee Vice President, and Wallace, Secretary. The plant manager was Arthur O. Olson. Plywood was made from the abundant Douglas fir logged in the surrounding hills.

18.11. Bellingham Plywood Corporation. Galen Biery Photographs #3358, CPNWS.

The peeler cores were sold to Adrian Yorkston, who had a small sawmill beside Padden Creek on the south side of Harris Avenue. Yorkston sawed the peeler cores into 2x4s, selling them for a tidy profit.

The Bellingham Plywood Corporation stayed in business until 1953, when it was sold to the Georgia Pacific Plywood Corporation, an offshoot of the giant Atlanta, Georgia, forest products company that would later have a major role to play in Bellingham's pulp and paper industry.

PEARL HARBOR

On December 7, 1941, the world changed for Fairhaven and the entire nation. Just days after the Japanese attack on Pearl Harbor, army trucks were rolling onto Bellingham streets. Fear of an invasion by the forces of the Japanese Empire was palpable. Machine gun nests were quickly constructed along the shore line. There were three or four on Larrabee's Edgemoor land. There were two built on the small rocky ledge that separates the over-the-water walkways south of Boulevard Park. The local kids playing at Easton Beach called that little ridge Bunker Hill, because of the gun emplacements.

The author well remembers a machine gun nest dug into the hillside in the 200 block of Garden Street. I used to ride up the street on my bicycle and loan comic books to the bored young soldiers manning the machine gun.

Young men were lining up at the recruitment centers. Those too old for military service volunteered as air raid wardens and were issued helmets, gas masks and armbands designating their official role. My father was a volunteer warden. I recall the fascination I felt for his new gear and his weighty responsibilities. Each evening at sundown he would leave the house to patrol the neighborhood. He was watching to be sure that all houses had their shades drawn and no light was showing to guide Japanese bombers to the city. The street lights were all out, the city was to be completely dark. Tarpaper was stapled over basement windows, shades were drawn down on all the upstairs windows. Invasion hysteria was rampant.

Even we little kids had our war duties. We towed our red wagons along the sidewalks canvassing the neighborhood in search of scrap metal. We would knock on doors asking residents to donate any unused possessions made of metal. Even the tinfoil from gum wrappers was collected, rolled into small balls and donated to the war effort. The family garage on the alley was my repository for metals. My friends and I soon filled it with castoff metal items. It was very difficult for a nine-year-old to be perfectly patriotic, as many of the items collected were marvelous metal toys no longer used by the generation going off to war. The temptation was to keep and play with many of those cast-off treasures.

The Pearl Harbor frenzy included the construction of aircraft watch towers, wooden structures rising perhaps 30 feet in the air, which were manned by volunteers trained to identify Japanese airplanes. A tandem effort was the distribution of small decks of airplane identification cards. I still recall a deck that I had, each card with a black and white drawing of and a description of a Nipponese war plane. Names like Mitsubishi and Kawasaki did not mean automobiles or motorcycles then, they were the deadly Japanese war planes painted with the dreaded "meatball" insignia.

Fairhaven, with the rest of the nation was at war.

19.1. Edgemoor as it began to develop, approximately 1941. Whatcom Museum.

0. Larrabee home, by the time of this picture, Mount St. Mary's Convent.
1. Erick Ekholm, 290 Brier Road
2. Charles Teel, 294 Brier Road
3. Lawson Turcotte, 298 Brier Road
4. E.B. Deming, 302 Brier Road
5. E. Brinson, 306 Brier Road
6. Harold Wahl, 310 Brier Road
7. George Keagle, 312 Brier Road
8. John Pierce, 402 Brier Road
9. Loren Wahl, 109 Middlefield Road
10. Jack Kilby
11. Claude Aubert, 215 Hawthorn Road
12. John Greene, 219 Hawthorn Road
13. Carl Sahlin

CHAPTER 19

After The War

As World War II ground to its exhausted close, a weary world entered a period of quiet repose and reconstruction. Gradual change came to Bellingham's southside village.

The heirs of C.X. Larrabee, led by his widow Frances and their eldest son Charles, began the gradual development of the family's residential acreage. They called their development Edgemoor.

The first few houses had been built along Briar Road in the late 1930s by prominent Bellingham families: Lawson Turcotte and Erik Ekholm, officers of Puget Sound Pulp & Timber Co.; John and Inez Pierce, owners of the Leopold Hotel; Harold Wahl, Wahls Dept. Store; E.G. Deming, PAF; Ed. Brinson MD; banker G.W. Keagle; and Charles Teel, MD.

By 1947 more streets were being constructed and building lots sold. Edgemoor was designed to be a prestigious neighborhood. The lots were large and the water views were impressive. Waterfront lots could be bought for the then princely sum of $10,000. Strangely enough, lots on the streets inland were also priced at $10,000, perhaps because they all had water views. R.H. Petterson, the Larrabee's realtor, did much of the selling for the Pacific Realty Company. In the post-war prosperity Edgemoor became a popular and upscale address for Bellingham's more affluent citizens.

19.2. The neighborhood in 1939 was growing. C.X. Larrabee II collection.

FAIRHAVEN BOATHAVEN DESTROYED

The Boathaven had been built in 1937 in the lee of the point of land forming Harris Bay, and was perfectly protected from the prevailing southerly winds and even from the occasional northeast winds that ravaged the northern county in the winter time. Piling driven into the mud of Harris Bay and cabled together was designed to protect it from the rare northwest winds—that every several years would roar out of the Straits of Georgia, over the lowlands of the Lummi Indian reservation, and pound the normally protected shoreline of eastern Bellingham Bay. 1947 was one of those years. In that year a major storm blew across the bay, uprooting and blowing down the protective pile barrier, damaging many of the boats moored inside it. The Port decided not to rebuild at that site and began planning for a major marina behind a rock breakwater on the former tide flats at the north end of Bellingham Bay near Squalicum Creek. Fairhaven had lost one of its financial engines.

FAIRHAVEN HOTEL BURNS

The once grand centerpiece of Nelson Bennett's dream had been in almost steady decline since its 1890 opening. By 1953 it was an ugly cement-grey building, long shorn of its ornamentation and its balconies. Its brick walls had been plastered over with cement. Even its grand tower had been removed. It was now owned by Whatcom County and hosted the Fairhaven Boys and Girls Club, a shooting gallery, and occasionally it was rented out for social events. On the night of July 26, 1953, a young people's dance club, Comus Club, had rented it for their monthly dance. Shortly after the dance was over fire broke out in the building. The fire, which started in an electrical junction box spread rapidly through the old structure. The building was gutted; only its brick walls remained.

19.3. Bob and Virgie Hayden. The Haydens brought a modern grocery store to the southside. Galen Biery papers and Photographs #1691, CPNWS.

The county decided to sell the property at auction, a condition of the sale being the complete demolition of the ruins. After the demolition the iconic Fairhaven Hotel was replaced by a Richfield gas station.

By 1957, population growth in Edgemoor and the entire southside attracted a modern supermarket—Bob and Virgie Hayden, allied with the Thriftway Food organization, opened their 20,000-sq.-ft. grocery in that year. In the former gas station space beside the Mason Block, just north of Hayden's Market, Winifred Walstrom opened her popular Win's Drive-in.

The Fairhaven industrial base began to change. Pacific American Fisheries (PAF), long the mainstay of the southside economy, began to show signs of weakening. Those businesses supplying it began to feel the slowdown. By 1958, the plywood plant now owned by Georgia Pacific (GP), was no longer meeting GP's financial expectations. Abruptly, GP announced the plant closure. Georgia Pacific left town and simply deeded the building and land to the Port of Bellingham.[1] The large plywood plant building sat empty for several years.

UNITED BOAT BUILDERS INC.

On the Squalicum fill at the north end of Bellingham Bay, a new boat building business had been growing. Art Nordvedt and John Thomas had gotten their start with Bellingham Shipyards. They were pioneers in the use of fiberglass for boats, and Nordvedt was a gifted designer. They called their business United Boat Builders. Their fiberglass "Uniflite" boats with innovative hulls designed by Nordvedt, were meeting great success in the marketplace. Their business had progressed until they had outgrown their manufacturing space. They were vying for government contracts, they needed to expand fast and the huge empty plywood plant with access to saltwater answered their needs perfectly.

In 1961 United Boat Builders moved into the old plywood plant. Their Uniflite product line was to have a long and successful run in the competitive, but boisterous and growing boating industry. United Boat Builders built a nationally popular line of pleasure boats. They won contracts to build numerous Annapolis 44 sail boats for the U.S. Naval Academy, and when the Vietnam War broke out, they were awarded contracts to build U.S. Army river patrol boats.

WASHINGTON LOGGERS INC.

1961 saw another successful business move to the filled tideflats below the bluff on 9th Street. Washington Loggers Corp. had been started by Eino Usitalo and Leo Simonsen in 1948. Its president Usitalo, was an engaging and hard working logger, who in 1961 had been able to unite a talented group of logging specialists successful in their own businesses and bring them together under the Washington Loggers name to form a formidable organization that

---

1   History was to repeat itself in 2005, when GP abandoned its pulp and paper mills and deeded the land adjoining Bellingham's downtown to the Port.

excelled in all areas of logging. Howard Hammer ran the logging operations, Vice President Oscar Johnson the log marketing. Norm Robertson was the road-builder, and Bill Moran the log trucker. Washington Loggers became a major player in Pacific Northwest logging.

The powerful corporation moved into a long narrow building just a few dozen feet north of the Uniflite plant. The building was dual purposed. The ground floor was a truck repair and machine shop. Offices of the corporation were constructed in a partial second floor. Washington Loggers also used the waterfront land and the water in front of it to dump logs, to receive logs and prepare them for export to Japan. Logs were trucked to the Fairhaven location and prepared for loading on ships.

PACIFIC AMERICAN FISHERIES CLOSES

1966 brought a terrible blow to Fairhaven and to the larger Bellingham economy when PAF announced its closure. The largest salmon canning company in the world had been a foundation industry for Bellingham Bay since 1899. Its closing rocked Fairhaven and its struggling retail businesses. Fairhaven began a decline that would take several decades to reverse.

THE DAVIS BROTHERS

Brantley Davis, a medical doctor new to Bellingham, had met Adrian Yorkston golfing at the Bellingham Golf and Country Club. The pair soon became friends. The affable fuel dealer offered the young doctor an invest-ment opportunity. Yorkston wanted to sell his idle mill and the two blocks of empty land that he owned along the south side of Harris Avenue. The ply-wood plant, his source of cheap Douglas fir peeler cores to be sawn into 2x4s, had closed and his mill was idle.

Dr. Davis declined the offer—being young, new in his practice, and knowing nothing about real estate investing. A few days after declining Yorkston's offer, he mentioned the opportunity to another friend who hap-pened to serve on the board of directors of United Boat Builders.

In the early 1960s, after their move into the new plant, United Boat Builders had enjoyed great growth and increasing sales. Management was concerned that they would not have adequate room on the leased Port property for their burgeoning business. The land offered to Davis was contiguous to the boat builder's plant, separated only by Harris Avenue. United Boat Builders sug-gested a mutually beneficial deal. If Davis would buy the land from Yorkston, United Boat Builders would lease it for a five-year period, with an option to either re-lease or purchase at the end of that term. In the meantime lease payments would be enough to pay off the land. Davis offered his brother Vincent Davis, a local orthodontist, a partnership in this remarkable deal, and on July of 1966 the sale was consummated. The Davis brothers found themselves in the real estate investment business. They now owned two blocks of Fairhaven. They would soon own much more land in the increasingly desolate village.

PAF had just closed its doors, Fairhaven land prices had plummeted. The Davis brothers met Roy M. "Pete" Petterson, the elderly realtor who had worked for the Larrabee family's Pacific Realty for years and was highly skilled and broadly connected in Fairhaven real estate. Soon Pete was bringing them deals—deals that the brothers could not refuse. Eventually they purchased 39 different pieces of property in Fairhaven, mostly vacant land and lots. They did not accept all of Pete's deals. They were offered all of Drydock Point from the railroad tunnel to its tip deep into Chuckanut Bay for $70,000. Eventually the point was sold by the Larrabees to Douglas Clark for $130,000. They were offered the Knights of Pythias building on 11th Street for $30,000. They did not have that kind of money. They did buy the land that the Tennis Club now sits on, and the land under the Harris Square, the large condo project in the adjoining block. They bought the land that Village Books now sits on, and fortunately for the entire community, they bought the land that later would become the Fairhaven Village Green.

By the end of the 1960s, the once grand dreams of Fairhaven becoming the *Imperial City* were long forgotten. Now it was simply a worn down, mostly vacant embarrassment to an otherwise growing and prosperous Bellingham, but the winds of social unrest were blowing and Fairhaven was in for a change.

Fairhaven in 1970

By the time Fairhaven entered its "Hippie Period" it had decayed to an alarming state. The land that had once held the exuberant buildings of the boom town of 1890 were now vacant lots growing weeds and untended grass, roamed by a large population of feral, or at least semi-domesticated cats.

There were seventeen buildings still standing in the eight key blocks of the city. Only seven of them had survived from the heady days of the Boom. Several of them had been built well after the boom along the Pacific Highway route. Most of the quickly erected frame buildings of the Boom Period had succumbed to age, weather and poor construction. Some of them were torn down by their owners because it was cheaper to pay taxes on empty lots than on empty old buildings.

We show the location of the existing buildings on the facing page taken from the 1967 Sanborn map. Conditions would not have changed between 1967 and 1970, the beginning of the hippie period.

1. Richfield gas station on the Fairhaven Hotel site, 1956
2. Shopping center on the Fairhaven Hotel site, 1968
3. Win's Drive-In, 1964
4. Mason Block, 1890
5. Fairhaven Pharmacy, 1929
6. Bellingham National Bank, 1969
7. Chuckanut Motors, 1919
8. Waldron Block, 1890
9. Nelson Block, 1902
10. Terminal Building, 1888
11. E.M. Day Building, 1890
12. Monahan Building, 1890
13. Knights of Pythias Building, 1891
14. Brown & Cole Grocery Building, 1890
15. Post Office Building, 1890
16. Morgan Block, 1890
17. Schering Building, 1903
18. Bellingham Bay Hotel, 1902

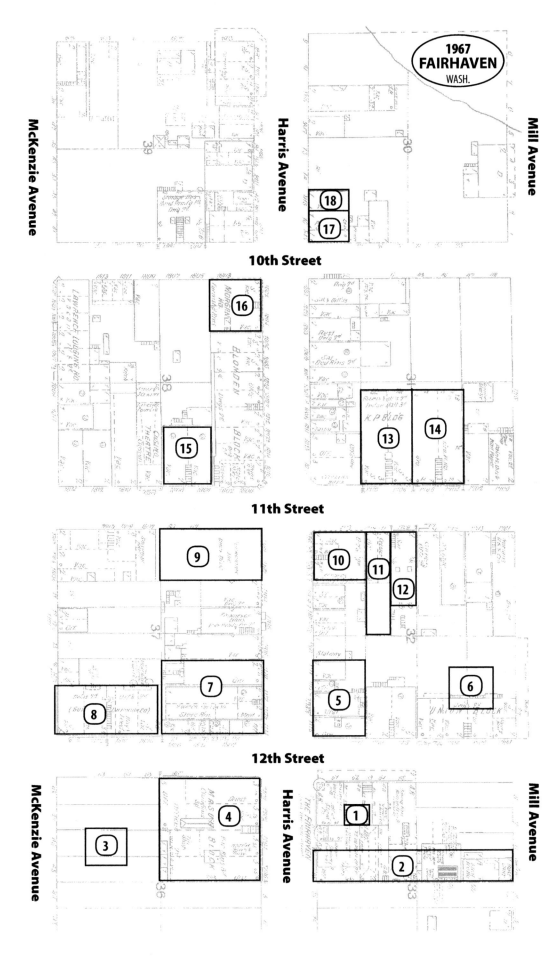

1967
FAIRHAVEN
WASH.

McKenzie Avenue

Harris Avenue

Mill Avenue

10th Street

11th Street

12th Street

20.1. The *Northwest Passage*; The front page of the December 4–18, 1972 edition. John Servais collection.

CHAPTER 20

The Hippie Era, 1966–1973

The early 1960s ushered in a decade of unrest among the young of America. Their malaise was perhaps a reaction to cold war tensions, the materialism of society, social inequality in the South, a weariness with the nuclear threats between east and west. Whatever the cause, the unrest became known as the Counter-Culture movement.

The assassination of John Kennedy in 1963 surely heightened the malaise among the youth of the nation, and the plunge of the United States into the war in Vietnam in 1965 was the final straw. Malaise turned into action. Opposition to the military draft became a powerful incentive to protest and "drop out." Many of the youth of America sought the answers to life's great questions by searching for another way of living. Protests against the war in Vietnam erupted on college campuses. The movement deepened.

In Bellingham, the Fairhaven district was staggering from the 1966 closure of its chief employer, Pacific American Fisheries. The few remaining buildings of its once robust business district along Harris and McKenzie Avenues were old and frequently dilapidated, and soon they were mostly empty. In the eight square blocks that comprised the Fairhaven business district only 18 buildings still stood. In 1890 there had been 75 buildings, and at least 119 separate ground-floor occupancies.

On the periphery of the business district there were numerous old frame houses (built during good times in the 1890s and 1920s) that were still standing, mostly vacant, but rented for as little as $50 per month.

In 1967, Western Washington State College opened a new liberal arts institution, which they called Fairhaven College. It presented a new and decidedly liberal approach to teaching and curriculum. Fairhaven College attracted both professors and students conversant with and supportive of the counter culture movement.

Noel Bourasaw was the editor of the college newspaper. Bourasaw, in a move that seemed to fit with the turbulent times, changed the name of the newspaper to *The Western Front*. One of the paper's regular columnists in 1968 was a student named Wally Oyen. Oyen's popular column "Oyen's Oyster" was heavily read, not only by Western students, but also by other young people in the community. Oyen was enamored of an old-time tavern called the Kulshan that occupied an 1890's bank location in Fairhaven's historic Waldron Building. Oyen featured the tavern in many of his columns. His cleverly written prose began to bring liberal-minded students of the college to the Kulshan and to Fairhaven.

Despite or perhaps because of its economic woes, the Fairhaven district of 1967 contained all that was attractive to these young people with a counter-cultural bent. In increasing numbers, they began to discover the decayed and decaying section of town. Then in March of 1969, a Californian named Frank Kathman, aided by Michael Carlson and Laurence Kee, launched a counter-culture newspaper that they called *Northwest Passage*. The paper, published every other Monday, was focused on lifestyle, politics and environmental issues. A "fort-nightly journal of ecology, politics, the arts and good healthy livin'," it featured such things as organic gardening and home canning, home-made beer and ginger ale, herbal cures, wheat germ enemas, yurt construction, and how to live a simpler laid back life. It was not primarily an anti-war publication and not primarily political in outlook, but it certainly included those topics.

The paper sold for 25¢ a copy and was produced by a passionate and unpaid staff which considered their labors an opportunity to right some of the wrongs of the world and lead society to a better future. Their message was received with enthusiasm among many of the nation's youth. The *Northwest Passage's* paid subscriptions grew to total more than 1,000 at its annual rate of $6. The *Passage* was sold on street corners in dilapidated used coin boxes and by youthful street vendors—who worked the streets of Vancouver, the U District in Seattle, and occasionally San Francisco—selling copies for 25¢ and retaining 12¢ cents for their commission.

In the beginning the *Northwest Passage* was written and put together in various houses, the rented dwellings of its staff. It was published from diverse places, such as the wet basement of the 1858 Richards' Territorial Courthouse building under Akers Taxidermy. Soon it settled into its long-time home on the second floor of the Good Earth Building, the hippie name for the Morgan Block. When a Bellingham printer could not be found, Kathman and crew took the first edition to Lynden to be printed by *The Lynden Tribune*. After that first issue, Kathman was told to take his business elsewhere. The *Tribune's* conservative advertisers had complained, said the *Tribune* owners.

The *Passage* found a printer in Mount Vernon and established a relationship that endured for the life of the paper. The Skagit County printer dictated a "cash on the barrel head" arrangement. He required payment for the entire issue before putting ink to paper, knowing that economically the paper was barely viable.

The *Northwest Passage* included feature stories on local environmental issues. One prominent story was written by Professor David Mason who, upon getting a tour of the Georgia Pacific Pulp mill, wrote decrying the mercury pollution that the mill was depositing in the environment. Another such feature was the *Passage's* thorough coverage of the fluoride emission lawsuit involving Intalco Aluminum and local farmers. They also wrote about the potential of oil spills in the Salish Sea caused by shipping oil to the local refineries. Their feature stories were not welcomed by the conservative community when they were written, but their concerns remain pertinent to this day. The huge cost of cleaning up the mercury contamination of the Georgia Pacific mill site is testimony to the rightness of their cause and the accuracy of their reporting.

The *Northwest Passage* had a large part in establishing Fairhaven as a hippie magnet. The paper celebrated the good life to be found among the quaint buildings and taverns of Bellingham, a little mill and college town in the far northwest corner of the country. The paper spread the word out to the Hippie communication network during the summer of 1969, and Fairhaven began to show signs of life after its recent economic doldrums. Fairhaven became a destination for the young. The word spread by the *Passage*, and by a highly mobile generation who hitchhiked or drove their VW vans about the nation—"the place to be on the west coast was either Haight-Ashbury in San Francisco, Eugene in Oregon, or the Fairhaven district in Bellingham."

Some of the new residents were attracted by or attended Fairhaven College, some were fleeing the draft and the Vietnam war. Some had been turned back at the border by Canadian authorities and just drifted back to Fairhaven to stay for a while. Others were disenchanted veterans having served their draft time in the military. Some were military deserters, who having served a tour in Vietnam, were due to be sent back to war. They were determined not to return to what they considered certain death, fighting for an un-righteous cause. Many sought to flee to Canada. An underground railroad operated out of Fairhaven carrying war resisters or deserters across the border to Canada.

The vast majority of the immigrants to Fairhaven were just young folks who had come from all over the country in their VW Kombi buses to taste the communal and counter-culture life they might find in Fairhaven.

1969 saw great growth in the Fairhaven counter-culture movement. Bill Heid, a Fairhaven College professor, had recently bought the old Morgan Block building. It was promptly renamed The Good Earth Building. It was to become one of the social centers of the *New Community*. It housed the offices of the *Northwest Passage*, its uphill retail space provided a home for the food bank, while the downhill space sheltered the Good Earth Pottery studio.

When Heid purchased the old brick-veneer frame building it was truly a wreck. He and friends held a celebratory party upon the purchase, but they held it on the roof, feeling that the lower floors were un-inhabitable. In the true communal spirit of the day, friends new and old helped renovate the 80-year-old building to make it usable. Heid and his family moved into the third floor.

•••

Among the most important 1969 emigres was a young John Blethen, who had taught school in the East, observed the Chicago riots of the 1968 Democratic Convention, and arrived in Fairhaven in his old Volkswagen bus after driving across the country without a battery. With a grin of remembrance, John relates that each night he had to find a hill to park on, so that he could coast-start the bus and resume his trip the next morning.

John got to Fairhaven in 1969 and recalls that the storefronts were mostly empty. There was Groom Hardware in the Knights of Pythias building, and Fairhaven Grocery at 1206 11th, where Paper Dreams now is located. Across the street at 1211 was Pluto's Tavern, but the Terminal Building on the corner was empty and for sale for $6,500. There was a tiny post office sub-station at 1306 11th inside the Southside Dry Cleaners, run by a couple named Finzel.

The Nelson Block across the street was vacant on the ground floor. The building remained economically viable only because of the ten elderly bachelors who lived in the former offices on the second floor for a modest rent.

Things looked a bit more prosperous on the heavily trafficked 12th Street up the hill. Of course, the Fairhaven Pharmacy anchored the northwest corner at Harris Avenue. The Richfield gas station occupied the old Fairhaven Hotel site across the street. On the southwest corner was an auto repair shop in the Chuckanut Motors Building, and across the street in the massive old Mason Block was the popular Cal's Tavern at 1303, and the Southsider Restaurant at 1305. Around the corner on Harris, was Mac's Barber Shop, a jewelry store, and the state liquor store.

Win's Drive-in, opened in 1964, occupied the lot south of the Mason Block. Across McKenzie was Bob and Virgie Hayden's very modern Thriftway supermarket. On the west side of 12th Street, next to the auto shop on the corner, was Art's Tavern at 1310 in the Waldron Building, and finally the Kulshan Tavern where the bank used to be in the corner of the Waldron Building.

That was about it. There were many empty lots where the old buildings from the boom days had either burned or been demolished because of the rigors of old age, cheap construction, and the tax burden during the Great Depression. Many owners tore down their buildings, but kept the land to reduce taxes. Those buildings that remained were for sale at very low prices. The Terminal Building had a price tag of $6,500. The Monahan Building could be had for $4,500, and the owner would throw in his shoe repair business. The fine old Bank building (the Nelson Block) had been for sale for $12,000 a few years before. It is thought that Leonard Lehman paid $18,000 for it.

John Blethen rented an ancient frame house down by Padden Creek where the Tennis Club is now. He paid about $50 a month. He and a friend, Jeff Winston, decided to rent the basement of the Nelson Block to begin a new venture. The building had just been bought by Leonard Lehman. The first-floor corner space (that had formerly housed the bank) was about to be occupied by Paul and Elizabeth Hansen who would start a bookstore called appropriately, Bank Books.

Blethen and Winston found the building's basement piled high with the detritus of the years. The young idealists swamped it out and created a community center, restaurant, and hippie hang-out which they named Toad Hall Coffee House. Toad Hall became one of the focal points of the Fairhaven hippie experience.

The partners built a stage with lumber from the remnants of the old building that had just been torn down next door on Harris. Jim Raines, a counter-culture antique dealer, living in the 1890's church on Mill Avenue and 15th Street, found them some castoff curtains and some very tired sofas and chairs. Tables were simply large cable spools that had been picked up for free. For about $500 they had created a nightclub and community center. About this time Jeff Winston decided the project had little future and departed for Guemes Island. Blethen soldiered on, working 100 hours a week to make Toad Hall work.

Blethen's commitment was to build a new community among the large crowd of young people that had thronged to Fairhaven. He was dedicated to the counter-culture mantra of peace and community. He molded Toad Hall to be a place intended to bring that community together.

John and his friends sought a menu to serve that would be cheap, healthy and a bit different. They experimented with various foods, seeking a menu that would satisfy and be economically feasible. For a while they adopted a cook-of-the-week program inviting various people to cook and serve their nomination for Toad Hall's *signature* dish. They tried Jewish food, Greek food, every kind of food imaginable, always with a bent toward organic, healthy and natural. They even tried macrobiotic food. When asked what macrobiotic food was, Blethen described it as, "beyond wheat germ, and sure to starve one to death in about two weeks."

20.2. John Blethen, 2015, after a long day in his cabinet shop.

Toad Hall finally settled on a unique pizza to be its every night signature dish. Their pizza, like everything else in Toad Hall, was organic. It was made from a recipe that included cottage cheese among its ingredients. A pizza was sold for $1, and could be delivered to any of the local taverns by a smiling waitress. Usually the attractive Beth Haley. Most of the food creation and cooking was done by Janice Soderberg, who would later marry John Servais.

Toad Hall community efforts included fund-raising for worthy causes. They hosted a weekly movie night showing old Buster Keaton-type films and charging 50¢ admission, which included a bag of popcorn. From time to time, touring bands were booked into Toad Hall and were offered at a small cover charge. Toad Hall made and sold organic root beer. Blethen related that it was sometimes called 12-hour root beer. You wanted to drink it within 12 hours of when it had been bottled, because if you waited as long as the 14th hour, the bottles might begin to explode.

Their activities included a fledgling food-sharing venture, which slowly grew to become the present day Food Co-Op. Blethen was proud to mention that the Crisis Center also had its beginnings at Toad Hall. The Food Co-Op soon outgrew Toad Hall and was moved to a storefront in the Good Earth Building down the street at 1002 Harris, now the location of the Artwood store.

A Toad Hall garden was begun by John Blethen on the vacant land beside the Nelson Block to provide vegetables for Toad Hall's kitchen. The garden stretched up hill to the corner of 11th and Harris. Blethen laboriously brought in topsoil to enrich the land and planted the vegetable garden that would soon be the scene of a classic confrontation between the hippie culture and the square community.

20.3. John Servais and Janice Soderberg, 2015 on Mt. Baker. She had been a cook at Toad Hall, and John is a long-time Fairhaven booster. John Servais collection.

•••

John Wesselink arrived in Bellingham in December of 1969. He was 25 years old and had just finished his four-year enlistment with the U.S. Navy, much of the time serving on an aircraft carrier stationed off the coast of Vietnam. John had been raised in the Washington DC area, and had been accepted at Western Washington State College. Upon his arrival in Bellingham he was charmed by what he saw as the rural nature of the community and the laid-back atmosphere of nearby Fairhaven. As a freshman he was housed in one of the dormitories of the new Fairhaven College where he was engulfed by the counter-culture folkways. He spent his leisure time experimenting with the communal laid-back atmosphere of its inhabitants including experimenting with the popular drugs of the day.

Wesselink recalls wonderful evenings at Pluto's drinking beer and listening to the name bands that frequently were featured there. Pluto's provided free peanuts with the beer. You were encouraged to throw the empty husks on the floor where they formed a permanent floor covering. The patrons of Pluto's had most likely been indulging in marijuana or some stronger mood changer and were a mellow audience for the blue-grass bands that played there. Wesselink recalls hearing such legendary musicians as Muddy Waters, Willy Dixon, and John Lee Hooker.

20.4. John Wesselink, in Hippie mode, 1973. This was John before he became the Columbia neighborhood postman and Bellingham's most knowledgeable tree taxonomist. John Wesselink collection.

He recalls Beat poet Gary Snyder reading his poetry among the peanut shells, and Ken Kesey on one of his Fairhaven visits chatting with the patrons and hanging out.

In June of 1970, Emily Eriksen and her brothers Kris, Tor and Bernt moved up from Seattle and bought Art's Tavern in the Waldron Building. They changed its name to The Fairhaven. The next year they expanded, taking over the vacant space next door and calling it Crazy Richard's Galley, a restaurant named for their cook. The Fairhaven became a funky, but popular drinking and eating place attractive to the entire community. It was here that their popular avocado, cream cheese and alfalfa sprout sandwich introduced *hippie hair* to Bellingham.

John Wesselink remembers the Fairhaven hippie experience as "a vibrant time that I was lucky enough to experience in the prime of my youth. Everything was so new and rule-breaking and exciting. ... And then Imus happened. ... It was an abrupt, rude, slamming shut of a hopeful, liberating utopian chapter in our cultural history, or at least that's how I saw it at the time. In retrospect I suppose it was inevitable, but it was heart-breaking at the time."

The Imus *happening* began in 1972, when the wealthy Bellingham native returned from his successful business ventures in California and began to rapidly buy up Fairhaven properties. He began with the Mason Block where Cal's Tavern was. Then the Waldron Building with the Kulshan Tavern and The Fairhaven restaurant. Soon he purchased the Nelson Block, which housed Toad Hall, and the Fairhaven Post Office building on 11th, which included a large vacant lot where the Blethen garden was planted.

Ken Imus was a typical conservative businessman of the day and probably represented the thinking of the vast majority of Bellingham residents regarding the hippie incursion into the southside. He had a vision of building a viable and robust Fairhaven attractive to tourists and the broader regional community. Hippies were anathema to him and he had no intention of including them in his vision. What followed was a classic and inevitable clash of cultures. Imus, who soon owned most of the village, held most of the cards.

He promptly evicted John Blethen and Toad Hall from the Nelson Block and established the offices of his Jacaranda Corporation in the old bank building. The leases for the Kulshan Tavern and The Fairhaven restaurant, both in Imus's Waldron building were not renewed. The Kulshan simply closed. The Fairhaven moved to a basement space at the corner of Harris and 12th, under what had been an auto repair shop. That building was not owned by Imus.

Blethen moved his Toad Hall across the street into an empty space just downhill from the Fairhaven Pharmacy. He tried to re-create Toad Hall there, but it never achieved the same ambiance. He soon sold it to the Martinez family who established the still successful Dos Padres restaurant.

The clash of cultures reached its crescendo on a Thursday morning in November of 1972, when a truck and trailer carrying a bulldozer pulled up in front of the Toad Hall garden. When several of the residents asked the driver what was going on, they were shocked to hear that he had orders to bulldoze the garden. Soon a crowd gathered and as the dozer crossed Harris Avenue, several of the more determined hippies stood at the edge of the garden in front of the dozer. The equipment operator shut off his engine and dismounted, walking across the street to a pay-phone beside Tony's Coffee. During the break in the action that followed someone built a campfire and began cooking soup in a large kettle using vegetables from the garden. Others played guitars and sang. The festive mood was soon broken when several city transit buses arrived, packed with Bellingham police officers clad in riot gear, complete with shields and batons. The Police Chief ordered the crowd to disperse.

Meanwhile John Blethen says he was trying to save his topsoil, urgently carting it off with a wheelbarrow to his waiting pickup truck.

When the crowd refused to disperse, the officers waded into the crowd making arrests. Later, the *Northwest Passage* dubbed the arrested hippies "The Fairhaven Eight." The eight were taken to the city jail for a few hours and then released. They were brought to trial later, charged with trespassing. They were found guilty and fined $25 each. The garden was gone, Ken Imus had won the day—and the hippie movement in Fairhaven rapidly began to fade. The center of the now-wounded movement retreated to the Good Earth Building.

1973 saw the beginning of the end for Fairhaven's, and for the hippie movement worldwide. The disillusioned youth were getting older. The military draft was ended in that year. The Watergate hearings captured the nation's attention. The *Northwest Passage* left Fairhaven and moved to Seattle, and the air simply went out of Fairhaven's hippie movement. Many of them drifted away to get jobs and begin families.

Some members of the *New Community* found another decayed small town in Skagit County and moved there to bring new life to the quaint waterfront town of LaConner.

Emily Ericsen married a successful attorney in Seattle. John Wesselink became a Bellingham mailman and spent 21 years delivering mail in the Columbia neighborhood while becoming Bellingham's premier tree taxonomist. John Blethen is still building custom cabinets in his New Whatcom Cabinet shop on Railroad Avenue, and remains actively engaged in his efforts to build community in the city he loves.

John Servais, who arrived on the hippie scene at its very beginnings and was a close observer and participant (although claiming to have always been a conservative), says that with the end of the draft and Ken Imus's efforts, the hippie era just ended almost overnight.

The hippies left an indelible mark on Bellingham and Fairhaven. Their idealistic dreams of changing the future were not in vain.

Their basic tenets of healthful food, organic diet, a cooperative community where people look after one another still thrive in Bellingham and are manifest in many surviving attitudes and institutions. The Community Food Co-op, the Crisis Clinic, The Food Bank, the Re-Store, the Bellingham Farmers' Market, all testify to the reality that the counter-culture moved our society to a better place in their brief Fairhaven era.

21.1. Ken Imus looking at the challenge, walking up an empty Harris Avenue, 1971. This desolate scene nicely illustrates the condition of Fairhaven upon Ken Imus's return. Brad Imus collection.

Ken Imus Returns

Ken Imus was born in Bellingham in 1926. His father was a construction worker, and built the family home in the 1930s on the Bakerview
Road, which was then a very rural location. Young Ken was educated
in Bellingham elementary schools and was a 1944 graduate of Bellingham
High School. He confesses to not being an athlete, a politician or a brilliant
scholar in high school. Music and automobiles were his passions. He played
drums in the Marching and Jazz bands and spent much of his time in the
school auto shop, where he became fascinated with automobiles and skilled
in repairing them.

Even then he was ambitious and a hard worker with a passionate desire
to get ahead. While still in high school he began buying old cars, repairing
them, and then selling them for a profit. He worked on his cars in an old gas
station that he rented "...out by the coal mine bridge." During those high
school years, 64 cars passed through his hands. He had discovered his way
to "get up in life."

It was war-time when he graduated and Ken joined the U.S. Navy. The
skills learned in auto shop gained him entrance to the Navy's engineering
school, where he received excellent grades. He graduated second in a class
of 128.

He soon found himself stationed on a 248-foot landing vessel in a flotilla
heading across the Pacific to the Marianas. The ship developed structural
damage in a severe storm during the crossing and had to return to the States
for repairs; repairs that kept it stateside until the war ended. Ken never saw
combat.

Imus was discharged in 1946 and eagerly returned home ready to get to
work. He first went to work in Maury Crocker's auto body shop. After a year
of experience with Crocker he opened his own body shop. In 1949, friends
convinced him that prospects were brighter in California, and he and his

wife Barbara moved to San Jose, where Ken quickly got a job in the body shop of the local Dodge dealer. Before long he was no longer repairing cars, but selling the dealer's used cars. He soon found himself the used car manager.

Ever moving upward, he then switched to a Ford dealership and became its sales manager. The owner of the San Jose Ford dealership learned of a dealership for sale in Dallas, Texas. He bought it and sent Imus to Dallas to manage the operation, providing him with an ownership interest. In the ensuing years, Imus parlayed hard work and his management skills into owning dealerships in Dallas and El Paso, Texas; Joplin Missouri; Greenville, South Carolina; and Sunnyvale, California.

As the profits mounted in those prosperous postwar years, Ken developed an interest in real estate investing and began putting his excess income into land and buildings. Before long he owned 12 properties across the south. He formed the Jacaranda Corporation to hold his real estate operations. By the end of the 1960s, after 24 years of extremely hard work, Ken Imus had become a wealthy man.

In 1971, he and Barbara made a trip home to visit relatives and become re-acquainted with their home town. The Imus's had become fond of antiques and antiquities. One day as they drove past the 1890 Mason Block at the corner of 12th and Harris Avenue, Barbara looked at the brick relic of Fairhaven's boom days and remarked, "We ought to buy that and fix it up." And that is exactly what they did.

The Jacaranda Corporation now had a northern investment and a growing commitment to Fairhaven. They bought the Mason Block—containing Cal's Tavern, the Southsider, Mac's Barbershop, and the liquor store—paying $150,000 for it. Then they bought the Nelson Block, with Toad Hall in its basement and Bank Books at street level—for $132,000. Next they bought the Schering Building at 10th and Harris for $12,000; then the Waldron Building with its two taverns, the Kulshan and The Fairhaven.

By now Imus's vision had matured. He wanted to transform the decayed, hippie-populated village of Fairhaven into "The Santa Barbara of the North." His buying continued with the Knights of Pythias building for $48,000; the adjoining old Brown & Cole Grocery building (where Paper Dreams is now located) for $23,000; and he bought every vacant lot that his realtor Frank Muljat could find for him. He continued buying buildings and land until he owned 42 separate properties.

It was a good time to invest. In 1971-72 Fairhaven was at a low ebb from a property value point of view. Many buildings were totally empty, most of the occupied buildings were continuing their gradual decay. In 1972, changing business conditions resulted in Washington Loggers moving their offices to the Hannegan Road area and their Fairhaven location was vacated. Only

Uniflite's boat building plant provided Fairhaven industrial payrolls.

The hippie movement was in full sway and what economic activity there was due largely to the hippie occupation. It was a propitious time to buy up a neighborhood. Ken Imus did a good job of it. Imus's buying spree was no doubt driving up Fairhaven prices, and he did not always get his property at the lowest historic price.

Ken Imus was and is a conservative business man, one who made his way in the world by smart management, hard work and long hours. The free-wheeling pot and LSD culture of the hippie movement was the last thing that he endorsed or wished to tolerate. He determined to get the hippies out of Fairhaven. A confrontation was inevitable.

His first action was to close Toad Hall. He evicted John Blethen. He chose not to renew leases for the Kulshan or The Fairhaven. Then he ordered the bulldozing of the Toad Hall garden, and fenced the scraped land to store the many antique doors, fences and lamp-posts that he had collected, which were awaiting installation in the Fairhaven of his vision.

Ken Imus won his battle with the counter-culture. By 1973 most of the long-haired youth had drifted off to more welcoming communities. Many of them found the quaint and almost forgotten town of LaConner, along the Swinomish Slough in Skagit County. Their counter culture energy soon began to transform LaConner into the active town that it is today.

Imus succeeded in large measure to dampen the hippie energy in Fairhaven, but his victory came at a cost. He had evicted the counter-culture folks from his newly purchased buildings—but the now empty buildings were slow to fill back up. The few Fairhaven buildings that Imus did not own were filled with counter-culture types and doing well in the 1970s and early '80s. Imus's buildings remained empty. He would not rent them to the counter-culture crowd, but the more conservative community showed little interest. The dispersal of the hippies had created a sort of vacuum of interest in Fairhaven. Consequently, the remainder of the 1970s were difficult ones for Fairhaven. Fortunately, Imus had the financial ability to weather the storm.

He quickly got to work promoting and renovating his acquisitions. He re-furbished the Mason Block, re-naming it the Marketplace and its grand opening was seen as a new beginning for Fairhaven. The community was excited about the Marketplace as an intriguing venue for boutique gift shops, artists studios, and craft sales. At its opening it was fully leased, the four tiered floors all visible from the central open space made it a unique and attractive building. The space on the third floor, occupied by the Cascade Club so many years previously was now a charming restaurant, Le Chat Noir. Also on the third floor was Phil McGruder's Fairhaven Book Store. It appeared to be a good beginning for Imus's renewal vision. Unfortunately, the public's interest in the Marketplace was short lived. Perhaps the rents were too high, perhaps too many of the shops were under-capitalized and lacked experienced management, perhaps the stairs were too steep or too high. There was no elevator at that time (imagine stocking a book store three flights of stairs above the ground level without an elevator). Perhaps it was the hippie image of Fairhaven that kept the bulk of the community away.

As shop after shop in the Marketplace failed, Fairhaven drifted back to its quiet ways. Imus kept investing. He owned the vacant land adjoining the Marketplace to the east. He had contracted with his old high school friend and building contractor, Stewart Heaton, to remodel the Mason Block. Now he extended the contract to construct a new building addition attached to the east side of the venerable brick building, that would house a department store or major retailer.

The building addition was to have a steel frame. Heaton began the project, installing the foundations and building the large structural steel framework. Then Heaton and Imus had a disagreement of some sort. The project stalled. They were unable to resolve their differences, and the troubles escalated to a legal battle. Stalemate occurred and the project was abandoned. The structural-steel frame stood in that vacant lot for 18 years, rusting and unused. Its gaunt structure an eyesore to many in Fairhaven. Unhappy locals began to call it "the skeleton." Imus had apparently lost heart for the project and just left it to rust.

The renovation of Fairhaven attracted the two Imus sons. Brad Imus moved to Fairhaven in 1978 to manage the day-to-day challenges for the Jacaranda Corporation. His father was still living in California where he was tending to his many other business interests. Brad and his family settled into the community where they live to this day, still managing Imus properties and supporting Fairhaven. Another son, Tim Imus, moved to Bellingham in 2000 and built the building at 2005 Harris Avenue. In 2007, Ken, Brad and Tim partnered in building the 711 11th Street building.

The difficulties of renting Jacaranda's Fairhaven properties began to diminish in 1980 with the arrival of Chuck and Dee Robinson, school teachers from Illinois. The Robinsons leased half of the first floor of the former Brown and Cole Grocery Store and opened Village Books. The opening of Village Books began a new chapter in the renaissance of Fairhaven.

Three years later, in 1985, four critically important businesses opened. Ray and Taimi Dunn opened the Colophon Café beside the book store. Across the street at the former Pluto's location, Jim Bolster opened the Dirty Dan Harris restaurant. On the 11th and Harris corner, the popular A Lot of Flowers blossomed.

21.2. Ken Imus in his office in the Nelson Block. ©John Servais photo.

The transformation of Fairhaven from a decaying counter-culture center to a thriving retail and restaurant urban village had begun to gather momentum. Its present day renaissance has been extremely successful. The community will always owe a debt of gratitude to the Imus family and their Jacaranda Corporation for the vision of a Fairhaven revival and for the huge part they played in beginning and maintaining it.

22.1. The first anniversary toast with Ray Dunn, Dee and Chuck Robinson, and Taimi Dunn. James A. Young photo.

CHAPTER 22

The Renaissance, 1971-2015

I t is fair to say that Fairhaven's modern renaissance began in 1971 with Ken Imus's return to Bellingham. Hundreds of people have contributed greatly to Fairhaven's post-hippie resurgence, but Ken Imus started it and perhaps no one has done more to perpetuate it. The present day condition of the Fairhaven district is truly remarkable when compared to the desolation of the village on the date of his arrival.

The Sanborn map on page 143 depicts the state of the eight key blocks of the business district in that time. The reader is urged to compare that map with the earlier Sanborn map on page 89, depicting Fairhaven in 1897 which shows the results of the great 1890 boom. The final Sanborn map on page 173 has been altered by the author to show the Fairhaven of today. It indicates the new buildings, the date which they were built and who built them. The transition from boom... to bust... to the robust Fairhaven of today is remarkable indeed.

While Imus began the village's return from desolation, a strong case can be made for Village Books being the true motor of the renaissance. In 1979 Chuck and Dee Robinson, grew weary of their Midwestern lives and decided to take a year off to travel the country. They sold their house and possessions, bought a motor-home, and headed west with $30,000 in their pockets. They were beginning their odyssey by heading to Tacoma to visit a friend. Somewhere along the route they settled on the idea of starting a bookstore on the West coast. This idea transformed not only their travel plans, but also their lives and the future of Fairhaven.

By the time they reached the coast, their trip had become a search for the town in which to start their bookstore. They searched from the Canadian border to as far south as Santa Rosa, California; but finally settled on Bellingham. The main business district of downtown Bellingham already had a book store, Fairhaven Books, which ironically had begun in Fairhaven on the third floor of the Marketplace, but moved to the downtown a few years before the Robinson's arrival. The Robinson's choice seemed obvious, if they wanted a bookstore in Bellingham they must open their store in Fairhaven.

Fairhaven was a rather sorry looking place in 1979. There were only 17 buildings standing, only eight of them survivors from the boom years. Several of them were completely empty. The surviving buildings were separated by weed-filled vacant lots. The Knights of Pythias building stood without a tenant in the center of the block on 11th, next to a struggling gift shop called Country Corner that occupied half of the former Brown & Cole Grocery building. At either end of the block were two sorry-looking empty lots. Across the street was The Picture Show, a tiny movie house beside an empty store that had just been vacated by Fairhaven Bicycle. At the corner was Tony's Coffee House, where what was left of the hippie crowd played hacky-sack on the street corner. At the north end of that block across the street from the Country Corner was another large and desolate empty lot. On the south side of Harris Avenue, the Nelson Block (the old bank) contained only a small gift shop; while across 11th Street the former Post Office/dry cleaners building was totally empty. Down Harris Avenue, the Good Earth Building held the Community Co-Op and the Good Earth Pottery Studio. Across Harris was The Chimney Sweep and another empty building.

Dake Traphagen was not yet making guitars in the ill-fated concrete block auto wrecker's store, that stood empty as the only building in the block below 9th Street. The building had been built by a former auto body man, Norm Fayette, to house an auto wrecking business. Fayette was unable to get a city permit to wreck cars on the lot surrounding the building. He had planned to sell the used parts from the wrecked cars in the building, but eventually sold the building to the Davis Brothers who purchased it with the entire block. Traphagen moved into the little concrete block building in 1982, and established a national reputation as a luthier for his exceptional guitars. He rented from the Davis brothers, who by that time owned much of the empty land in Fairhaven.

In one of the few new buildings to be constructed in Fairhaven in many years, Brantley and Vincent Davis partnered with CPA Harvey Tebrich to build the Tennis Club on their property bordering Padden Creek, in the block below 9th Street. The Tennis Club building was built in 1971, but not built without controversy. Their contractor was having a dispute with labor unions. He was refusing to use union workers in the Tennis Club construction. Two-thirds of the steel frame construction had been erected when, one morning passerbys found the building collapsed. Unknown persons had during the night removed all of the nuts from the bolts holding the framework together. The framework came apart and fell to the ground. The vandalism made big news in the local newspaper, but the culprits were never identified. New steel had to be ordered, and the building was completed without further incident. The Davis/Tebrich partnership also constructed outdoor tennis courts across McKenzie Avenue in front of the building. The Davis brothers soon bought out Harvey Tebrich, and they operated the club for the next 16 years.

Things were not quite as desolate up the hill on the busy 12th Street arterial. The Richfield station was still pumping gas on the historic site first occupied by The Fairhaven Hotel. The Mason Block, then called the Marketplace, had failed to become the shopping metropolis that Ken Imus had envisioned, but it still held a few shops and a restaurant on the upper floors. Its street level shops included Cal's Tavern, a tobacco shop, a barbershop, and a few other little shops.

Adjoining the Mason Block on the lot up hill was the 'skeleton'. A reminder of the failed dream of Ken Imus to build a department store building connected to his remodeled Marketplace.

Of course, the venerable Fairhaven Pharmacy was busy filling prescriptions on their corner, and their neighbor Dos Padres was building a good business selling Mexican food and Margaritas.

Across the street in the old Chuckanut Motors building, which was perhaps the most successful Fairhaven building at the time, was Brenda Young's gift shop The Wicker Basket; Joanne Hanesworth's candy store; Gallery West on the corner; and in the basement, the popular Fairhaven Restaurant and Bar that Ken Imus had evicted from his Waldron Building. Sofie's Restaurant was the key tenant on the 12th Street sidewalk. The building was owned by Sehome High School Vice Principal Larry Young, his wife Brenda, Cliff McKee and Phyllis McKee, the Sofies, and Steve and Linda Winterburn.

Adjoining the Chuckanut Motors Building to the south was the empty Waldron Building. Empty because Ken Imus had bought it and refused to renew the leases of the two taverns of hippie days, the Kulshan and The Fairhaven.

Undaunted by the surrounding desolation, the Robinsons chose a location for their book store across 11th Street from the Picture Show (which was in the Monahan Building). Ken Imus leased them the south half of the old Brown and Cole Grocery store, just half of the present Paper Dreams store. From February 20, 1980, when they signed the lease, to June 20 when the store opened, they frantically built book shelves, attended the booksellers convention in Detroit, and learned all they could about the book-selling business.

They must have learned their lessons well. They immediately began authors' readings, advertised aggressively, and stayed open long hours seven days a week. The business grew rapidly. By 1982, they needed more room and knocking out part of a wall, they expanded into half of the first floor of the Knights of Pythias building.

Three years later, in 1985, they convinced their friends Ray and Taimi Dunn to open the Colophon Café in the other half of the Pythias building, and again they knocked out part of a wall to connect the two businesses. The synergy worked. You could buy a book and take it into the connected restaurant to read it as you dined.

Perhaps most importantly, two new creative entrepreneurs had arrived to promote Fairhaven in the persons of Ray Dunn and his wife Taimi.

In a late evening planning session, aided by a glass or two of wine, the four friends searched for a good name for the new restaurant. Chuck proposed Colophon, the word for the publisher's mark at the end of a book. Taimi and Ray were seeking a word that was alliterative with Café, and so Colophon Café was the perfect name for a café beside a bookstore, and history was made. The Colophon was busy from its opening day selling only ice cream, desserts and lattes.

Inspired by their visits to Paris, the Dunns were the first Bellingham restaurateurs to seat customers at outdoor tables on the wide sidewalk in front of the café. In a move uncharacteristic of Paris, they were also the first restaurant in Bellingham to ban smoking.

By 1988, both businesses needed more space. They convinced Ken Imus to knock a hole in the floor of the Knights of Pythias building and build a large staircase to the basement of the building. Ken's son Brad built the staircase using antique newel posts and balusters that his father had collected during his antique buying trips. The stairs led down to an enlarged Colophon Café

22.2. The birthplace of Village Books, 1980. Village Books began here in half of the old Brown & Cole Grocery location beside the Knights of Pythias Building. Galen Biery Photographs #1396, CPNWS.

22.3. Colophon Café grand opening ribbon cutting. Chuck, Dee, Mayor Tim Douglas, Taimi and Ray. James A. Young photo.

and kitchen on the basement level, where you could also access the new and substantially larger Village Books.

Village Books and the Colophon had become the anchor businesses for the entire village. Their success encouraged others. Ken Imus and his family began to build buildings on some of the unsightly vacant lots. The first of them was the Quinby Building, built in 1992 on the north side of Harris. Its back wall would become an outdoor movie screen and enclose the Village Green that would be developed 11 years later.

A major development came to Fairhaven in 1991, when realtor Sharon Lipscomb filled the large empty lot across the street from Village Books by building a brick retail and residential building. She named it Judson Plaza after her forbears, Holden and Phoebe Judson, pioneers of Lynden. Her building completed the east side of the block.

In 1995, Imus's Jacaranda Corporation built two more buildings across the street from their Quinby Building, at 1006 and 1010 Harris, adjoining and uphill of the Morgan Block. These new buildings filled the gaps on the street and portrayed a sense of growth and prosperity. Meanwhile on the corner across the street, a vacant lot slowly morphed into the popular A Lot of Flowers. In 1982, Mary Cain had rented the vacant lot at the corner of 11th and Harris to sell Christmas trees. Her location evolved into the ever-popular garden and florist shop. After Mary's unfortunate death the business was successfully carried on by a young employee, Penny Ferguson.

Meanwhile, Imus renovated the old dry cleaners/ Post Office building and it became the Cobblestone Kitchen, now Skylarks. The ball was rolling. Even John Blethen's notorious garden lot of hippie days became useful with the addition of the Imus's red London bus dispensing clam chowder and fish and chips.

Another major step forward was made in 1998 when Ken Imus made an important decision based on his belief that Fairhaven needed a hotel. His Jacaranda Corporation constructed the

22.4. A Lot of Flowers, 2001. Kate Weisel photo.

22-room Fairhaven Village Inn with its three street-level retail locations. The Inn would become an important element in Fairhaven's growth and maturity. The Village Inn was soon joined by the upscale Chrysalis Inn built on the site of the McEvoy Oil Company's tank farm beside the Taylor Avenue Dock. The Chrysalis was the dream of Ellen Shea, who guided it to completion. Fairhaven now had two quality inns and the ability to become an upscale destination for travelers.

In the year 2000, the ever-creative Taimi Dunn opened a most unlikely store in the Quinby Building. A devoted dog lover, Taimi conceived the notion of a store devoted to pampered dogs and their solicitous owners. The Doggie Diner provided special treats, doggie biscuits and doggie muffins, specially baked in the nearby Colophon Café kitchen. Dog owners could sit with their dogs at tables or a counter and dine with them. The humans were served on plastic dishes, their canine friends received their food on paper plates. Doggie birthday parties were held daily and doggie birthday cakes were served to all guests human and canine. Of course, Taimi stocked her store with all sorts of expensive dog gear, collars, blankets, leashes etc. That was where the profit was.

The Doggie Diner was such a unique concept and it was so successful that news media from around the world flocked to Fairhaven. Television crews were an almost daily sight in the store and the business was featured in *People Magazine, Readers Digest, Good Housekeeping*, almost every national magazine. Taimi recalls being awakened at 3 AM one morning to do a radio interview for

22.5. Taimi at the counter with Mattie at the Doggie Diner. Courtesy photo.

a station in Gibralter. The Doggie Diner publicity was also calling attention to Fairhaven and adding to the growing awareness of this quaint neighborhood in Bellingham.

Taimi rode the whirlwind for two years, but running the Doggie Diner and her role in the Colophon Café were simply too much. Exhausted, she sold the Doggie Diner in 2002. It took only six months for the new owner to fail. It was a unique business and it needed an owner with the unique creative and promotional skills that Taimi possessed.

The Colophon Cafe and the Doggie Diner were not the only contributions that this amazing woman has made to Fairhaven. Taimi can be credited with envisioning a park where the Fairhaven Village Green now sits.

David Ebenal must be included among those having a major role in bringing Fairhaven to its present state of health. Ebenal is a general contractor with a fascination for history and a love of Fairhaven. He has been a key contributor to Fairhaven's success. He began by buying Ken Imus's failed *skeleton* structure beside the Mason Block.

The unsightly abandoned steel framework had stood on its weed-infested lot for 18 years. Using the old structural steel, Ebenal was able to build the four-story brick-faced building called Fairhaven Square in 2006. The skeleton that was Ken Imus's failed eyesore now supports a modern building with residences above a ground-floor restaurant, and parking for residents in the basement. His next project, also in 2006, was a small retail/residential building at 13th and Mill, beside the empty lot where E.L. Cowgill's house once sat.

In 2007, he built the attractive Fairhaven Gardens on the corner of 12th and Mill, which currently houses several restaurants, a toy store, and other 11th Street shops. The building has two upper floors of residential condominiums.

Ebenal then made a commitment that will forever endear him to Fairhaven history buffs. He bought the historic 1891 Waldron Block from Ken Imus. The building was empty and badly deteriorated. It appeared that demolition was in its future. In 2011, Ebenal converted the old building to luxury condominiums and retail space and was even able to entice a bank to occupy the corner space that C.H Waldron's Bank of Fairhaven originally occupied. In a companion project, he built the adjoining Young Building on the vacant lot west of the Waldron Building. The Young Building is another combination residential and retail structure at the corner of 11th and McKenzie.

Another Fairhaven building was a 2004 collaboration with Chuck and Dee Robinson on the bookstore building at the corner of 11th and Mill. Ebenal built and owned the Village Books building to the Robinson's plans, trading them the building lot for one of the two luxury condominiums on its top floor. David Ebenal has made a huge contribution to Fairhaven's present success.

22.6. The Waldron Block in 2001. On the right is the Chuckanut Motors Building. On the left side, part of Chuckanut Square can be seen. Kate Weisel photo.

22.7. The 'saved' and remodeled Waldron Block, with the Young Building shown behind and below to the west. 2015 photo by the author.

An additional pillar of Fairhaven vibrancy has been Phyllis McKee, who with her husband Cliff and three other couples, bought the Chuckanut Motors Building at the corner of 12th and Harris in 1972. Cliff McKee built his art

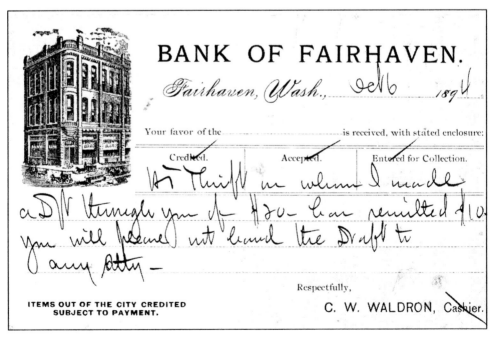

22.8. Bank of Fairhaven transaction card.

22.9. Chuckanut Square. The Bellingham Housing Authority built this low-cost housing apartment building in 1971 across the street from Hayden's Thriftway. Galen Biery Photograph #1404, CPNWS.

gallery in the corner by enclosing what had been the drive-through gas station portion of the building. In the mid-1970s the McKee Gallery on the corner was transferred to David Lucas who has operated Gallery West since then.

By 1980, the other partners had been bought out and the McKees and Youngs owned the building. Sofie's 1312 had gone out of business and Stan Velas had leased the space for his Venus Pizza restaurant. Velas would later change the name to Stanello's and establish a long and successful restaurant tradition in Fairhaven.

When Ken Imus bought the Waldron Block and evicted the Fairhaven Tavern, Emily Eriksen and her brothers moved their operations to the basement of the McKee's building and opened the *new* Fairhaven—a restaurant and licensed premises.

By the year 2000, Phyllis McKee was single and the sole owner of the building and its adjoining parking lot on Harris Avenue. In that year she constructed the large retail and office structure called Finnegan's Alley on the parking lot. With excellent foresight she designed the building with a passageway through the building, which now connects to the walkway surrounding the Young Building, creating what is indeed an alley-like shopping experience. Finnegan's Alley is a fitting name.

As Fairhaven grew in charm and business vitality in the early years of the new century, its attraction as a residential location became apparent. The Bellingham Housing Authority had built Chuckanut Square, a low income housing development conveniently across 12th Street from the Hayden's Market, back in 1978. Now visionary developers began building large residential structures on the periphery and in the Fairhaven Historic District as well. The 12th Street Village condominiums and commercial center were built along Padden Creek at the 12th Street bridge in 2005. The large three-building Harris Square condominium complex was built a few years later covering the entire block between 9th and 10th on Harris.

Another large retail and residential building was soon built on 9th Street south of the McKenzie corner. In 2015, the Shannons, present owners of the Village Inn, have completed a handsome apartment building with a restaurant and retail space next door to the inn. The building has water views and faces the busy trail leading to the Taylor Avenue Dock and north to Bellingham's central business district. Just weeks before publication of this book it was announced that more residential buildings were to be built on land in front of the Tennis Club and farther west along Harris Avenue toward the water.

Fairhaven has become a true Urban Village, more than just a place where businesses thrive, but also a place where hundreds of people live. Its renaissance has been remarkable.

Fairhaven in 2015

The renaissance of the Village has been remarkable. To illustrate its current health we have again indicated its current buildings by overlaying their borders onto the Sanborn Map of 1897. Builder, construction date, and present occupancy of the buildings are indicated below.

1. Site of Fairhaven Hotel contains the now-vacant Richfield gas station, 1956
2. Retail strip, William Wood, 1968, credit union, retail
3. Fairhaven Square, David Ebenal, 2006, restaurant, residential
4. Mason Block, Allan C. Mason, 1890, restaurants, retail.
5. Win's Inn, Winifred Walstrom, 1964, Drive-in restaurant
6. Chuckanut Motors Bldg, 1919, retail, restaurants
7. Waldron Block; C.W. Waldron, 1891, bank, residential, remodel 2011
8. Fairhaven Pharmacy Bldg., Geo. Finnegan, 1929, retail, restaurant
9. Bellingham National Bank, 1969, Key Bank
10. Terminal Bldg., Evans & Fick, 1888, restaurant, coffee shop, offices
11. E.M. Day Bldg., Milton R. Straight.1890, Dirty Dan's Restaurant
12. Monahan Bldg., Thomas E. Monahan,1889, retail
13. Judson Plaza Bldg., Sharon Lipscomb, 1991, retail, residential
14. Finnegan Alley Bldg., Phyllis McKee, 2000, retail, offices
15. Nelson Block, James P. Nelson, 1900, restaurant, retail, offices
16. H. Dale Young Bldg., David Ebenal, 2011, retail, residential
17. Rocket Bldg., Jim Swift, 2014, restaurant, retail
18. Knights of Pythias; 1891, restaurant, retail
19. Fairhaven Cash Grocery, 1891, Paper Dreams, retail, office
20. Village Books, David Ebenal, 2004, retail, restaurant, residential
21. Quinby Bldg., Ken Imus, Jacaranda Co., 1992, restaurant, retail
22. 1025 Harris Bldg., Ken Imus, Jacaranda Co., 1995, retail
23. Fairhaven Village Green, City of Bellingham, 2003, public park
24. Morgan Block, Phillip Morgan, 1890, retail, restaurant, offices
25. 1006 Harris Bldg., Ken Imus, Jacaranda Co., 1995, retail
26. 1010 Harris Bldg., Ken Imus, Jacaranda Co., 1995 retail
27. London Bus on lot, Ken Imus, 1992, restaurant
28. Post Office, 1890/1911, retail, Skylarks Restaurant
29. 1012 12th St. Bldg., Ken Imus, Jacaranda Co., 1997, retail
30. Automobile parking, Ken Imus
31. Fairhaven Village Inn, Ken Imus, 1998
32. Schering Block, Charles Schering, 1903, retail, office, studio
33. Bellingham Bay Hotel, 1902, retail and offices
34. Tim Imus, 2002, retail, offices
35. 905 Harris, 1979, retail
36. Dharma Juice Bldg., 1991
37a,b,c. Harris Square. 2005, 3-building retail and condominium complex

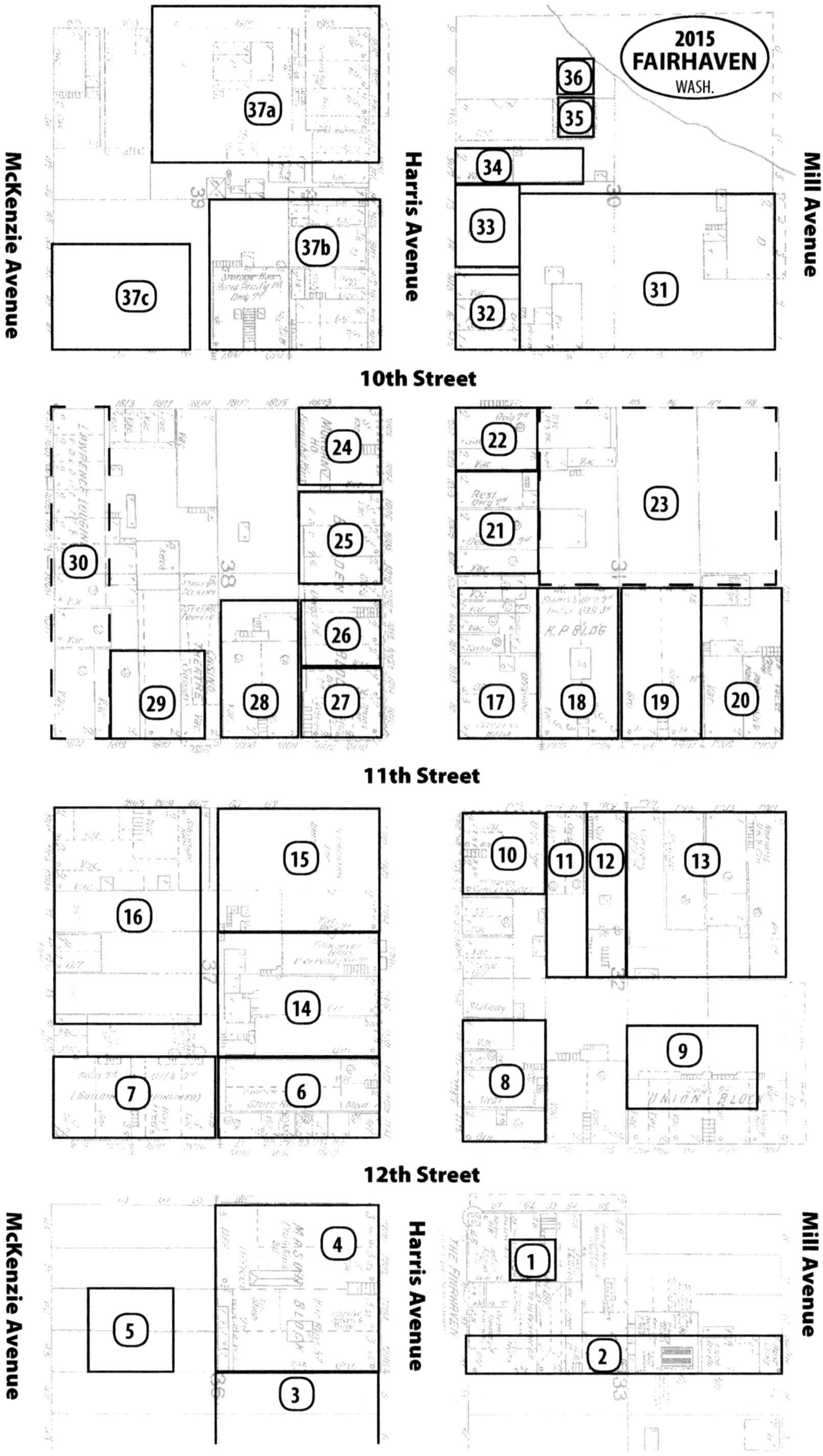

2015 FAIRHAVEN WASH.

McKenzie Avenue

Harris Avenue

Mill Avenue

37a

37b

37c

36

35

34

33

32

31

10th Street

24

25

26

27

28

29

30

22

21

23

17

18

19

20

11th Street

15

16

14

7

6

10

11

12

13

8

9

12th Street

4

5

3

1

2

McKenzie Avenue

Harris Avenue

Mill Avenue

23.1. Chuck and Dee Robinson, The founders of Village Books and the legendary "Builders of Community" in Fairhaven and in greater Bellingham. ©John Servais photo.

CHAPTER 23

Modern Boomers

It would be a disservice to history and to scores of devoted Fairhavenites to fail to credit the efforts of those who have brought Fairhaven back from the depths.

It is not quite accurate to refer to those scores of people whose energies have fueled Fairhaven's 21st century renaissance as *boomers*. Perhaps it would be better to categorize those stalwart merchants and volunteers and investors as *believers*. They surely displayed their belief in Fairhaven's future with their efforts and their investments. I write this chapter with a certain amount of dread, as I am sure I will leave out many who deserve to share the credit for Fairhaven's present charm and economic success. Those I have missed will know in their hearts the role that they played, and I am sure feel a rewarding warm glow as they view the Fairhaven of today.

Fairhaven was at the bottom in the late 1960s. PAF had closed in 1966, one after another, the small merchants struggled and closed their doors until the village was replete with vacancies. Fairhaven's woes happened to coincide in time with the great societal upheaval of the Vietnam War years. The counter culture revolution was aflame across the country, and its idealistic youth found the empty old buildings and quaint setting of Fairhaven to their liking. The word spread across the west coast and the nation that Fairhaven was the place to be. In a way the counter culture movement established Fairhaven as a special sort of place, it endowed the village with a certain aura adding to its charm.

Among the leaders in those long-haired days was John Blethen. John is a member of the prominent and conservative Blethen family, owners of the *Seattle Times* newspaper. He was perhaps typical of many in his generation, rejecting the dictates of family and society and seeking life's answers in other ways. But the family entrepreneurial blood ran in his veins, for soon after his arrival in Bellingham he discovered the large basement under the Nelson

Block and established his Toad Hall restaurant and hippie hang out. John, now the owner of a respected cabinet building business, has continued his community building in countless ways in the four decades since his arrival.

John Servais who came to Fairhaven in 1969, was an active observer during the hippie days, and has been a devoted board member of the Historic Fairhaven Association since 2002. He saved the summer outdoor movies when the Pickford people withdrew from Fairhaven. He has created and carried on a number of Fairhaven annual events that brought wide attention to the village, including Dirty Dan Days and the Bocce Ball Tournament. For many years he was the owner and operator of a commercial website, Fairhaven.com, which spread the news of Fairhaven far and wide. John has been a fountain of creativity and energy and has served the village in innumerable ways. Trees, benches, gazebos, the flag pavilion and more can be credited to his devotion and tireless effort on behalf of the village.

Kenneth Imus. We have written much about his role in earlier chapters. His pivotal role cannot be minimized.

Brad Imus, Ken Imus's eldest son who came to Fairhaven in 1978 to be the resident manager of Jacaranda's holdings. For much of the 1970s and '80s, his father was still living in California and making only periodic visits to Fairhaven. It was Brad who managed the business. It was Brad who solved the problems. He has always been the positive, steady, reliable, helpful influence that has kept Fairhaven moving forward. He remains the everyday manager of Imus interests in Fairhaven, and is now the President of the Jacaranda Corporation.

Tyrone and Penny Tilson, for many years this couple published the *Fairhaven Gazette*, a monthly publication filled with Fairhaven lore and history. Their efforts did much to publicize the village.

The Davis brothers, Brantley and Vincent, a medical doctor and an orthodontist, invested in much of the vacant property of the decayed town. They built the Tennis Club. They agreed with the need for a public park in Fairhaven, and were willing to wait to sell their property until the Greenways levy had passed and the city could buy the land for Fairhaven Village Green.

Taimi Dunn Gorman. Taimi Dunn and her then-husband Ray Dunn, opened the Colophon Café, making it a Fairhaven institution. The ever-creative Taimi then opened the Doggie Diner, drawing national publicity to Fairhaven. Taimi was a long-time leader of the Historic Fairhaven Association and a village booster in so many ways. She can share credit with Phyllis McKee for convincing the Davis brothers to sell the Village Green land to the City.

Chuck and Dee Robinson, these legendary figures have led, pushed or assisted every forward-moving effort since their arrival in 1980, opening their marvelous stores, Village Books and Paper Dreams. No one has done more.

Gordon Tweit, who was born and raised in Fairhaven, is the very soul of the village. Gordie's 49 years of photographing Halloween kids, and any little thing that has happened in Fairhaven, has strengthened a sense of community. His incredible museum under the pharmacy is a gold mine of history, collected with loving interest over the years. His knowledge of families and events of the Southside is unparalleled. Gordie has shared his knowledge of Fairhaven history with the community for many years, opening his basement museum on Friday afternoons to all comers.

23.2. Gordon Tweit. Whatcom Museum.

Stanley Velas opened his Venus Pizza restaurant in the Chuckanut Motors Building and grew it into a successful draw for the village. Later Stan moved south a block or two and built his handsome new Stannello's restaurant which continued to draw customers to Fairhaven for many more years.

Ellen Shea had a dream, a boutique inn on the Fairhaven waterfront. She found a partner to help with the financing and built the Chrysalis Inn and Spa on the old McEvoy Oil property at the Taylor Avenue Dock.

David Ebenal, a general contractor with an evident love of history and high risk. Ebenal has built five modern buildings in Fairhaven. While clearly done for profit, his buildings have fit well into the ambiance of the village and have made a huge contribution to the renaissance of Fairhaven.

Sharon Lipscomb may have been the first *boomer* to build a new building in the still struggling Fairhaven. She was a realtor with family roots deep in Whatcom County history. She constructed the large building directly across 11th Street from Village Books and named it Judson Plaza, honoring her forebears, the founders of Lynden, Washington.

Jody Finnegan, the owner of 12th Street Shoes, who has served for ten years on the board of directors of the Historic Fairhaven Association and been its president for three. She is a leading merchant who has provided steady leadership and marketing skills

Jack and Dawn Weatherby, who in the 1990s published *TV Facts* and advertised Fairhaven with energy and success.

23.3. Fairhaven's oldest and newest buildings. The Terminal Building and the Rocket Donuts/Fat Pie Pizza building, 2015.

Tip Johnson is a former Bellingham City Councilman who started Fairhaven Boats—the forerunner of the Community Boating Center. Johnson played Dirty Dan Harris for the Fairhaven Village Green opening ceremonies, and rowed a boat from Victoria to Fairhaven as a promotional stunt for the event.

John Hauter is perhaps the Fairhaven merchant with the most seniority. Hauter opened his Fairhaven Bicycle shop in October 1971 in the uphill half of the Terminal Building. His opening coincided with Tony Campbell's opening of Tony's Coffee. The bicycle shop was moved in 1975 to a location farther north on 11th Street, where it remained until 2004 when he moved to the new building he had constructed up the street at 1108 11th Street. John has been a constant supporter of the Village and the Historic Fairhaven Association.

Anna Williams, the steady hand at the helm of Fairhaven's premier annual event, the Ski to Sea finale, originally known as 'It All Ends in Fairhaven'. This event largely funds the annual activities of the Historic Fairhaven Association. Anna was for many years the owner of The Fairhaven Restaurant. She continues on the board of the Association and is the chairman of its major fund-raiser.

There are literally hundreds of others whose efforts to boost the village deserve mention, it is impossible to mention them all.

PART TWO

FAIRHAVEN
Anecdotes & Recollections

F airhaven history is enlivened by many interesting anecdotal stories that were difficult to fit into the preceding chronology. We offer a few of those historical tidbits, stories or recollections in the following pages in the hope that they will enrich the reader's understanding and enjoyment of Fairhaven.

Whatcom county was a forest primeval. The trees were huge, and men quickly set to work to turn those trees into railroad ties, boards and shingles. Galen Biery Photographs #3090, CPNWS.

The empty lot at 10th and Mill in June 2001. Kate Weisel photo.

Fairhaven Village Green

T his charming and popular city park functions as the beating heart of Fairhaven Village. It is the site of public celebrations, summer movies, a weekly farmers' market and most importantly, a place to meet people and experience the warmth of community.

For most of Fairhaven's history the land was undeveloped, simply a vacant lot behind the mercantile buildings on Harris Avenue and the Knights of Pythias building on 11th Street.

We believe that the only structure ever built on this lot was an outhouse behind one of the Harris Avenue buildings. Ironically it was the desire to build a modern outhouse which resulted in its current development as the heart of the Village.

In the 1980s, the vacant property was purchased by the Davis brothers. It was just one of the 33 vacant properties they had accumulated. By the early 1990s, the Colophon Café had established itself in the Knights of Pythias building, and the restaurant had joined with Village Books in expanding into the basement. Ray and Taimi Dunn, remembering a Parisian experience, began having thoughts about outdoor dining at the edge of the vacant lot outside their back door. One day to Taimi's dismay, Dr. Brantley Davis mentioned to her that the brothers had a prospective buyer for the property and that the buyer would likely build a building on the site. Taimi's dream of outdoor dining with a view was threatened.

A few days later Taimi was invited to attend a Beyond Greenways committee planning session at the studio of artist Jody Bergsma. The meeting was devoted to considering potential park land purchases should the Greenways levy be passed by the voters. Taimi suggested the Davis land behind her restaurant as a potential park. The committee agreed and added the site to their list.

Phyllis McKee and Taimi, concerned that the site would be sold before the levy could be passed, invited the Davis brothers and their wives to dinner at

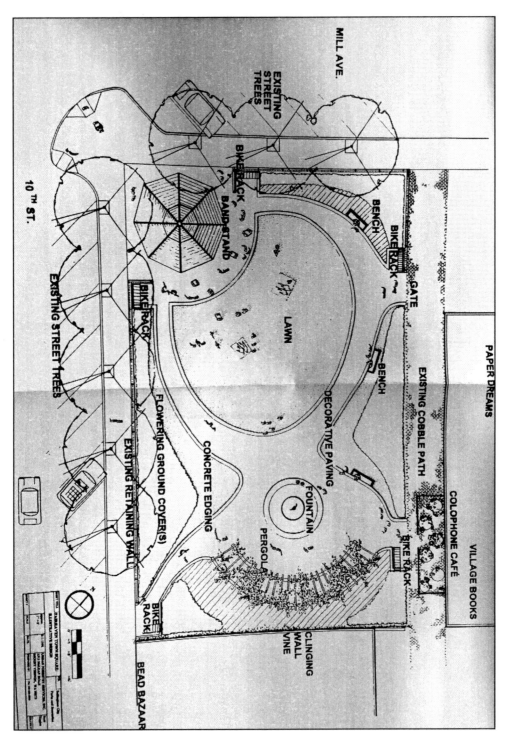

The first park design was called Fairhaven Town Square and resembled an English garden with paths and flower beds and a small public restroom under a bandstand gazebo at the corner of Tenth and Mill Avenue.

Bellingham's finest restaurant, Il Fiasco. The two women pleaded with the Davis's asking them not to sell the land until the results of the levy were known. They convinced them that it would be in the public interest if their land could become a public park. The Davis's agreed to wait for the levy.

The 1997 Beyond Greenways levy passed handily, and after appraisal the property was sold to the City of Bellingham. The City had offered $350,000 which was less than the appraised value. The brothers decided to accept the low offer considering that the community would benefit.

The Historic Fairhaven Association had hoped to see the property immediately developed into a public park which would include a public restroom, an amenity badly needed in the Village.

Jointly, the merchants' group and the city came up with a park development plan designed by Urban Forestry Service of Mount Vernon. The park design was called Fairhaven Town Square and resembled an English garden with paths and flower beds and a small public restroom under a bandstand gazebo at the corner of Tenth and Mill Avenue. There was little enthusiasm for the plan and neither the merchants association nor the City were able to find the funds to construct the park. The land lay fallow, an undeveloped grass field, mowed occasionally by the City Parks Department.

Some public activities were being held on the newly acquired park property. The most notable of which was the Pickford Theater's idea. In 1996, the Jacaranda Corporation had allowed the merchants' association to paint a white movie screen on the back of the Quinby building, and the Pickford Theater people began showing outdoor movies on the wall on summer Saturday nights. This became an extremely popular use of the grass field.

The increasing business and recreation activities in Fairhaven placed a glaring light on the village's most pressing need, public restroom facilities. The park property was a perfect place for such facilities, but getting the funding to build them was another matter. The stalemate continued for several more years.

One day in March of 2001, Chuck Robinson, co-owner of Village Books, and Denise Dibb, a stockbroker at Edward Jones, both representing the Historic Fairhaven Association asked to meet with this author. They proposed that I assume the leadership of a campaign to fund the earlier design plan and accomplish the much needed public restrooms. I was flattered at being asked, but not excited about the prospect of building public restrooms for Fairhaven merchants. I declined their offer. They would have to look elsewhere for their restroom builder.

Over the next several days my mind kept returning to that tiny little open space in the heart of Fairhaven. The challenge of doing something with the sloping grass field would not leave my mind. I began to think of the small pocket parks that I had so admired in Europe. Small parks and public places which seemed to be the central focus of neighborhoods in great cities like Paris and Amsterdam and Rome. I began to visualize what we could do with a similar central meeting place in Fairhaven. I became intrigued by the possibility of creating a park in Fairhaven where 'community' could happen.

Three days later I called Robinson and agreed to lead a task force to develop the space. He agreed to serve on the task force. He would be important in dealing with the Fairhaven merchant community and for his many other skills.

Seeking people with the necessary skills and experience to put such a project together, I recruited the team. Chuck Robinson, leader in the Fairhaven merchants' organization and respected community member; J.C. Hickman, recently retired publisher of the *Bellingham Herald*, a veteran businessman with communication and media skills and a influential citizen; Kate Weisel, a graphic artist, publishing expert, savvy with computers; Barbara Evans, organized, hard worker, ardent lover of Fairhaven; her husband Howard, retired WWU professor, willing to work hard at any aspect of the project; Evelyn Bell, recently retired, competent organizer; Charles Onion, former organizer of the Garlic Festival in California, a lover of Fairhaven and eager to work. A small but talented group of dedicated people, a task force, not a committee. We met weekly.

The first task was to design the project. I immediately turned to an old friend and gifted architect, John Stewart. John, seeing the exciting potential of the project and its community value agreed to design the project without a fee, an incredibly generous donation to begin our campaign. We quickly discarded the earlier English Garden plan, and in short order Stewart came up with a new design guided by our remembrances of the parks of Europe. The task force was delighted with his results. He had designed the community center that we had envisioned and committee enthusiasm ran high.

We debated the selection of a name for our projected park and could think of no better name than the one first used by Taimi Dunn when lobbying the City to buy the land—Fairhaven Village Green. Now we needed a cost estimate. Pete Dawson of Dawson Construction Company generously spent the time to calculate an expected cost of Stewart's plan. $500,000.

Now it was time to go to the City.

Bellingham had just hired Paul Leuthold as their new Parks Director. I clearly remember the crucial first meeting with Paul and his assistant, Leslie Bryson. If we could not convince them of the virtues of the plan our project would be over. We met for lunch at the Colophon Café beside the grass field we hoped to develop. I found the new director to be a positive and enthusiastic person. He immediately saw the opportunity. Leslie Bryson, was interested and favorable, but professionally cautious. She had seen over-enthusiastic citizen committees before.

We unveiled John Stewart's preliminary sketches. I revealed that he was providing the architectural work without cost. We proposed a partnership approach to this project. The volunteer committee would raise $150,000 of the project. It would raise those funds to pay for the above-ground assets of the park—such as the pergola, pavers, fencing and benches. The city would contract for the earth work—the grading, concrete construction, lawn, restrooms, etc. We would work as partners making all design and construction decisions together. The committee would retain control of the money it raised, and would individually pay for those elements of the park that the partners agreed upon.

Director Leuthold agreed to the deal. He assigned Leslie Bryson as the City's project manager. We shook hands on our agreement and together we set to work.

This unusual approach meant that the committee would have to raise, account for and dispense $150,000 or hopefully more. Needing the fund raising help of a tax-exempt 501c-3 organization, we went to Don Drake, Executive Director of the Whatcom Community Foundation. With them we forged a working agreement, which was to be the first of many such agreements that the Community Foundation has since partnered in civic advancement.

The Community Foundation agreed to accept all funds raised by the Fairhaven Village Green Committee. Contributions were to be made to the Community Foundation, Fairhaven Village Green Fund. Thus the contributions would be tax deductible to the donor. The Foundation would safeguard and account for the monies and pay the invoices that the committee presented for the Village Green amenities. The Foundation charged a modest 3% fee for their services to cover their expenses. This placed all of the fiduciary responsibility with the Community Foundation and left the Committee with the challenge of raising the money.

Now we needed to get the project into the Parks Department budget in time so that it could be incorporated in the city budget. Failure to meet the time requirements would mean a one-year delay and a major set-back for our fundraising campaign and our momentum. John Stewart and his architectural firm did yeoman's work completing the plans. The committee met with Leslie Bryson weekly, planning the moves ahead and making decisions. The Park Board met and quickly approved the deal and the plans and finally, at a memorable City Council meeting, the project was approved and placed in the City of Bellingham budget. The City budgeted $350,000 contingent upon the committee successfully raising their $150,000 pledge. We had met the deadlines and were free to move forward.

Cooperation and success began immediately. The Jacaranda Corp. loaned us an empty storefront in their Fairhaven Village Inn building on 10th Street where we could set up our sales office and mini museum of Fairhaven history. We staffed it with volunteers to tell the story, take contributions and sell the various fundraising schemes we had developed. The walls were filled with historic Fairhaven photos loaned by Whatcom Museum and the Mayor's office. We displayed a number of historic items: the silver service from the Fairhaven Hotel, a tulip water fountain that had stood beside the Terminal Building for years. The historic displays were aimed at getting visitors in our door, so we could sell them something.

We sold engraved names on yet-to-be purchased pavers. The Parks Dept. agreed that names could be engraved on 10,000 of the eventual 44,000 pavers put into the park. We charged $35 to engrave one paver, or four for $100. We solicited families and businesses offering to put their names on large blue-stone tablets that would be grouped around the Knute Evertz Tulip Fountain. Solicitations were made to persons and families known to be supportive of community projects. Fairhaven Merchants contributed, money came unsolicited from unexpected sources. We sold 232 bowler hats to the newly formed Bowler Hat Society. The community responded with enthusiasm, and by January of 2001 we had reached our $150,000 goal. Our achievement validated the city's budget requirement, and the project could now be put out to bid.

The low bidder was Colacurcio Brothers Construction Company of Blaine. We were relieved that they had bid just below the estimated cost. The construction contract did not include construction of the wood and glass pergola, the purchase and construction of the iron fence, the bollard and chains along the east side, or the purchase of the pavers and benches. Those tasks were reserved for the Committee.

At some point during this time the idea of a statue of Fairhaven's founder Dirty Dan Harris came forth. I knew of a local sculptor who had done nice work in bronze. I also had an acquaintance, a retired university administrator who was doing sculpture as a retirement hobby. The Committee decided on a competition. We asked each of these men to do a maquette—a miniature version—of how they would portray Dirty Dan, and to quote us a completion price. The winner was Robert McDermott, a retired industrial project manager with considerable artistic talent. His price for Dan Harris sitting on a bronze bench would be $35,000. A contact was made with the Conoco Phillips Refinery manager Gary Goodman. With Goodman's support, Conoco Phillips agreed to fund the entire project and pay for the iron railing around the park as well. Their contribution totaled $50,000.

McDermott's sculpture of Dirty Dan has become a beloved feature of Fairhaven Village Green and truly a community icon.

One of the big expenses for the Committee was the purchase of the brick pavers. We contracted Kenadar Corp. of Seattle, who performed the paver engraving, and also represented Whitacre-Greer, the makers of fine clay pavers in Ohio. We considered purchasing less expensive pavers made of colored concrete, but chose to commit to quality. We carefully chose Whitacre-Greer pavers in five different colors, being advised that they would look far better than a field of identically colored pavers. We ordered 44,000 pavers to be delivered to Bellingham by rail.

Then the challenge became where we could unload and store these pavers until they were needed. They would have to be stored for several months until the contractor was ready to install them. The pavers would be shipped in three boxcars, their handling seemed a huge problem to solve. Our good fortune continued and the good people of the

The Knute Evertz Tulip Fountain with Dirty Dan statue on the Village Green, 2011. Taimi Gorman photo.

community stepped forward to help, as happened again and again in this project.

Georgia Pacific had just ceased their pulp mill operations and were slowly moving out of their waterfront location. The man in charge of this removal operation was Tom Spink. Immediately upon hearing of our need Spink offered to store the pavers in the fenced yard beside the Great Northern spur at the GP receiving warehouse. His men unloaded the scores of pallets of heavy pavers with their forklifts and stacked them in the lot, where they sat for several months until we were ready for their installation. Spink's generosity made a huge contribution to the project and lifted a great burden from the Committee's shoulders.

Soon the heavy equipment of Colacurcio Brothers moved onto the park site and construction began on this property that had never before seen a building. The excavation began for the restrooms, which would be at the 10th Street level under the new stage. The backhoe operator was digging, taking great bites of dirt as he began the excavation. Suddenly he found evidence that there had been a building there before. The big backhoe was digging easily through soft and sandy gray soil when the excavator claw revealed a very different column of rich dark soil three or four feet wide. As the shovel filled with this contrasting rich soil a number of glass bottles were seen.

The operator stopped his dig for a moment to salvage the old bottles. We could see several small medicine bottles and more than a couple old whiskey bottles. Those bottles and the dark soil were sure signs of an ancient outhouse on that site. Any bottle collector can tell you that in the old days medicine bottles and booze bottles were frequently disposed of down the hole of the outhouse. We think that the outhouse on the Village Green site had served one of the 1890 buildings facing on Harris Avenue. A review of old Sanborn Maps going back as far as 1890 indicate that no larger structures had ever occupied the Village Green site.

The equipment operator was apparently a bottle collector. He quickly got off his machine, picked up the bottles and secured his finds beside his lunch bucket in the cab. I happened to be standing by watching the dig and at my request he gave me a small medicine bottle with a tiny chip at its opening. It still commands a position of respect in my office as a treasured memento of the Village Green's construction and of Fairhaven history.

One of the high points of the project was the construction and installation of the glass-covered pergola that surrounds the Green and protects the occupants from inclement weather. Knowing that we were blessed with two extremely community-minded and competent wood-working companies, we contacted both GR Plume Company and Cascade Joinery, asking for help and suggesting they both take a part in the project.

In a thrilling display of community generosity, Jeff Arvin of Cascade Joinery and Gordon Plume owner of GR Plume, both enthusiastically joined the cause. Plume agreed to make the vertical posts with their internal threaded rods, Arvin took on the horizontal pieces. Each company did their part at extremely competitive low-profit or no-profit prices.

The original plan called for concrete plinths under each of the posts. Gordon Plume pointed out that concrete would look cheap and suggested we find stone that could be cut to make proper plinths. I happened to know that the Parks Department had a large pile of beautiful granite curb-stones that had recently been removed from downtown Bellingham streets. It was not a large task to talk the Parks Department out of a truckload of them, and soon several of us were learning to cut granite at the GR Plume yard on the Bakerview Road. It was a lot of work, but well worth it to see historic granite that had been placed as curbs in Bellingham's downtown in 1909, now supporting the beautiful posts in Fairhaven Village Green.

Finally the day came when we could raise the pergola. It turned out to be an old-fashioned barn-raising. Cascade Joinery and GR Plume each volunteered six professional wood workers to erect the structure. The Committee provided 12 volunteers to carry the materials to the professionals and hoist them up. Sarah Dawson at Birch Equipment donated hand-operated lifts that would raise the heavy beams up to the professionals. The Colophon Café, unasked, offered a free lunch for all 24 workers.

At 8 AM on a cool fall day, all of the parts of the pergola were trucked to the site and were stacked on the Mill Avenue empty lot where Village Books now stands. The volunteers began to pick up and deliver the beams and posts to the professionals. Two men to a beam, up to the shoulder and away we go! The beams were heavy and most of the men were up in years and not used to such labor. The beams were carried to the lifts and cranked up to the professionals on ladders. It was hard work. Gordon Plume applied the mortar to the concrete foundation pad and set the granite plinths upon them, aligning the stone plinths and the threaded rods in advance of the professionals with the upright posts. He was on his knees for the entire day, until he could hardly rise to go to the next post.

As the morning progressed new volunteers appeared, asking if they could help, and the aged and out-of-shape beam carriers welcomed their help. Robert Keller walked down Mill Avenue, saw the activity and taking off his coat, pitched in for the rest of the day. Perhaps the best unexpected volunteer of the day was Bellingham Mayor Mark Asmundson, who surprised us all by arriving early and working very hard until the job was done. We all agreed he may have been the best worker among us.

It was indeed an old fashioned barn-raising. Almost 30 men working with joy and community pride can accomplish an incredible amount of work. At noon as we were finishing the Colophon's much appreciated lunch, I challenged the crew, announcing that if we got the last section of pergola erected by 3 PM, I would host an open bar at Archer's Ale House across the street. They did it. I have long forgotten the bar bill that afternoon, but I will never forget the camaraderie and pride that we all felt that day.

With the pergola now up, the project progressed with remarkable good fortune and few problems. The partnership spirit between the City and the Fairhaven Village Green Committee was marvelous. Leslie Bryson, the Parks Department's project supervisor, and the committee chair worked together in a collegial fashion that saw few differences of opinion and an easy concession to the other's view. A supportive Mayor and City Council and an excited populace made the project progress almost without controversy. A few critics were concerned that the wall along 10th Street would be too high. Some felt there should be more grass and fewer pavers or vice versa, but there was remarkably little contention over this seemingly blessed project.

One of the few contentious issues was the Dirty Dan Harris statue. Art installations on city property must be vetted by the City Arts Commission. This is a wise and necessary step to assure quality and consistency of the cultural climate in any community. Procedural matters, and the subjective opinions of individual Arts Commission members, however made problems for the Harris statue. At the time, Commission procedure called for public art to be proposed only by the Arts Commission, a Call for Artists issued, and a selection made from those artist submissions. This was not the procedure followed in the case of Dirty Dan Harris.

The Fairhaven Village Green Committee had conceived the idea, held their own artist competition, made the selection, raised the money to pay for it and then presented it as a *fait acompli* to the Arts Commission. Some of the Commission members were not happy about that. Adding fuel to the fire, in making the presentation to the Commission I read a brief history of Dirty Dan, mentioning that he had been a crewman on a sailing ship headed to China to pick up *coolies* to work the gold mines of the California Gold Rush.

The presentation devolved into a heated discussion. Several commission members, upset by the procedural lapse, their lack of involvement, and the fact that we proposed honoring a blackguard such as Dirty Dan, whose pursuit of coolies was akin to being a slaver, moved to deny permission to use the statue. Fortunately, cooler heads on the commission prevailed, and the Dirty Dan Harris statue was narrowly approved by the Arts Commission by a 5 to 4 vote.

A few weeks later, another dust up with the Arts Commission occurred when the Fairhaven Village Green Committee received a letter from the Commission informing it that the Arts Commission would execute its right and responsibility of deciding where in the new park the statue would be placed. This time the Village Green Committee was not happy. After some consideration it responded that the statue had not yet been gifted to the City, and was still the property of the Fairhaven Village Green Committee. We had designed the park and intended to continue our design responsibility by placing the statue. If we were prevented from doing that, we would consider placing the statue on the eight-foot strip of private land adjoining the park alongside the buildings. There was no further communication with the Arts Commission on the matter; however, the conflicts with the Commission made the Committee wary.

In the contract deeding the Harris statue to the City of Bellingham for a token $5, the Committee required a condition that should the statue ever be removed from the Fairhaven Village Green, the City title to it would be nullified and ownership would be transferred to the Whatcom Community Foundation. A signed copy of that agreement is preserved among the 'Fairhaven Village Green' papers in the Center for Pacific Northwest Studies at the State Regional Archive.

Soon after the Pergola was completed, the pavers were laid, and then came the great day when the grass arrived. Now it truly was a Village Green. Benches were purchased and installed. Iota Metalworking installed the railing they had built in their Fairhaven workshop. Louis Auto Glass placed the glass on the Pergola, and the community was invited to a great opening dedication ceremony.

The Fairhaven Village Green on an August farmers' market day, 2013. Kate Weisel photo.

To celebrate the event, and the history of Fairhaven, Tip Johnson, a former City Councilman rowed a boat from Victoria dressed as Dirty Dan Harris. His arrival was timed with the opening ceremonies. Mayor Mark Asmundson cut a ribbon which spanned the stage. The Bellingham High School Alumni Band belted out Sousa marches, vendors sold food under the pergola, speeches were delivered and a tour of three historic homes was conducted. The Gamwell House, Wardner's Castle, and the old Church on Mill and 15th (now converted to a residence), were open to the public for a fee.

The celebration was a huge success as waves of people visited their new park for the first time. The home tour, chaired by Mary Hickman, raised an incredible $15,000 to add to the Committee's contribution to the construction costs.

In its final report to the City, the Fairhaven Village Green Committee reported that it had raised $269,964 in cash. It valued pro bono contributions of architect fees, lent equipment, labor, etc., at $122,477.59, bringing the total private contribution to the park to the total of $392,441.59. City records indicated their costs at $462,000.

Fairhaven finally had its restrooms. The citizens of Bellingham have a place where community happens.

The Croatians of Fairhaven

A s the salmon canning industry developed in the Pacific Northwest and on Bellingham Bay, an opportunity was created for experienced fishermen and seamen. For the first time since the days of the fur trade a major industrial opportunity was developing that focused on the sea. Before salmon could be canned they had to be caught and delivered to the cannery. In the beginning years of the canning industry salmon were primarily caught by the highly efficient stationary fish traps that dotted the inland waters. From the beginning, there was a need for men familiar with fishing and the sea.

As early as 1895, a small cannery in Brookfield, Oregon, on the Columbia River advertised in Croatia seeking the ancient skills of a hardy race of fishermen who lived on the numerous islands in the Adriatic Sea off the Austrian Empire's Dalmatian coast. These islanders had earned their living from the sea for countless generations. By the time salmon canning had begun on Bellingham Bay, word about the opportunities in the new world had reached the outermost island off the Croatian shoreline, the island of Vis. The small mountainous island contained two villages, Komiza and Vis. Their inhabitants had been fishermen and seamen since pre-Roman times.

This was a period of mass migrations from Europe to an expected brighter future in the New World. The fishermen of the island of Vis were not immune to the hope of a better life. The difficult economics of the day and the constant threat of conscription into the armies of the Austrian Emperor provided ample motivation for a young man to leave home.

It is thought that the first Slav fishermen to immigrate to the Northwest fishery were Nick Bozanich and Barto Fadich. Probably the first Slav to come to Bellingham Bay was Antone Glenovich from the village of Komiza in the year 1896. Before long, others from his village came until eventually most of the Bellingham Slavs could proudly claim their origin as Komiza.

Like all immigrants of the time these hardy fishermen were rather clannish. They gathered together in this new land for security and social ease. The

Map of Adriatic Sea. Arrow points to the island of Vis.

large population of Croatians in Anacortes, also fishermen, were largely from the villages of Vela Luka and Blato on the island of Korcula, or the town of Splitska on the island of Brac. In a perfectly natural progression, a young man would arrive, work hard fishing in the summer and in the lumber mills in the winter. He would write home telling of the good life in the New World and others of his village would be encouraged to come. Frequently he would send for a bride from his home town, or if he had been frugal, he would buy passage home to marry and then return with his bride to Fairhaven or Anacortes.

The Croatian population of Fairhaven grew quickly. Pacific American Fisheries operated a salmon camp on the Cattle Point beach on San Juan Island. After a day of fishing on the rich salmon banks just offshore, the fishermen would ride the flood tide each evening through Cattle Pass to shelter in Fish Creek for the night, sailing or rowing out again on the morning ebb to set their nets. At this time most of the salmon to be caught were caught in fish traps.

In 1935, when salmon traps were declared illegal, purse seining became the primary way to catch salmon. In the early years the purse seine boats were powered by oar and sail. Now the Croatian's fishing skills gave them a great opportunity and immigration increased. Soon there was a major enclave of perhaps 500 Croatians, occupying mostly the lower streets of Bellingham's South Hill convenient to their fishing boats in the Fairhaven Boat Haven,[1] and to the canneries where many of the women worked. Staunch Roman Catholics, they attended the Sacred Heart Church at 14th and Knox. They attended Lowell Grade School, and Fairhaven High School and even after Consolidation, proudly called themselves *Southsiders*.

When the first generation had arrived in Fairhaven, few of them could speak any English. Most of them learned the language from their children who were taught English in school. The old 14th Street School, and its 1914

---

1   The Fairhaven Boat Haven was built in 1937 with a voter approved bond issue of $75,000. Tide flat land was purchased in front of the plywood plant.

replacement Lowell School, had a large number of students whose names ended with I-C-H. Names such as Evich, Zuanich, Elich, Zorodovich, Valich, Derpich, and Vitalich. They formed a distinctive cultural community. In the early years teaching English was a major curriculum subject in the 14th Street School.

Like immigrants from any culture, it was natural that they sought others of their kind to live beside. Many of them were related and almost all of them had come from the same tiny village of Komiza, connected by blood and friendship. They shopped at Slav grocery stores where they could find their familiar foods. They took care of each other. Many are the stories of a Slav family taking in a newly immigrated family until they could fend for themselves. They were a tight and cohesive community.

Wine was an important part of their culture. Many Slav families, perhaps most Slav families, made their own wine each year. Each summer the community's wine makers would select two trusted representatives and pay their way to California, where they would negotiate for and select the best Zinfandel grapes they could find in the Napa area. The grapes would be ordered and paid for and transportation arranged. Then on a propitious day in the fall the word would flash through Fairhaven, "The grapes have arrived!" Dozens of wine makers would descend on the train station, or to the Pacific Fruit and Produce warehouse on York Street to pick up their annual order. The heady smell of fermenting grapes would soon fill the air along 11th, 12th and 13th Streets. The precious grapes were crushed in large wooden fermenting barrels in cellars and basements and woodsheds.

When the 'first wine' had fermented and was racked off into clean barrels or glass carboys, the 'second wine' would be started. To extend the second usage of the grapes, dried raisins, sugar and water would be poured onto the grape mash exhausted from its first fermentation. All stirred together in the proper mixture, a second wine of equal volume and alcoholic power, but of less quality, would begin its fermentation.

Wine was an everyday drink among the Croatians. Every fishing boat leaving for the fishing grounds had its cask of wine stored safely in the lazerette. The author has fond memories of calling on southside families to discuss their insurance renewals and sharing the ritual glass of wine offered to every guest in Slav homes. The wine was usually not very good, but the hospitality was sincere and warm.

When the Croatian immigration began prior to the First World War, the immigrants were usually called *Austrians*. They had arrived as Austrian citizens, subjects of the Austro-Hungarian Empire. They were sometimes called *Dalmatians* having come from that region of Croatia. With the outbreak of the First World War Austria became an enemy of the United States, and the immigrants began to call themselves *Slavs,* as they are a Slavic people. That name was used by them until after the post cold-war collapse of Yugoslavia. After that event the use of *Croatian* to describe their heritage and ethnicity become most common. Old timers around the southside still call them Slavs, and many of them call themselves Slavs. It is not a term of derision, but a proud declaration of their ancestry.

By the time of this writing, the strong and visible Slav enclave in Fairhaven has largely dispersed into the melting pot that is modern America. There are still a great many Slavs in residence, but they now live in every part of the city. They are no longer clannish, most of them have married *foreskes,*[2] few can speak the old language, but they all share the treasured memories of their fisherman past and the stories of their homeland on the Island of Vis and its village of Komiza.

With his permission, I have included a personal narrative written by Steve Kink, a third generation Slav, entitled *Bellingham's Croatian Roots.* I have edited it slightly for publication in this book.

BELLINGHAM'S CROATIAN ROOTS

Much of the Croatian immigration to Bellingham came from a tiny little island called Vis located near the coast in today's Croatia. The Island of Vis, then as today, consisted of two towns called Vis and Komiza, plus several small villages.

Among those immigrants were my grandfather Paul Kinkusich, and my grandmother Marie Evich. Marie came from Komiza and Paul came from one of the small villages. They came to Bellingham around the turn of the century. I had always wondered about the roots of this Croatian culture, would the customs, occupations and traditions be the same in the *old country* as I experienced growing up in Bellingham? What would it be like in Croatia a hundred years after my grandparents left. If I went there what would I find? With this curiosity my wife Joann and I decided to go to Komiza.

We took a ferry from Split to Vis. As Vis appeared in the distance we could see a small rounded island. The shore was rocky with a few sandy beaches. It was green with small pine trees, bushes, olive and fig trees, vineyards and gardens spread among the rocky landscape.

We got off the ferry in Vis town and took the community bus over the island to Komiza. As we traveled over a small mountain Komiza came into view. There were many terraced gardens and vineyards seen from the road above. It was a beautiful serene little town located on a small bay. The small houses had red or tan tiled roofs, and white or tan sided walls. A few trees were scattered among the buildings. St. Nicholas Church stood majestically

---

2   The Slav word for anyone who is not a Croatian.

above the town surrounded by trees and vineyards. The waterfront was filled with a variety of fishing boats, some anchored and some tied to the promenade and a pier. The pier stretched about a quarter of a kilometer into the bay providing excellent protection for the small boats in the harbor. The setting and beauty was far more than we had expected.

It became very clear that this was primarily a fishing town. There were large purse seiners with nets and skiffs, like those found in Bellingham, Anacortes and Gig Harbor. Although designed only slightly different than those of Puget Sound and Alaska, they had virtually the same type of fishing gear and used the same techniques. Seeing the gear and boats brought back memories of purse seining in Puget Sound and Alaska. There were a variety of small boats separately outfitted to catch lobster, calamari or octopus. The small boats were used for day fishing, leaving in the early morning and returning in the evening with their catch. Komiza fishermen were tending their boats and fishing gear. They were talking and laughing and I suspect sharing fishing stories and recent gossip. This again reminded me of the many hours I spent in Bellingham working on nets, doing maintenance work on purse seiners, and listening to the stories shared by the sons of the first immigrants from Komiza.

We strolled the narrow streets of the town. Groceries, hardware and nautical supplies were sold out of little shops. A few people sold vinegar, wine and olive oil out of their homes. It seemed that everyone had their own family recipes. It reminded me of what Fairhaven was like when I was growing up. No large supermarkets, no big chain stores and my grandmother making wine, Slav spaghetti, and Slav sauerkraut from family recipes she remembered as a child in Komiza.

Each evening grandparents, parents and children would stroll along the promenade. It was a friendly and open atmosphere as people stopped and chatted and laughed. During the day several men would sit in front of bars and talk, laugh and then suddenly some would stand up and start singing. They were extremely good.

We visited the cemetery beside Saint Nicholas Church. The names we found could have been the same as those found in Bayview. Stanovich and Repanich were without the 'h' in Komiza. That can be explained by the fact that 'ic' is pronounced like 'ich' or 'itch'. Immigration officers were known to spell the names like they sounded, as thousands of immigrants filed through customs. Other names like Zanchi and Kuljis were exactly the same.

The hill above the town was terraced halfway up the mountain. There were several vineyards producing grapes for all those family wines. This brought back memories of smashing grapes in large vats in my grandmother's basement as she, my dad, uncle and aunts made the family wine.

We found Komiza to be a wonderful place that has maintained its culture and customs for centuries. It Is somewhat sad that you now have to go to Komiza to see what the fishing culture and Slav community life was once like in Fairhaven on Bellingham's southside.

THE MARDESICH LEGACY

Andro Mardesich was born in the year 1878 in the village of Komiza on the island of Vis. Andro, like many of his contemporaries, chose to leave his home island and risk a new life in the *new world*.

Andro arrived in the U.S. in 1903, and he became a naturalized citizen in 1912. He married and divorced early. In 1910 the U.S. census finds Andro living at 2230 29th Street in Tacoma. Age 34, he is listed as a salmon fisherman on the sound. The census also shows him to be a boarder in the home of a Katie Stanovich, who is listed as the head of the household. Katie is listed as a widow, living with her three children, Ellen age 14, Joseph age 13, and Grace age 8. The final member of the household is shown as brother-in-law Martin Sponorich age 18.

Katie Stanovich, 36, had immigrated from Komiza in 1896 and become naturalized that same year. She married a man named Sponorich, who died leaving her a widow with three children. Always a strong and capable woman, Katie chose to return to her maiden name.

We know that by 1914 Andro and Katie had married and were living in Bellingham. They had leased the store building at 1008-1010 11th Street and started the South Bellingham Grocery. They lived above the store in some of the sixteen rooms of the former lodging house and they had company, presumably tenants who were subletting from them. The 1920 census shows a total of eleven people living in the upstairs rooms. There was Andro and Katie and their 8-year-old daughter Catheryn. Down the hall were Tony and Mary Bakulich and their infant son Frank. In other rooms were Katie's daughter Ellen and her two children, Anthony 6 and Dorothy 5. Ellen had married a man named Milosevich and divorced. Also living above the store were Katie's son Joseph Sponorich 22, and a boarder Chris Radisich.

This photo shows Andro, a huge man for his time at six foot four, standing in the doorway of the store with Joe Sponorich. Sponorich helped in the store waiting on their primarily Croatian customers and delivering groceries to homes and fishing boats. He would eventually Anglicize his name to Joe Spencer. Andro's daughter Catheryn at age 13, drove the delivery truck for another store employee, Mitch Karuza, who carried the groceries into customers' homes and onto fishing boats.

Andro Mardesich, in front of his South Bellingham Grocery on 11th Street. Whatcom Museum.

The Mardesich family successfully operated the store for about 20 years. As soon as they were able they moved out of the lodgings above the store and into a house they built across the street at 1115 11th street. Finnegan Way was constructed in 1935 connecting 11th Street with 12th Street. The Mardesich house was in the path of the new road and was moved up to 1108 12th Street where it stands today.

The Mardesich's never owned the 11th Street store building, but in 1924 they did buy the adjoining lot (lot #2 in block 12). In 1917 or '18, a small warehouse was built on the north half of that lot. It is not known if the Mardesich's built the building, but it is probable that they did, needing storage for the considerable foodstuffs with which they provisioned the Slav purse seine boats. They bought the lot from a long-time Fairhaven grocer, Nels Anderson, who had begun the Fairhaven Cash Grocery on Harris Avenue in 1903. We do know that on Nov. 17, 1943, Andro and Kate

The Warehouse Building. The old building's last usage was as an antique store. R. Aiston drawing.

Mardesich sold the small warehouse building and the still-vacant south half of lot 2 to Homer F. and Marguerite A. Aiston. Eight years later, in 1951, the Aistons sold the property to the Fairhaven Townsend Club who used it for their meeting hall for many years. Finally, it was operated as an antique shop. In 2001 David Carlsen bought the lot, demolished the decrepit old building, and constructed the present day Eclipse Book Store. His book business had begun in 1989 in the Schering Block at the corner of Tenth and Harris.

The old grocery store building was demolished sometime in the mid 1940s. It had been built in 1890 in the midst of the Fairhaven boom by Philip Morgan. Morgan was a developer who had constructed several other buildings—the most notable of which was the Morgan Block that currently houses the pottery shop and Artwood. He had built the 11th Street building on a post and block foundation with wood-frame construction. It had two store fronts and 16 rental rooms above the stores. Its distinctive upstairs windows thrust out over the sidewalk in the front, as was typical for the time.

Immediately after its completion, Morgan entered into a one-year lease with Robert Heney who agreed to pay rent of $140 per month in gold coin for the north half of the building and all of the upstairs rooms. He negotiated the lease with the intent of operating a restaurant and lodging house. This paragraph from the lease document found in the State Regional Archive succinctly tells the story, "It is understood that the store is to be used for a restaurant business and the upstairs portion of the house is to be kept respectable as a lodging house." This was a period when there were many houses of ill repute in Fairhaven and Morgan did not want that activity in his building.

Heney's restaurant must have led a short life, as the Sanborn Map of 1897 shows the 1108 half of the building being used by an undertaker and the 1110 storefront was empty. In a few more years, the Mardesichs would move in and occupy the building for the rest of its history. Like most of the small wood-frame commercial buildings built in Fairhaven during the boom years, it was built very quickly and very cheaply. There were no building codes in effect or city inspectors to satisfy. In later years, Catheryn Mardesich Elich was to recall for her son Peter Elich, that the old building would sway so much in a windstorm that braces were installed on the north side for fear the building might fall over. Such braces are seen on other frame buildings in old photos of Fairhaven (see page 64).

Catheryn Mardesich married Anthony Elich in 1930. Elich was a Komizan who had immigrated to America at age 10. He was a fisherman for many years, crewing for several of Bellingham's best purse seine skippers, Peter Zitco and Nick Vitalijic (who had married Elich's sister Fanny Elich). With them he fished the Salish Sea and Alaska for salmon, and for sardines in California. Eventually Elich quit fishing and began working in the plywood plant in Fairhaven, and finally the Mt. Baker Plywood plant from which he

In these early days on 11th Street the sidewalks were planked and the fire department rushed to fires drawn by a troika of beautiful white horses. This photo shows the fire rig in front of 1108 11th Street, which would become the Mardesich grocery store. Whatcom Museum.

retired in 1962. Catheryn was known for her many years as a volunteer at St. Joseph's Hospital.

The American melting pot was at work as many of the third generation Croatians married *foreske*, their word for those who were not Slavs. The Elich's son Peter married a fellow 1950 Bellingham High School graduate, Margaret Ann Shagren, a blond of Icelandic heritage. Peter became an educator of considerable stature. He ended his long career in education as a professor emeritus and Dean of the College of Arts and Sciences at Western Washington University.

The next generation of the Mardesich legacy included four children, among them, Matthew Elich, a current Whatcom County District Court Judge.

Five generations of Mardesichs have worked and achieved and contributed to their community and nation, as have so many others descended from those immigrants from the island of Vis. In final testament to the success of the American melting pot and the Croatians of Vis, it must be told that a third generation Croatian descendant is serving her second term as Mayor of Bellingham, the city that her grandfather immigrated to in the early years of the 20th century. Mayor Kelli Kuljis Linville is the daughter of Martin Kuljis Jr., the son of Martin Kuljis who had been born in Komiza, Island of Vis, Croatia.

>―◦―◦―◦◦―◦◦―<

The Name Game

Poe's Point/Post Point

Clarks Point/Drydock Point

Chuckanut Island/Dot Island

Fairhaven has a number of confusing or mis-used place names. We shall attempt to clarify the confusion and provide evidence to support the correct name for several well known but mis-labeled geographic locations.

POE'S POINT

The oldest and most contested issue is the Poe's Point/Post Point confusion. Both the City of Bellingham and the Port of Bellingham have contributed to the problem with erroneous signs and careless naming practices. The Port has erected a large sign at the foot of Harris Avenue which proclaims that you are at 'Post Point'. Then, as if the point had a second name, in smaller letters below Post Point are the words in parentheses 'Poe's Point'. This sign suggests that Post Point and Poe's Point are the same place and that they are both at the shipyard at the foot of Harris Avenue. Wrong!

Let's find the truth by looking to history.

On September 17, 1853, Alonzo Poe filed on 303 acres under the Oregon Donation Land Act. His claim included the great mound of glacial till which had been left by that last glacier approximately 13,000 years ago. The great moraine was 80 to 90 feet in height and extended from its prominent tip at the salt water, eastward perhaps 500 feet towards the high land above the adjacent marsh. Poe built his cabin on the bayside western slope of that moraine. The prominent point that provided much of the protection for the deep water cove (that would become Harris Bay) was immediately called Poe's Point. That was a logical choice, Poe owned it and had built his house upon it.

Several years later, in 1857, a party of northern Indians, probably Haida or Yakutat, made a revenge attack at Coupeville on Whidbey Island, killing and decapitating Colonel Ebey. They sought to revenge the death of one of their chiefs who had died the previous summer at the hands of white men.

Word of the killing quickly spread north to the handful of settlers on Bellingham Bay. They were warned that the *Northerns* were headed towards the bay on their way home with their grisly trophy. The settlers gathered at the stout log cabin of William Pattle at Pattle's Point (now the site of The Woods coffee shop at Boulevard Park). Two men, Melville and Browne, were sent down to Poe's Point to mount a lookout on top of the high moraine and fire a warning shot if the Indian canoes were seen. Unfortunately, the lookouts took along a bottle of whiskey to ward off the night chill and perhaps to bolster their courage. The story goes that the whiskey put them to sleep, that the Indians found them that night and added two more heads to their trophy bag. An accidental rifle shot from Pattle's cabin convinced the raiders that additional trophies would come at a high price, so they paddled their canoes across the bay and headed home. The next morning two headless bodies were found and Poe's Point gained an additional name, 'Deadman's Point'.

In 1858, Alonzo Poe moved to Olympia, assigning his land to his brother Americus. In August of 1861, Americus Poe sold 43 acres, the majority of the point, to Dirty Dan Harris. Dan promptly sold four acres of his new property to Whatcom County who wanted to use it for a graveyard. The point acquired a third name, 'Graveyard Point'.

It is believed that all three of the names were in common usage, depending on who you were talking to. There is a charming early map at the Center for Pacific Northwest studies which shows all three of the names for the prominent point. (See map in chapter 5.)

It was not until 1918 when Pacific American Fisheries moved their shipyard from Eliza Island to its north flank that the point began to be called 'Shipyard Point'. Later, after PAF had carved down the great gravel mound to create more land for the shipyard, the point picked up yet another name, 'Commercial Point'.

There can be no doubt that the Port of Bellingham's sign at the foot of Harris Avenue sits squarely in the center of what used to be a great glacial moraine—called variously Poe's Point, Deadman's Point, Graveyard Point, Shipyard Point or Commerical Point, but never Post Point.

POST POINT

Three hundred yards south of Poe's Point there was another prominent point, also owned by Alonzo Poe. This one was a rocky point and was adjacent

The last vestiges of Poe's Point being removed. Whatcom Museum.

to a shallows off shore that created a serious hazard to ships. Between the two points the land curved inward in a crescent shaped gravel beach which was backed by a large tidal marsh that flooded with brackish water during high tides and winter rains.

That early beach was closed off from the sea by the 'first trestle', built by the Great Northern Railroad in 1902. The tidal marsh has been filled and is the site of Bellingham's Sewage Treatment Plant called The Post Point Water Treatment Plant.

The southerly point was a logical place to install a warning to mariners of the dangerous shoal offshore, so the settlers erected a tall pole on the point and painted it white. The point came to be called 'Post Point'. When the Federal government began installing navigation aids in the Salish Sea, a prominent red bell buoy was anchored off of Post Point to warn of the shoal— and the marine charts named the buoy, Post Point Buoy. The name remains on the charts to this day.

The City of Bellingham can perhaps be forgiven for naming its sewage plant Post Point Water Treatment Plant. It is not on the Point, but it is at least close to it. The Port of Bellingham has no such excuse and really needs to correct its nomenclature and recognize Alonzo Poe's point for what it is and where it is and what it was. Marine Park, the Port's shipyard buildings and the Alaska Ferry Terminal are all firmly ensconced on Poe's Point—unless you prefer to call it Deadman's Point, or Graveyard Point, or Shipyard Point. Just don't call it Post Point.

FAIRHAVEN, A HISTORY

CLARK'S POINT

C.X. Larrabee, the grandson of Fairhaven pioneer C.X. Larrabee, would become outraged when he heard anyone use the term Clark's Point to describe the beautiful timbered sandstone point that forms the northern arm of Chuckanut Bay. His family had owned the land since the 1890s, and he knew the rocky point as 'Drydock Point'. X, who died in 2014 at the age of 90, heatedly argued in correspondence to the author that Doug Clark, the Bellingham grocer, was a newcomer to the scene. X reported that Clark only bought the point from the Larrabee family in 1958, surely not having earned the right to have the point named for him. Incidentally, he revealed that Clark had paid $103,000 for the property.

Larrabee insisted that the point had long been called Drydock Point because of the two natural dry docks on its shoreline. These dry docks were two shallow narrow inlets with sloping sandy bottoms that had been used in the old days by mariners. Ship owners would bring their ships into the inlets, tying them off to trees on either side. When the tide went out, the ship would be high and dry with the keel sitting on soft sand. The ship's bottom was available to be worked upon until the tide rose again to float it.

Doug Clark destroyed the smaller of the dry docks on the east side of the point when he dynamited an opening in its sandstone leg. Using the dislodged stone to close its former entrance, he created a small boat harbor near his house at the end of the point. The larger dry dock inlet remains just west of the house.

Common usage calls the point Clark's Point. The author sides with C.X. Larrabee and the flow of history and prefers the old name Drydock Point.

DOT ISLAND

The small timbered island that sits in the middle of Chuckanut Bay has been called Dot Island by locals for many years. The name, while descriptive of the roundish island seen so clearly from Chuckanut Drive, is incorrect. The correct name is found on maps and marine charts as Chuckanut Island. It is owned by the Nature Conservancy under that name. Its common name, Dot Island, apparently is a corruption of Dodd's Island. The island was owned by a man named Dodd many years ago. Names have a way of being twisted to conform with community usage. Dot Island is surely one of those names, and we must confess it is easier to say than Chuckanut Island.

14th Street School. This photo can be accurately dated to 1896 because the trees, planted by the students on that date are visible, supported by their wooden stakes. The trees in this photo still grow in front of Lowell School. Lowell was built in 1914, behind the 1890 14th Street School which was then torn down. Galen Biery Photographs #1403, CPNWS.

Arbor Day Trees

While reading Rosamonde Ellis Van Miert's massive compendium, *The Fairhaven Hotel Journal*, I came across a quote from the *Whatcom Reveille* of 1896 that caught my eye. It was from an article declaring that Fairhaven Mayor Eli Wilkins had proclaimed April 15, 1896, to be Arbor Day in Fairhaven.

On March 2, 1896; the Mayor announced a resolution to plant shade trees on the streets of the city and appointed the following citizens as members of the commission; J.J. Donovan, Chairman; J. Wayland Clark, E.M. Wilson, G.W. Gillette, Cyrus Gates, J.M. Scarseth, B.W. Huntoon, J.O. Sharpless, T.E. Monahan.

The article went on to quote his proclamation:

"Whereas only seven years ago the forest impenetrable forest was slashed and burned and whereas Fairhaven, phoenix-like rose from the ashes, on the ashes of the old stumps, 290 young trees will rise making Fairhaven the fairest city on the West coast."

"J.J. Donovan, president of the Arbor Commission, has collected $166.80 in donations to buy the shade trees."

And then the paragraph that grasped my attention,

"On 11th and Front Streets, which promises to be in the future the main thoroughfare between Fairhaven and New Whatcom, we will plant 119 cork bark elms to beautify 3,500 lineal feet."

"Cork Bark Elms," I had often observed the old trees along State Street above the old gas plant site (now Boulevard Park). Those old trees have very thick cork-like bark, many of them so old that the centers of the tree's limbs (which the power company frequently prune) are hollow. And the article had gone on to mention that they would be planted 25 feet apart. I wondered, could those tortured old trees along State Street be the very trees planted on Arbor day in 1896?

I hurried back to the Center for Pacific Northwest Studies at the State Regional Archive, to read the 1896 editions of the *New Whatcom Daily Reveille*. In the Sunday, April 26, 1896, edition I found this article entitled "Fairhaven Arbor Day."

"A month or more ago an arbor commission of eleven, including members of the city council and two ladies, was appointed and the preparations for tree planting began in Fairhaven on Arbor Day.

"By popular subscription money was raised to buy four hundred trees of different classes, and many who preferred to do so bought and planted their own trees. All work was done in a systematic way under the directions of the Arbor Commission whose intention is to have trees every twenty-five feet throughout the residence portion of the city.

"The work was opened Thursday afternoon when 117 cork bark elms were set out on Front Street along which the street railroad runs between the two cities. Everybody in town was interested in the move. Several teams and the work of many men were contributed."

Now confident that I was on to something, I drove to State Street, formerly called Front Street in the 1883 plat of the original Bellingham. Sure enough, there they were, the surviving 35 cork bark elms standing 25 feet apart in a long line of survivors, their tops heavily pruned and spread wide to prevent them from interfering with the high voltage power lines directly above them.

That evening I phoned James Luce, the long-time City of Bellingham arborist. Luce confirmed that they were very old, that he thought they were elms, and that the progeny of those old trees had spread down over the bank toward the railroad tracks and were a constant threat to the view from the road. The City had for many years, cut down the spreading volunteer saplings to preserve the view. He pointed out that some of the progeny of the old elms had been allowed to grow naturally and stand tall just to the west of the sidewalk.

The next day I stopped at the site and found a recently cut stump of one of the elms that apparently had been in the way of a power company operation. I returned with a magnifying glass and counted its annual growth rings. It was very difficult to distinguish the rings due to the chain saw cut, but I easily got to a count of 100, convincing me that these are indeed the trees planted 118 years ago on April 23, 1896, Fairhaven's Arbor Day.

There is an amusing side note to this story. The *Reveille's* editor went on to congratulate Fairhaven on not only "setting out the finest grade of shade trees all over the city, but to have protected every tree with an ornamental

Cork Bark Elms on State Street, 2015. Collection of the author.

and durable framework." It seems that the greatest threat to the survival of the young trees were the cows that, in 1896, were still allowed to roam freely in Fairhaven. The city ordnances allowed cows to roam free only if they wore a cowbell. The bells created their own problems as the wandering cows with their bells interfered with residents' sleep causing frequent complaints to the City Council.

An additional point of historical interest was revealed by the article. It mentioned that at 9:30 the morning after the planting of the 117 cork elms along the trolley line on the waterfront, "the Arbor day exercises took place at the Fourteenth Street School, when a large number of trees were planted in front of the school grounds by the children of the school." In 1914, Lowell School was built behind the Fourteenth Street School and the old school was demolished, but those old trees remain on the parking strip in front of Lowell to this very day

St Joseph's Hospital, 1891. The new hospital was built on 17th Street high on the hill. Whatcom Museum.

St. Joseph's Hospital

airhaven was the birthplace of Peace Health St. Joseph Medical Center, today's pre-eminent health care provider for this Pacific Northwest region. The Peace Health story began in the year 1887 in Tacoma, Washington Territory, with two young Irish sisters from New Jersey. The Farrelly sisters had made the long journey from their East Coast home to visit a married sister in Tacoma. The sisters were devout Catholics and apparently filled with missionary ardor. Seeing the dire need of religious training in the rude surroundings of the recently settled Pacific Northwest, they called on the Very Reverend Peter Hylebos, the Vicar General of the Diocese of Nisqually and the pastor of Tacoma's St. Leo's Church. The sisters suggested that he might look for missionary help from a new community of Catholic sisters recently founded in England, and had even more recently established itself in New Jersey. They volunteered to communicate his request to the Order if he should care to invite them.

Father Hylebos was intrigued with their proposal and promptly commissioned the Farrellys to present the matter to the Superior of the new Order upon their return to New Jersey. Immediately upon their return, the young ladies laid their story before Mother Ignatius and her community of nuns, The Sisters of St. Joseph of Peace.

Several months later Father Hylebos himself traveled to the East Coast on a double mission of appealing to the Bureau of Indian Affairs for a much needed appropriation for the Catholic Indian Missions, and also to make a personal appeal to the nuns that he had invited to his diocese.

His tales of life on the distant frontier and the urgent need for medical help for the small outlying communities struck a chord of sympathy among the sisterhood, and he left with the hope and expectation of success. It took two more trips east, and several more years before he finally learned that the Order would send two nuns to the distant Pacific shores as an experiment.

There were 28 members of the Order in New Jersey. Sisters Mary Teresa Moran and Mary Stanislaus Tighe were selected for the western challenge and both eagerly volunteered for the mission. These young nuns, charged with the mission of bringing medical help to the hinterlands, were not trained nurses. To provide some rudimentary medical training they were sent to St. Mary's Hospital in Brooklyn where they were given a crash course in nursing. They began their long journey by train to the wilds of the northwest on August 3, 1890. Upon their arrival at Tacoma five days later, they were met by the reigning prelate Father Peter Hylebos. He promptly assigned the Sisters to the rapidly growing town of Fairhaven with the challenge to build a hospital there.

The sisters arrived in Fairhaven by steamer on August 14, 1890. On Sunday, August 17, they sought help for their mission by meeting with Father Boulet, the Indian missionary priest and pastor of the Church of the Assumption located at Cedar and Elk Street (now State), and John Joseph Donovan, the most prominent Roman Catholic in the booming new town. Donovan was able to convince his superiors at the Fairhaven Land Company to donate a full city block in their newly acquired town of Bellingham for the Sisters' hospital. The free land comprised the entire block between 16th and 17th Streets, and Adams and Jefferson (now Ferry) Streets high on the South Hill.

With the land secured, the Sisters, Donovan, and other local Catholics began fund-raising to get the necessary money for building their hospital. While Donovan and his committee sought contributions from the community, the sisters visited logging camps and outlying communities offering hospital care for an entire year in return for a contribution of $10.

The architects Longstaff and Black were hired to design the building. They designed a grandiose hospital structure that was estimated to cost $50,000 to $70,000, a huge amount of money for that time. Despite the best efforts of the fund-raisers it quickly became obvious that they could not raise that kind of money in the fledgling community and the architects were directed to redraw their plans for a much less ambitious building. Only $3,500 could be raised. For that amount a simple frame 35-bed hospital was constructed.

Just a few weeks after the Sisters arrival in Fairhaven the town was visited by a serious and deadly outbreak of typhoid fever. The *Whatcom Reveille* of October 8 reported, "There have been six funerals from the fever since Saturday. A little daughter of Mr. & Mrs. Hostetter of Fairhaven and F.T. Wood, a young man age 27 years, died yesterday of the fever." The next day the paper reported "Andrew Lind, a Scandinavian, died at Fairhaven yesterday of the fever. Just why the victims will persist in using the Padden Lake water surpasses ordinary comprehension. The Health Officers should examine into the matter. If the fault is not the water of Lake Padden, the water company is being injudiciously censured."

The disease found its victims amongst all classes of society. The *Reveille* reported on October 25th, Mr. E.W. Purdy is confined to his room treated with the fever. He has not been able to attend to business for a week past. The fever also struck E.M. Wilson the Mayor of Fairhaven and one of the stalwarts of the Fairhaven Land Company. Purdy survived and went on to become the president of the Bellingham Bay Improvement Company and later president of the Bellingham 1st National Bank. Wilson also survived, but was bed ridden for the majority of his one-year term of office and unable to perform any of his mayoral duties.

Twenty-two unfortunates did not survive the typhoid epidemic. The pollution which caused the epidemic was never identified, but the City of Fairhaven completed its sewer system later in 1891 and the problem went away. The maligned waters of Lake Padden had been declared sanitary by a chemist from an Oregon company hired to test the water supply. Lake Padden water would continue to safely supply the dwellings of South Bellingham for many years until the city consolidated the water systems and made Lake Padden a park in 1968.

Perhaps it was coincidence, perhaps it was in response to the typhoid epidemic, but in July or August of 1890, Doctor C.P. Thomas established a temporary hospital in a former blacksmith/wagon repair shop at 1109 Douglas Avenue. The old building, long-since converted to a dwelling, remains on Douglas Avenue to this day, now a rental dwelling.

Fairhaven Hospital, 1890. This was the first hospital on Bellingham Bay. Now a residence at 1109 Douglas Avenue. Collection of the author.

We were able to identify it as the first medical building in Fairhaven and probably the first on Bellingham Bay, in what was an exciting bit of historical research by the author and friends. In 2009 the author was doing an oral history video about the Croatians of South Bellingham with Peter Elich, a third generation resident of the Croatian community. As we walked past an old house at 1109 Douglas Avenue, Elich remarked that his father had once mentioned that he had been told the house had been used as a hospital "in the early days."

Over years of doing historical research, I have learned that memories passed down orally are not to be ignored, and Elich's remark piqued my interest. I sought the aid of fellow historians Gayle Helgoe and Neelie Nelson to see if we could verify this oral memory.

The first revelation came when Gayle talked with an acquaintance who owned the house. The owner confided that several years previously he had installed a gas furnace in the building and had needed to dig a pipe trench in the earth of the crawl space under the floor. He had been astounded when he found amputated human limbs buried in the dirt, fingers and hands that had clearly been amputated. Further inquiry told us that it had been common practice in the medical world of the 1890s to bury amputated human parts on hospital campuses. In fact Dr. John Arnold told us that the Yale Medical School, which he had attended, had a consecrated section of the basement in their old Medical School building for just such burials.

This revelation seemed to add credence to the hospital story, and we began to think we could make a case for the fact that the old house had indeed been the first community hospital. Then one day Gayle found the proof positive while glancing through an 1889-1890 *Fairhaven City Directory* at the Center for Pacific Northwest Studies at the State Regional Archives Goltz-Murray building. There it was, the perfect proof. The listing was simply "Fairhaven Hospital, 1109 Douglas Avenue." It was a sublime moment for the three historians.

Fairhaven Pharmacy, H. K. Stewart manager, 1700 Twelfth street.
Fairhaven Hospital, 1109 Douglas avenue.
Fairhaven World Publishing Company, 1310 Eleventh street.

The proof. Polk Fairhaven City Directory, 1890. CPNWS.

Further investigation revealed that this lot 8, block 9, town of Bellingham had been owned by a succession of Irishmen, probably Catholics all. Patrick McLoughlin sold it to Malcolm McKechnie in 1889. McKechnie sold it to Thomas L. Farrell on Sept. 5, 1890; and Farrell added the west quarter of lot 8 by buying it from Joseph P. Cummisky on Sept 19, 1890. If Cummisky was not an Irishman at least his wife was a hospital advocate. We know that because the incorporation papers of the hospital executed in 1892 show Annie Cummisky as a witness of the signing, as was J.J. Donovan. We are confidant that the building was on the lot during these transactions.

Dr. Thomas was a graduate of Oregon State University and had been a student in the San Francisco Sisters Hospital and the Portland General hospital. He had been a surgeon for the Northern Pacific Railroad Company in Eastern Washington and had come to Fairhaven and established his office in the Blonden Block. I surmise that he leased or borrowed the old blacksmith and wagon shop from Farrell for his Fairhaven hospital. The hospital had opened in July or August of 1890, and was used when the epidemic of typhoid fever broke out. The crude hospital housed as many as 25 patients at times. A newspaper source mentioned that "about January 1st, 1891, the 15 patients now in the Fairhaven Hospital would be transferred to the new Sisters' Hospital, where Dr. Thomas would continue to treat them." The article continues by mentioning that it had two rows of beds, and that the Sisters lived in the upstairs of the building.

The 1891 Sanborn map shows the building as vacant. By that time its former occupants would have moved to new quarters in the new hospital on 17th Street.

Fundraising efforts continued while construction began on the new hospital. By the end of 1890 the hospital was completed. The dedication ceremony was held on January 9, 1891. Father Hylebos bestowed its name, Saint Joseph's Hospital.

The modest two-story frame building accommodated about 30 patients. The first floor had an office, a pharmacy, a general ward for ten beds, one private room, a dining room, kitchen and lavatory. The second floor consisted of a ward of the same size as that on the first floor, two single rooms, a dormitory for the Sisters, a chapel, linen room and lavatory. The laundry and mortuary would later be built in a separate building. Construction had taken only three months.

The founding sisters moved into the building in December and on January 6 were joined by four additional nuns sent out from New Jersey. Sisters Monica, Scholastica, Benedict and Gabriel arrived just in time for the opening ceremonies. Sister Mary Teresa Moran was the Superior, Sister Mary Stanislaus Tighe headed the nursing staff. Dr. H.A. Compton was the principal medical advisor, and J.J. Donovan continued in his role as business advisor and supporter, a role that he would continue for the remainder of his life. The hospital became commonly known as Sisters' Hospital and served the community at its location high on the South Hill for the next ten years.

As the century ended, the consolidation of Whatcom and Fairhaven loomed on the horizon. Competition from the Protestant hospital, St. Luke's, was reducing income, and the St. Joseph's location high up the hill made for difficult access. It became apparent that a better location was necessary. The Sisters again turned to J.J. Donovan who negotiated a land trade returning the land and buildings to the Fairhaven Land Company in return for a new site fronting on State Street which was served by the trolley. The new location was almost exactly on the border between Fairhaven and Whatcom. The property, sandwiched between State and Forest Streets proved to be an excellent choice. A new frame building was completed in 1901 that provided 53 beds. St. Joseph's remained in that location through many years and six expansions and remodels. The hospital finally outgrew its State Street site and moved to its present location at the north end of Ellis street in 1966.

St Joseph's Hospital was the second medical facility on Bellingham Bay, Dr. Thomas's infirmary being the first. The third hospital, St. Luke's, had its roots in the religious and community competition spurred by the presence of the Catholic sisters and their arrival in Fairhaven. Only four months after their arrival and the start of their fundraising, prominent Whatcom Protestants began to organize their own hospital project. On December 18, 1890, just weeks before the dedication of the new St. Joseph's Hospital, articles of incorporation were filed at the County courthouse for the Bellingham Bay Hospital Company. Its stockholders were Wm. B Brengle, physician, Whatcom; J.J. Brenneman, physician, Whatcom; J.H. Stenger, hotel owner, Whatcom; and F.B. West, physician, Whatcom. Each man owned 500 shares of the for-profit corporation. They soon opened their hospital in Whatcom in a rental building and not to be outdone in the religious sense they called it St. Luke's Hospital. Much of its support came from parishioners of St. Paul's Episcopal church.

St Joseph's Hospital did not file its incorporation papers until September 14, 1892, 21 months after their opening. They incorporated as 'The Saint Joseph's Sisters of Peace'. Their declaratory statement shows the incorporators as Sister Mary Teresa, Sister Mary Benedict, and Sister Mary Stanislaus who "have associated themselves together for the purpose of forming a corporation for charitable purposes."

Article III of the document reads, "The objects and purposes of this incorporation shall be to establish and maintain hospitals, orphanages, homes for young women, homes for the aged, the blind or the infirm."

St. Joseph's Hospital built on State Street in 1901. Galen Biery Photographs #3127, CPNWS.

Witnesses to the document were J.J. Donovan, Annie Cummisky and Margaret T. Byrne.

The two hospitals served the soon-to-be consolidated City of Bellingham for the next 97 years, until changing economic realities for all hospitals resulted in the sale of St. Luke's. At some point in history, St. Luke's had changed from a for-profit corporation to a community-owned organization. In 1982 the St Luke's Board of Directors, faced with major financial challenges to keep pace with modern medical advances, chose to sell to a large California health organization, Health West. The parties agreed to a selling price of about five million dollars which was payable on a 30-year contract at 12.5% interest. The monies would be paid into a "conversion foundation dedicated to the community health of Whatcom County." The foundation was called The St. Luke's Foundation.

The St. Luke's Hospital Board of Directors had the expectation that in selling to the large California group the hospital would have access to the capital necessary to keep up with hospital modernization needs. From 1982 to

1989 St. Luke's Hospital was owned and operated by the Health West group.

The rapidly changing medical scene continued to require huge capital investments by both of Bellingham's hospitals if they were to stay current. St. Joseph's announced a major expansion in 1988. Health West concluded that it made no economic sense to duplicate that expense in a community the size of Bellingham. Negotiations began in 1988 and culminated in 1989 with Health West selling St Luke's Hospital to the Sisters of St. Joseph of Peace.

Since 1982 the St. Luke's Foundation, established at the original sale and benefiting from good management and the excellent interest rate of its sales contract was living up to its promise. The foundation, now called Chuckanut Health Foundation, has grown its original five million dollar endowment to approximately $14,500,000, while returning $16,500,000 to the community funding a myriad of worthwhile health-related causes.

Whatcom County's surviving hospital is Peace Health St. Joseph Medical Center. Its size, reach and healing abilities would surely be considered miraculous to those two young nuns who arrived on Bellingham Bay by steamer more than 100 years ago.

>━┥◆❯━O━❮◆┝━<

The Fairhaven Hotel

The standard bearer for Nelson Bennett's great adventure in Fairhaven was to be a truly grand hotel, a larger-than-life structure that would shout to the world that here on Bellingham Bay would be a great city to rival anything on the West Coast. There would be no better way to encourage investors and immigrants than to build a spectacular hotel that would rise amidst the stumps and mud of the recently logged and graded streets and building lots of his township; its ornate tower visible for miles at the high corner of Harris Avenue and 12th Street. Already his friend and fellow Tacoman, Allen Mason, wanting to be in the vortex of the great building had committed to building a large retail and office block across the street at the vital intersection. The two massive buildings would rise together to offer assurance and confidence to all who would arrive and invest here.

Bennett had initially looked close to home for his design. The Tacoma firm of Proctor & Dennis were engaged to draw preliminary plans, and Bennett had considered building his centerpiece hotel on top of the great alluvial mound of Poe's Point. However, he soon changed direction and hired both Longstreet and Black to design and supervise construction and to add design elements to the original plan. They conceived the great dome that gave the hotel such distinction. He decided to build his grand hotel at the high point of his projected business district at 12th and Harris. There it would reign like a regal crown atop the great city yet to be built. Both Frank Longstaff and A.N. Black were brought to Fairhaven by Roland Gamwell to build his mansion. They found Fairhaven an exciting opportunity and a ready market for their professional skills. They designed and supervised construction of a significant number of Fairhaven's houses and commercial buildings in addition to the iconic hotel.

Bennett would call the hotel 'The Fairhaven'. Construction began in late 1889. One million bricks were ordered from the new brick works in nearby Happy Valley. Hard sandstone was ordered from the Chuckanut Quarry. Choice redwood was ordered from California mills to add a touch of elegance to the hotel that the abundant and equally lovely, but too familiar Western Red Cedar surrounding Fairhaven, would not. By late January 1890, the 12th and Harris corner was alive with brick masons, carpenters, laborers of all sorts, horses and wagons all working on the huge hotel and the massive Mason Block across the street.

The Fairhaven would be built with four floors of rooms, a full basement, a crowning tower, grand wooden porches and balconies supported by great round wooden columns reminiscent of the temples of ancient Greece. It would have electric lights, a barber shop, bar and a billiard room, a modern kitchen and an elegant dining room, and furnishings that were simply the best money could buy. It even boasted a hydraulic elevator that ran from the basement to the fourth floor and cost $4,125.

Bennett's First National Bank would occupy the southwest corner on the ground floor, while on the third floor there would be two special corner suites complete with the great luxury of private baths. The Fairhaven was built with 75 rooms and luxurious public parlors opening onto broad balconies, the magnificent structure was constructed and furnished at the incredible expense of $150,000.

In August of 1890, the First National Bank moved in and by the 15th of September the building was ready for its grand opening extravaganza. Hotel manager Fred L. Presbrey presented a magnificent meal prepared in the hotel kitchen and served by white-gloved black waiters. The women of Fairhaven were decked out in fine gowns imported at considerable cost from San Francisco and beyond. There was dancing to the Silver Cornet Band led by W.A. Langdon. It was a celebration of this epic achievement in city building.

But a dark cloud hung over the event. Nelson Bennett who had started all this development was not present. The rumor mill was saying that Bennett was having trouble with his partners in the Fairhaven Land Company, Larrabee, Wilson, Cowgill and others; that Bennett might be divesting himself of his Fairhaven interests and giving up on his vision. The rumors were soon proven to be correct. Within weeks it was announced that Larrabee would be buying out most of Bennett's interests in Fairhaven, including the hotel.

A local newspaper reported the rumor that Bennett had been too Napoleonic in his dealings with his partners, and that had created the rift. Others wondered if Bennett had received private information about J.J. Hill's Great Northern Railroad plans that had convinced him to abandon his Fairhaven investments. On August 12, 1891, Larrabee's bank draft in the amount of $495,954.50[1] was delivered to Bennett. The hotel and the Fairhaven Land Company were thereafter controlled by Larrabee.

On October 4, 1890, just days after the purchase was announced, Larrabee

---

1   Grandson C.X. Larrabee II revealed in a 2009 letter that he had seen the canceled check in that amount.

closed the hotel bar. There was to be no consumption of alcohol on his premises. He was adamant. This was surely a foolish business decision considering the hard drinking days of the 1890s, but Larrabee had seen the terrible results of 'Demon Rum' in his days of copper mining in Butte, Montana. It is also thought that his conviction resulted from a difficult childhood with an abusive alcoholic father.

C.X. Larrabee was a man of high principle, rock solid in his convictions, fair in his dealing with others, generous and impeccably honest. His banning of alcohol from the premises surely did not help business at The Fairhaven. Manager Presbrey immediately quit the job and moved to Tacoma, where he was reported to have taken a job as manager of Bennett's other hotel interest, The Tacoma.

C.X. Larrabee moved into one of the third floor suites of the hotel and got on with the business of the Fairhaven Land Company. Real estate sales were robust, the boom was in full bloom. Daily steamers were coming to the Ocean Dock filled with newcomers and tourists. Housing was scarce, frame buildings and homes were being built on every street, as the new city's inhabitants struggled through the clinging mud of the streets, awaiting the relief of planked streets and sidewalks that were soon to come.

The Fairhaven was, of course, the center of the city's social life. Weddings, parties, celebrations, conventions were hosted there. Family life arrived as well in 1892, when Larrabee returned from a trip back east with a handsome young woman at his side and registered in the hotel as Mr. and Mrs. Larrabee. He had married Frances Payne of St. Louis and brought her home to his third floor suite. Three years later, on August 13, 1895, their first child, Charles Francis Larrabee was born in the hotel. He would be the first of the four Larrabee children, all born in the Fairhaven Hotel.

The Fairhaven boom died in the 1893 depression and with the Great Northern's decision to cross the Cascades through Stevens Pass into Everett and Seattle. The fortunes of the hotel suffered along with those of the city. The hotel was likely an economic failure from the date of its opening. Larrabee's decision to ban the sale of alcohol was surely a part of the problem, but the economic tide had turned for Fairhaven and the hotel's future was destined to be plagued with continual ups and downs.

In the summer of 1895, Bellingham Bay was vibrating with excitement anticipating the arrival of the great humorist Mark Twain, who had included a performance in Whatcom on his world tour. Twain was speaking at the Lighthouse Theater on Whatcom's Holly Street, and was spending the night in the bridal suite at the Fairhaven Hotel. The local papers urged the community to make him welcome as it was thought that his favorable opinion would create national publicity important to the city's future. Unfortunately,

The Fairhaven, 1902. The great hotel had been shorn of its upper balcony and its colorful bricks had received a protective, but unsightly coat of cement. Galen Biery Photographs #1394, CPNWS.

numerous forest fires in that hot dry summer created an extremely smoky atmosphere. The mountains and Mt. Baker were obscured by the smoke. The air was thick with smoke. Twain was not pleased.

History records that his lecture went well, but that afterward his host Roland Gamwell had to take him to the Cascade Club on the third floor of the Mason Block, because he could not get a drink of whiskey to soothe his weary throat at the Fairhaven. He later commented only on the bad air of Bellingham Bay.

Larrabee stubbornly kept the hotel open for years despite what must have been significant losses. Finally, in September of 1897, he ceased hotel operations and closed the restaurant. For most of seven years the hotel had struggled just as Fairhaven had struggled. The traveler and tourist activity had dropped to almost nothing. There were a small number of permanent tenants living as roomers, and the Larrabee family still occupied its third floor suite. But its life as a hotel was almost over. It reopened for a brief period in the brighter economic times of 1898, but by December of 1899 it was closed again.

By 1902, the building was showing signs of wear. Porous brick was absorbing rain water on the south walls. The wooden railings and posts of the second balcony were beginning to show signs of decay. The decision was made to remove the balcony and to apply a coat of cement to the brick to seal it from the weather. Critics bemoaned the "destruction in the name of restoration," pointing out that the beauty of the brick and the aesthetic balance of the balcony were essential to the success of the hotel. The 'restorations' were done and the Fairhaven took another step to its eventual demise.

In 1904, Larrabee's Pacific Realty announced that the Fairhaven Hotel was for sale. There had been several offers in the past to lease the hotel, but in each case the lessees wanted to open a bar. In each case, C.X. Larrabee turned away the prospective operators. In 1907, the newspapers were full of the news that Pacific Realty had a buyer. The hotel would be reopened with experienced new owners to a new era of prosperity. On May 10, 1907, the *Herald* reported, "Negotiations for transfer of the South Side hostelry from C.X. Larrabee to Mrs. White of Vancouver and Victoria, will probably be concluded today. Price is about $100,000." Mrs. White owned hotels in Vancouver and Victoria and claimed nine years of experience in the hotel business.

Once again Larrabee's iron clad scruples damped the Fairhaven Hotel's future. Upon learning that a grandiose bar was included in Mrs White's plan for the rejuvenation of the hotel, Larrabee immediately ceased negotiations. He had sworn that liquor would never be served in the hotel.

On September 19, 1914, Charles X. Larrabee was entering the Harris Avenue entrance of his storied hotel and home when he was seized by a massive heart attack. He slumped to the stairs and there he died. It was sudden and unexpected. He was 71 years of age. He had lived an incredible life. Suddenly the future possibilities for the hotel had changed.

The Larrabees had been planning to move out of the Fairhaven to a new home being designed at the high point of their land south of town. At her husband's death, Frances Larrabee rejected the couple's architectural plans and redesigned her home. Her new home at #1 Hawthorn Road was soon underway. When construction was completed in 1916, she moved her family out of the third floor suite in the hotel where each of them had been born. The hotel was left partially occupied by a handful of residents on monthly rentals.

On January 16, 1922, the building was sold to Yoghurt Sanitarium Inc., for a mere $30,000. This corporation was operated by Henry M. White, a former Bellingham city attorney and immigration commissioner, and a partner, H.R. Fischnaller. The Sanitarium purported to combat "All diseases attacking organs of the body which are nourished by food going into the stomach," with the ingestion of yoghurt.

Its optimistic advertising perhaps best describes its mission:

YOU NEED NOT TRAVEL HUNDREDS OF MILES AND
SPEND HUNDREDS OF DOLLARS TO OBTAIN THE BENEFITS
OF A FIRST CLASS SANITARIUM.

The Yoghurt Sanitarium is complete in every respect. We are not bound by any set rules governing the method of treatment. Our staff of twenty specially trained physicians, diagnosing the ailments of each patient, pursue the treatment or series of treatments best suited to the patient's needs.

Here you may obtain everything from the simple rest cure to the most thorough systems of body rebuilding, embracing the use of electro-hydro and mechano-therapy — the celebrated milk cures and the world famous YOGHURT TREATMENTS — THE MINERAL SALT TREATMENT AND THE PHOENIX CURES.

Our rates are reasonable and our service and accommodations leave nothing to be desired.

The Yoghurt Sanitarium, despite its grandiose claims, did not appear to be a rousing economic success, but the very large building apparently offered additional opportunities for White and Fischnaller. In May of 1923, it was announced that the building would be re-named the Hotel Victoria with the opening of the "Victoria Caberet on June 1st." Their ad proclaimed:

"A $1.00 cover charge, the best maple dancing floor in the city, excellent music, genuine entertainers. Reservations can be made by calling phone number 2888."

Soon a large electric light sign was hung on the 12th Street wall reading 'Hotel Victoria'. The building was now open for regular hotel business as well as long-term residential apartments. The old Fairhaven had become a multi-purpose building. The Yoghurt Sanitarium was still operating, local organizations such as the new Washington Club were holding their weekly luncheon meetings there. It was operating as a hotel and an apartment house, and the former bank location on the southwest corner of the first floor was still the office of the Larrabee's Pacific Realty and their Roslyn-Cascade Coal Company.

The frantic activity of the Yoghurt Sanitarium and the Victoria Hotel were not successful. By February of 1928, the Pacific Realty Company was filing suit for foreclosure of their $40,000 mortgage to the Victoria Hotel Company; and by April, the old hotel was returned to the Larrabee family. Charles Larrabee declared that the hotel would remain open.

The building was showing serious signs of decay. That summer, in actions designed to prevent structural collapse, the heavy central tower and the remaining lower balcony were removed. A local paper wrote:

> "Passersbys who see the Fairhaven in renovation can easily imagine its final destruction made easier by these partial plunderings, the siege of the renovation. The memory of those who built The Fairhaven is dishonored."

Its remaining beauty and dignity were taken from it that year, but at least its name was restored. The electric Hotel Victoria sign was removed, and it was again the Fairhaven Hotel. The now featureless cement-coated old structure remained open for public and club meetings. It advertised "reasonable rates by day, week or month with or without board." The Polk Directory of that year showed 21 residents, including a number of female teachers at Fairhaven High School.

Terminal store, and the Fairhaven Hotel in background without its tower. Whatcom Museum.

The Depression crashed into the struggling Fairhaven Hotel and provided a death blow. By September of 1931, it was vacant, only the Larrabee's Pacific Realty office remained in the corner space. The Mason Block across the street was also vacant.

In 1935, the Whatcom County Commissioners opened negotiations to buy the building for use as a tuberculosis hospital. Applications for Federal aid for the project were made and there were discussions of a $3,827.80 sale price. Of that amount all but $2,000 was for delinquent taxes and interest. Obviously, the Larrabees had not been paying the taxes on the old structure. Federal funding did not come through and the hospital plans were dropped.

In 1936, the Work Projects Administration (WPA), opened a sewing project in the building. "Approximately twenty women will be employed in the manufacture of garments and articles used by the county's charity department, materials will be furnished by the county."

In February 1937, the Fairhaven hotel got a new lease on life. The WPA took over a portion of the basement of the building to open a recreation center for the boys of Fairhaven. The next month, Mrs. Larrabee signed a quit claim deed giving the building and property to Whatcom County for a token consideration of $1.00. Now consideration was given to making it into the county hospital. Those plans were eventually dropped, but the old hotel did find one final use. The WPA provided funding for a recreation center for teenagers. The Fairhaven Boys Club was opened in the basement of the building. Soon membership was broadened to include girls and the Fairhaven Boys and Girls Club became a community center for the youth of Fairhaven. For 16 years the basement of the old building was a positive influence on a generation of south-side teens. The building also housed a rifle club that ran a 22-caliber shooting gallery in the basement. The upstairs was frequently rented for community meetings and social events.

On the night of July 26, 1953, the youthful members of the Carousel Dance Club met for their monthly dance. As the dance ended at 1:30 AM, the lights flickered and smoke alerted the dancers to a fire. Jack Frazier and Robert Marr ran upstairs to the second floor and discovered smoke pouring from an electrical junction box. Fire extinguishers were ineffectual, the fire was in the wall. "Moose" Zurline ran two blocks up Harris Avenue to the fire hall to turn in the alarm. By the time the firemen arrived minutes later, the flames had broken through the roof and the fate of the old building was sealed. The wooden interior was consumed, the roof collapsed, and by morning only the brick walls and stone arches of the monarch of Fairhaven remained.

Demolishing The Fairhaven Hotel

After the fire of July 26, 1953, the opulent grand hotel that had been the crown jewel of Fairhaven's boom period stood a total loss, its massive brick walls and stone arches still standing, but its roof collapsed onto the charred timbers of what had been its central core. Its complete demolition was the only course open to the County commissioners. They promptly advertised for demolition and purchase bids. The successful bidder would own the land conditioned upon his complete demolition and removal of the wreckage.

In 1953, Richard Johnson was a student at Washington State University in Pullman, Washington. Dick was in the habit on Sunday mornings of going to the university library to read his hometown newspaper, the *Bellingham Herald*. One Sunday morning in that year he was startled to read that the owner of a local florist shop, Arthur T. Johnson, had been the successful bidder at the County Courthouse. He had purchased and would demolish the fire damaged Fairhaven Hotel. Arthur Johnson was Dick Johnson's father.

Dick hurried to a phone booth and called home. His mother answered and Dick excitedly told his mother of what he had just read. There was a long, dead silence on the phone line. Ethel Johnson was in shock, she had not been told of the purchase.

As Dick's story unfolded, he related that his father had, on a whim, put in a bid of $1,500 for the old ruin and the 17 lots it stood on. As the days and weeks before the bid opening passed he began to worry. He realized he would have to demolish the huge building. "What if I win this bid? Then what do I do?" Weary of the sleepless nights, he went to the Courthouse and reduced his bid to $1,200. Now he was sleeping better, temporarily.

On the fateful morning of the bid opening, October 21, 1953, Arthur Johnson discovered that he was the only bidder. The longtime Bellingham florist was now in the demolition business. His wife was very unhappy with him.

The Last Arch. Dick Johnson is seen atop the ladder at the final arch to be removed. Perhaps with some irony, this is the Harris Avenue entrance arch under which C.X. Larrabee had collapsed and died in 1914.Galen Biery Photographs #2997, CPNWS.

Dick Johnson returned home for summer vacation and took on the demolition project for his father. He recruited an old high school friend, Dave Brozovich, and together they began the huge job. The inexperienced young men began the daunting task of knocking down the brick walls and Chuckanut stone foundations, selling what they could to people who were building chimneys, patios or outdoor barbecues. They were daily climbing ladders and scaffolding, pushing over heavy stonework and operating heavy equipment. Dick recalled that it is a wonder that the two inexperienced friends did not kill themselves.

As the demolition progressed, the unusable wood was thrown into the center of the building until the basement was filed with a huge mound of charred timber. The partners decided that the easiest way to get rid of it was to simply burn it. One morning, without a permit, they poured a few gallons of gasoline on the pile and tossed a match. The resulting fire was memorable. A huge column of flame rose between the standing walls. It was a massive bonfire that sent smoke and ash high into the sky to settle on the surrounding neighborhood. Their fiery solution would be highly illegal today, but it apparently caused them no great problems in 1956. Now the last of the walls could be knocked down into a huge pile of rubble. The next challenge was to find a suitable dump site for the rubble.

The solution was found nearby. Another high school acquaintance, Richard Falk, had returned from military service and had started a small dump truck business. His headquarters and truck garage was the old steam turbine building on the E.K. Wood sawmill site on the waterfront. His parents had purchased a building lot from the lumber company in 1947 and built their State Street home on it. The mill property lots extended from State Street, down over the bank and across the railroad tracks to the water. The Falk property included the old steam turbine building ruins. Young Falk had put a roof on the surviving concrete walls and operated his business from it.[1]

The Falks and their neighbors had no particular use for the waterfront portions of their State Street lots and encouraged the dumping of demolition rubble among the hundreds of pilings that had previously supported the mill. Here was the perfect place to dump the remains of the great hotel. The Johnsons hired Richard Falk to haul and dump the Fairhaven Hotel rubble on the mill site. In an interview with the author, Falk reported hauling more than 1,100 dump truck loads to the land providing much of the under-pinnings of what we now know as Boulevard Park.

Finally in 1956, the demolition was completed. The now vacant lot at the corner of 12th and Harris was sold to Ted Harmer who built and operated a Richfield gas station on the site. Richard Johnson reported that after all of the anxiety and family discord resulting from his father's impetuous gambit, the family actually made a small profit on the project. However, his mother never quite got over it.

---

1   The old steam turbine building exists today as The Woods Coffee Shop at Boulevard Park.

The Bank Building Dream

It began in 1968. Pacific American Fisheries had closed its doors two years previously. Fairhaven was empty and desolate. Only a couple of businesses opened their doors each day, the Fairhaven Pharmacy, Cal's Tavern, maybe one or two more.

I was a young man with a family and a mortgage and not much of an income but always with healthy optimism and an over-active imagination.

One day, for reasons long forgotten, I found myself at the intersection of 11th and Harris in Fairhaven's decaying center. I may have been taking a Sunday morning stroll.

I found myself fascinated with the old building at the corner with the word BANK boldly engraved in the stone lintel above the front door. Although I had seen the old building for most of my life, on this particular morning I really looked at it carefully for the first time. I was struck by its solid construction and its handsome brick exterior. Unlike most of Fairhaven's buildings, it was not entirely vacant. The former bank premises with its corner entrance was occupied by the Whatcom County milk testing laboratory. The retail store location facing Harris Avenue was being used to store old gasoline pumps and unused equipment by McEvoy Oil company. Only the 11th street store front appeared vacant.

The door to the upstairs opened to my curious tug. Inside I was greeted by a marvelous wooden staircase with massive turned balustrades beckoning to the ten upstairs rooms. Those former offices were now being used as rental living quarters with a sign advertising 'Bank Apartments'. I was to learn that most of the old offices were occupied by elderly single men. I wandered the upstairs hallway thrilled at the woodwork and craftsmanship of the building, completely unchanged since its construction in 1902. Then descending from the upstairs, I followed the elaborate staircase down and to my delight found an open door to a full basement that just begged to be used as an entertainment place of some sort.

A dream began to form in my mind. Surely from a construction stand-point this building was excellent. It was still in good condition and had to be the best building standing in Fairhaven. If I were to find it was for sale, it could not be very expensive considering the distressed state of the surrounding business district. I envisioned a variety of exciting uses for the building, a rollicking tavern-restaurant in the basement. Perhaps I could entice a bank to open a branch in the old bank corner, as there was no banking to be done in Fairhaven at the time despite it being surrounded by good residential districts and a considerable population. There were two good ground floor retail locations, and the upstairs could again be rented for offices or art studios. My excitement grew. The next morning, after a fitful night filled with visions of leading a Fairhaven renaissance from this building with brass bands and other promotional hoopla, I determined to buy it if I could. I went directly to the County Courthouse to see who owned the building.

I learned that it was owned by a widow who lived in Edmonds, Washington. After finding her telephone number and with fingers crossed I called her.

Yes, she would sell the building. She and her now deceased husband had owned it for many years, but she was getting older and Fairhaven was not doing well. She would sell the building for $12,000. She welcomed my interest and invited me to visit her to learn the details. I spent an anxious week massaging my dream and the next Saturday drove to Edmonds to meet the owner. I carefully examined her income and expense records and concluded that the present income would support a selling price of $9,000. Which I offered her.

She insisted on her price of $12,000. I did not have $12,000. In fact I did not have the $9,000 that I had offered her. I returned to Bellingham to consider my options. Were I to withdraw my savings, empty my checking account, sell what I could of my unnecessary possessions and borrow the cash value from my life insurance, I could maybe come up with $9,000. I needed a mortgage loan.

That Monday I walked in the door of the Bellingham National Bank and recognized a loan officer whose son had been a classmate of mine in Bellingham High School. He walked to the front of the bank to greet me, and when I told him of my desire to buy the old Bank building in Fairhaven I can still remember his words, "Young man, come back to my desk, I am going to tell you about the value of the dollar."

He led me to his desk, sat me down and gave me a lecture that I have not forgotten to this day. He berated me for my lack of good judgment, and turned down my request for a loan in a most demeaning fashion. I walked out the door promising myself to never cross that doorstep again.

He had succeeded in deflating the dream. I telephoned the widowed owner and told her I could only afford to pay her $9,000. That perhaps in a year I would be able to meet her $12,000 demand and that I would call her one year later.

Twelve months later, now able to put together $12,000, but hoping that the widow would now look favorably on my $9,000 offer, I placed a phone call to Edmonds. To my great disappointment, I learned that she had just sold the building for $18,000. So much for that dream. So much for that good idea.

But now things began to change in Fairhaven. The hippies had discovered the decrepit and mostly empty old buildings. Life began to return to the neighborhood. John Blethen rented the basement of the old Bank to start his restaurant, hippie hangout, Toad Hall. The Fairhaven Restaurant opened in the almost empty Waldron Building. A brighter future began to reveal itself. And then things changed again. Kenny Imus returned to his home town and saw a different future for Fairhaven. He first bought the Mason Block and began to remodel it into the 'Marketplace', at the same time he began his campaign of buying property and buildings in Fairhaven.

One of his early purchases was the Nelson Block, the old bank building. He paid $132,000 for it.

I always wanted to return to the Bellingham National Bank and have another discussion with that short-sighted banker, but I never did.

>─┼─◆>─•─O─•─<>─┼─◄

Fairhaven City Water and Power Co.

It was April 24, 2008. At the invitation of Joel Douglas, owner of the historic Larrabee home (now known as Lairmont Manor), I went to visit him at his office. Joel had called me to offer what he described as "the papers of the water company." Not knowing what was before me, I entered his office and was immediately presented with a cardboard box filled with old ledgers, record books, blank stock certificates, and the corporate minute books of old Fairhaven's water company.

Joel explained. Sometime in the late 1960s he had been enjoying a beer in the Kulshan Tavern (the tavern that occupied the old Fairhaven 1st National Bank corner in the 1890 Waldron building). The tavern owner, knowing that he had just bought the Larrabee property said to him, "Mr. Douglas, I have some old papers upstairs that you would like to have." Joel followed him up the rickety temporary stairs at the back of the tavern to the second floor of this historic building. There he was given a cardboard box containing the corporate records of the Fairhaven City Water and Power Company.

Douglas had no idea why the documents were in the Waldron Building. He stored them away at Lairmont Manor for many years before learning of my commitment to write this Fairhaven history. He thought I should have them. I have pledged that when I am through with them they will be gifted to the Center for Pacific Northwest Studies at the State Regional Archive.

I was able to solve part of the puzzle of why the records had been abandoned in an empty room on the second floor of the Waldron Block. My research has revealed that the last office of that historic company was indeed on the second floor of the Waldron Block at 1314 12th Street. Apparently, when the water company was sold to the City of Bellingham in 1935, the records were simply abandoned in the old office.

One of the very first challenges for Nelson Bennett, C.X. Larrabee and their Fairhaven Land Company was to provide a reliable source of water for the thriving city they hoped to build. Their townsite was well chosen, for just two miles to the east at an elevation well above the highest hills of the town, was the 160-acre Lake Padden. The lake was large enough to satisfy the needs for a considerable population and high enough at 447-feet elevation to provide the gravity water pressure necessary to deliver water to any of Fairhaven's streets. Nestled between two mountain ridges it was constantly being refreshed by the abundant rainfall on the watershed. Its excess water spilled into a canyon leading through Happy Valley, and finally met the sea where the Harris Avenue bridge crossed the stream at the edge of the salt water.

Bennett assigned his capable lieutenants to the task and in true entrepreneurial fashion they organized a stock company to raise the money for this major undertaking.

Incorporation papers were filed on October 19, 1889, and the first organizational meeting was held on November 4, 1889. Attending that first meeting as the corporate trustees were the Fairhaven Land Company stalwarts E.M. Wilson, E.L. Cowgill, and George A. Black, plus the wealthy, influential and flamboyant banker James F. Wardner, who had committed to a large amount of the initial stock. At that meeting, Wardner was elected President, Cowgill was elected Vice President, Black would be the Secretary/Treasurer. The Company was called the Fairhaven City Water & Power Company.

The stock was priced at $1.00 per share and 100,000 shares were authorized. It was thought that the waterworks could be built for $100,000. Stock was offered to the community. Its buyers were a compendium of the leaders of the Fairhaven community.

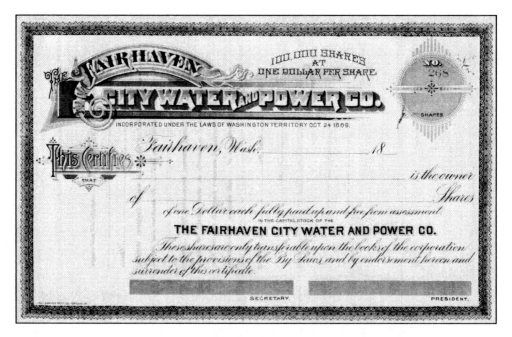

Stock Certificate, 1889. A blank stock certificate found among the Water Company records.
Collection of the author.

T.W. Gillette at lake Samish. Gillette was the long-time manager of the water company. Here he appears to be inspecting the condition of the water supply. Galen Biery Photographs #1729, CPNWS.

The four trustees of the new company wasted no time getting started. The system was promptly designed and the project advertised. At the trustees meeting of January 15, 1890, construction bids were opened. The contract for constructing the water system was awarded to the John Barratt Company of Portland, Oregon, who had bid $49,000. The contract stipulated that the waterworks must be completed by the 15th of May 1890, only four months away.

The original plan called for water mains serving the city west to 20th Street. In March the plan was expanded to lay pipe one block further east on 21st Street. This expansion added $2,250 to the contract. Upon Cowgill's motion at a later meeting, the trustees also voted to extend the water pipe north through Bellingham to service the Bellingham Bay Mill Company,[1] that had recently been purchased by the Fairhaven Land Company.

Other important business in these early months was the arrangement to purchase one acre of land, at the outlet end of the lake at the Padden Creek mouth, from Hugh Eldridge. He had verbally agreed to the deal and construction proceeded without finalizing the sale.

Other important business was preparing the franchise documents to be proposed to the new Fairhaven City Council.

---

1   This was the Eldridge and Bartlett mill on the present site of Boulevard Park.

The trustees hired a Water Superintendent, T.W. Gillette. Gillette would shortly thereafter submit his calculations of the water rates to be paid by Fairhaven citizens.

Fundraising commenced with the offer of stock to the public subject to the purchaser paying 60% of the stock value in cash at point of purchase.

On June 2, 1890, at a trustees meeting held in the offices of the Fairhaven Land Company, a representative of the John Barratt Company pronounced the water works contract completed.

The corporate minutes contain any number of curious entries which allow the reader a glimpse at the activity of the time.

- The initial water works included 26 fire hydrants. The city would pay to install up to 50 more hydrants and would pay the water company for each installation as well as a monthly rental.

- A contract was signed with the Fairhaven and Southern Railroad for 30,000 gallons of water daily at an annual cost of $1,000.

- September 1890 financial report, total sales of water $1012.60
  Amt. collected $617.40
  Amt. uncollected . . .$395.40
  Expenses. $379.91

- Superintendent's report; the lake has been cleared of the brush and logs which is now being burned. The water is clear and pure.

- The domestic water pressure ranges from 50 lbs to 100. There are now ten miles of pipes of all sizes. There are 23 city hydrants all in good working order.

- There are constant demands for extension of pipes and service.

- From August 8 to September 26 the lake level fell seven inches, since that time it has not fallen at all. He recommends the installation of a timber dam at the outlet, so as to raise the lake level two feet at the outlet, at a cost of $225.

- In 1891, they bought an additional 20 acres of land on the east side of the lake around the outlet for $4,500. They still did not have the deed for the one acre at the outlet and were having troubles getting the "long promised deed" from Hugh Eldridge.

- Hugh Eldridge now wanted $1,000 for the deed to the one acre. Trustee Cowgill moved to deny his request and to instruct their attorney to press for conclusion of the original purchase arrangement. Later they offered him $500. Eldridge refused. Black met with him later and Eldridge agreed to settle for $450. This time the Water Company declined agreement.

- October 1890, they hired a chemist from Oswego, Oregon, to analyze the water (this would have been during the typhoid epidemic when Padden water was suspect).

- Company offices were in the Montezuma Block at the corner of 14th and McKenzie, sharing the office with Fairhaven Electric Light Power & Motor Company.

- The pressure valve was at 21st and Donovan. The company rented a house nearby for an employee named Van Houten to live in. He was to open the valve in case of fire to double the water pressure in the system. The monthly dwelling rent was $4.00. "Appliances for electrical communication were being prepared" (that must have meant a telephone was being installed).

In October of 1891 a stockholders meeting was held and the corporate minutes published the roll call of stock.

W.R. Albee	1,000 shares
Geo. A Black	900 shares
Annabell Black	5,000 shares
John Black	500 shares
Nelson Bennett	390,000 shares
Blackwood	1,000 shares
E.L. Cowgill	10,000 shares
J.J. Donovan	1,000 shares
W.J. Diehring	5,500 shares
T.N. Gillette	500 shares
Alex McKenzie	500 shares
Metzner	100 shares
Charles Schering	5,500 shares
R.C. Vanderford	1,000 shares
E.M. Wilson	15,000 shares
William O. Wright	4,000 shares
John H. Ware	9,000 shares

The 1890 franchise agreement with the City of Fairhaven gave the water company the right to operate its waterworks for a period of 50 years and provided that the city would have the first right to purchase the water company in 20 years should it wish to do so.

After the 1904 consolidation of Fairhaven and Whatcom, the Fairhaven Water and Power Company continued business as usual, selling its Lake Padden water to south Bellingham under their original franchise. The franchise had simply been transferred to the new municipality.

Just after midnight on Sept 30, 1924, the watchman at the Bloedel Donovan Box factory at the foot of Cornwall Avenue called in a fire. Sparks from the Morrison Mill trash burner had ignited a fire in the 12-million-board-feet of lumber that was stacked between the mill and the box factory. The huge fire that resulted consumed the box factory and the 12-million-board-feet of lumber belonging to both companies. The Morrison Mill reported a loss of $40,000. The box factory was destroyed. The Bellingham Fire Department was woefully under manned. The water supply to the fire hydrants was inadequate, a desperate call for help went out to surrounding communities. Fire trucks came from as far as Anacortes. Fortunately it rained that night.

Three days later, J.J. Donovan appeared before the Water Board to read and deliver the following letter. He made the following plea for improved fire protection:

> *"Bellingham, with 35,000 people, has two independent water systems, one private, one public, relics of the old days of two cities. Both are like Topsy-"they just growed." Neither is perfect. Both need many changes. They should be united, improved and under one management with the same rates and same policy for the whole city. I advise these things:*
>
> 1. *Immediate physical temporary connection of the two systems with valve to be opened only in case of serious fire.*
>
> 2. *Completion of the new Lake Whatcom line with all possible speed.*
>
> 3. *Acquisition of the Fairhaven system forthwith.*
>
> 4. *Separation of the two systems except in case of fire, the Fairhaven system to supply all domestic and the upland fire service, the Lake Whatcom system to furnish the factories of the water-front.*
>
> 5. *Open Lake Whatcom to the public.*
>
> 6. *Develop both systems as the business of the city warrants."*

Donovan's plea was apparently coordinated with a Chamber of Commerce initiative to improve City fire protection. On August 11, 1925, a blue ribbon committee of the chamber appeared before the City Council to request purchase of the Fairhaven system. The committee included many of the city's most influential citizens; E.B. Deming, President of Pacific American Fisheries; Frank I Sefrit, Publisher of the Bellingham Herald; E.W. Purdy,

President of the 1st National Bank of Bellingham; F.F. Handschey; C.S. Beard; Cyrus Gates; C.K. McMillin; H.B. Paige; J.L. Easton; and R.A. Welsh, owner of the Bellingham Canning Company. It was a list of powerful business and industrial leaders. They reported to the council that they had negotiated with the Fairhaven City Water and Power Company a sale price of $165,000. They delivered to the city the water company's offer to sell for $165,000.

As though the fire gods were trying to influence the Bellingham Water Board, another catastrophic fire broke out in September 1925. The E.K. Wood lumber mill burned in a huge fire that consumed the entire mill, except for the concrete steam turbine building (now The Woods Coffee Shop at Boulevard Park). The city officials were finally convinced, and with the aid of several bond issues, improvements to the city's fire protection was begun.

The purchase of the Fairhaven City Water and Power Company was consummated on February 27, 1926. On that date the water company president, W. A. Gillette and its secretary, A.C. Miller, signed the final documents which surrendered their city franchise and hydrant rental contracts and transferred ownership of the land, the riparian rights, the 1890's grants of water rights to both Ruby Creek and Chuckanut Creek, the rights to use the water of Lake Padden, the water mains, pipes and hydrants—the entire waterworks of the old company. The purchase price was the $165,000 that the Chamber of Commerce committee had negotiated.

The City operated the former Fairhaven company's waterworks using water from Lake Padden until 1968. By that time, a diversion dam had been built directing water from the south fork of the Nooksack River into Lake Whatcom. A new filtration plant on Lake Whatcom went into operation in 1968. The south Bellingham water pipes were connected to Lake Whatcom, and for the first time, south-side residents who had drunk Padden water since 1890, began drinking Lake Whatcom water.

In 1968, the protective fence around the lake was taken down and by September of that year, the Bellingham Park Board was making plans to include Lake Padden Park development in the Park Bond Issue that they were preparing. Soon the idea of building a golf course on Lake Padden land gained acceptance. In 1969, the Park Department got permission from the Water Board to log land to clear it for a golf course. By 1970, the park was a reality and the golf course was under construction. Lake Padden and its surrounding lands had become a part of Bellingham's Park system.

The Power Plant along Padden Creek. The 1891 Fairhaven Birdseye depicts the coal-powered steam-generating plant located in the Padden Creek canyon 150 feet upstream of the 12th Street bridge. The coal smoke is seen rising from its stack.

Fairhaven Electric Light, Power and Motor Co.

Electric lights were perhaps not as essential to a modern 1890's city as an adequate water supply, but the Fairhaven Land Company was intent on building an up-to-date city. Even before they incorporated the Fairhaven Water Company, Bennett's lieutenants incorporated the Fairhaven Electric Light, Power and Motor Company. The Articles of Incorporation are dated October 19, 1889, five days before the incorporation date of the water company. The trustees were Pierce Evans, lawyer for the Fairhaven Land Company, George Black, and James F. Wardner.

Stock Certificate, 1889. A blank stock certificate found with the Water Company records. They shared office space for many years. Collection of the author.

Electricity to power street lights, homes, and perhaps even street trolley cars was the goal and because they located their power plant alongside Padden Creek, is it reasonable to believe that they gave some thought to developing hydro-electric power from the waters of the stream. The certain source of energy to power their steam generator was coal from the Bennett and Larrabee owned Cokedale mine near Sedro.

The Fairhaven and Southern Railway track from Sedro ran along Padden Creek. The power plant was located about 150 feet east of 12th Street on the south side of the creek. Its location is illustrated on the 1891 Fairhaven Birdseye.

The company's first customer was the City of Fairhaven, as evidenced by a contract dated January 5, 1891, and signed by Pierce Evans, company president, and Mayor pro tem, J.J. Donovan. The contract language follows:

> "for the consideration hereinafter mentioned agrees to furnish to the said City of Fairhaven thirty five all night 2000-candle-power lamps. Said lamps to be placed in position as soon as possible. Said lamps to be used for street lighting and run on the moonlight schedule. That when there are bright moonlight nights the lights are not to be turned on. The lamps are to be hung at intersections of streets, suspended from poles so that lamps hang over center of streets. Poles not to be less than forty-feet-high above grade. In consideration whereof, the said City of Fairhaven agrees to pay the said Fairhaven Electric Light Power & Motor Company the sum of ten dollars per month for each and every light so furnished."

The Fairhaven Electric Light, Power and Motor Company was sold in the first decade of the 20th century, as scores of small community power companies in western Washington were consolidated into what would become Puget Sound Power and Light Company.

The Electric Company had shared office space with the Water Company and perhaps did so until their closing, as a book of blank stock certificates was found in the box of Water Company records found on the second floor of the Waldron building in the 1970s.

$\succ\!\!-\!\!\leftrightarrow\!\!-\!\!\bigcirc\!\!-\!\!\leftrightarrow\!\!-\!\!\prec$

Town Marshal Winfield Scott Parker

THE SAGA OF A FAILED LAWMAN

The law in cities of the 1890s was enforced by town marshals. One of the first acts of the fledgling City Council of 1890 was to select a town marshal. The marshal would be the commander of the tiny police force of four policemen, he would be responsible for enforcing the ordinances passed by the council, would collect fines generated by violators of the various laws, and would pursue tardy tax payers and collect their unpaid taxes. It was a job with considerable financial responsibility and, in their prudent wisdom, the Fairhaven City Council established the requirement that the town marshal post a penalty bond of $1,000, guaranteeing the faithful performance of his job. In the modern world, public officials are required to post similar bonds and the guarantor of those bonds are typically insurance companies, which charge a premium for their commitment.

In the 1890s, the guarantors of these fidelity bonds were typically well known persons who would sign documents assuring the bond holder, in this case the City of Fairhaven, that they had the financial capacity to guarantee such bonds and would pay the penalty should the bond principal fail in his prescribed duties. Whether they charged for their risk was entirely up to the parties involved. In many cases, the guarantors simply backed an office holder's bond out of respect and friendship with no consideration. In the case of a bond in a large penalty amount there would be numerous volunteer sureties. We found one example in 1896 of 18 sureties for the $15,000 City Treasurer's position. Among them were many notable persons, including J.J. Donovan for $1,000, and Nellie Padden, spinster, for $500.

In that first Council meeting of 1890, the Council majority elected Winfield Scott Parker as Town Marshal and established a bond amount of $1,000.

A REWARD

— OF —

$1,000.00.

Will be paid by the City of Fairhaven, Washington, for the delivery to the Sheriff of Whatcom County, Washington, of

WINFIELD SCOTT PARKER,

late City Marshal of said city. Parker is wanted on the charge of embezzlement of public funds.

Height, 6 ft. 2 or 3 inches. Age, 38 years. Very red face with cheeks full and prominent; small veins in cheeks give them a crimson purple color. Weight, about 245 lbs. Wore, when he disappeared (Thanksgiving Day, 1891,) jet black mustache and narrow chin beard. His black hair and swarthy complexion suggest a trace of Spanish blood. Of powerful frame and the type of perfect health. Erect carriage, with shoulders slightly stooping.

Forehead full just above the eyes but slopes toward the top, leaving top of head very small. Wears a number 10 shoe. Inveterate smoker and steady drinker of whiskey, but not to intoxication. Liberal spender of money, of a jovial disposition, with a very hearty laugh when amused. Member of Knights of Pythias, Elks and Knights Templar. Is a lover of horses and ordinary sports.

For further information address A. McKenzie, Mayor of the City of Fairhaven, Washington.

This wanted poster was found among the treasures from the trunk, the J.J. Donovan papers found in Long Island, New York, and gifted to the CPNWS by the Donovan family. Donovan Family Papers, CPNWS.

We have no information on the marshal's background, nor why he was considered qualified for the job, but choosing Parker as marshal would prove to be a very costly mistake by the new Council.

Parker took office in August of 1890, served for eleven months, and then suddenly he simply disappeared. City officials soon realized that also disappeared was the money that he had been collecting. After considerable investigation, it was estimated that as much as $15,000 was missing. A huge amount of money for the fledgling city. No trace could be found of the errant marshal.

Five years later, in December of 1895, a Mr. Sauls of Seattle, and J.C. Dyer of Fairhaven located Parker in far-off Buenos Aires. It seems that he had fled to Argentina, invested in mining opportunities, become an Argentine citizen and prospered in some degree. Parker indicated a willingness to clear his accounts and his name. He was willing to settle the matter with the City of Fairhaven and initially offered the sum of $15,000. Saul and Dyer wanted a fee of $4,500 for their investigative services and a successful completion of the negotiations with Parker. A long negotiation with the City began and eventually their relationship with Saul and Dyer faltered. A Seattle lawyer named J.A. Kerr was contracted to do the negotiation. Negotiations were done through an extremely diligent U.S. Legation member in Buenos Aires, William Buchannan. Negotiations began at $15,000. Page after page of the City Council minutes of the spring of 1898 record the complex and lengthy communications through telegrams and letters. Finally Kerr was able to report on April 4, 1898, the final agreement had been reached. He had received a settlement of $10,203.10 from Parker. After his commission of 25% Kerr was able to tender a check to the City of $7,652.35. For this settlement Parker was relieved of all debt and responsibility to the City. The case was finally closed, the bond guarantors finally off the hook.

Consul Buchannan who exhibited remarkable dedication to the challenge summed up his activity in a lengthy statement which begins as follows:

> Legation of the United States of America
> Buenos Aires, Argentine Republic
>
> To All whom it may concern, Greeting
>
> I William I. Buchanan, Envoy Extraordinary and Minister Plenipotentiary of the United States of America to the Argentine Republic, hereby certify that under telegraphic authority from J.A. Kerr, the attorney for the City of Fairhaven, State of Washington, United States of America, I have today received from Winfield Scott Parker, now of this city and formerly City Marshal of the said City of Fairhaven the sum of two thousand pounds sterling (2,000) and that in compliance with said telegraphic instruction, as below set out. I have in return delivered to said Parker for said sum a release from the said City of Fairhaven signed by J. Wayland Clark, Mayor of that city for any and all claims of whatever character which the said City of Fairhaven has or may have against said W.S. Parker.
>
> Case closed.

The Movable House

Edgar Lea Cowgill was one of Nelson Bennett's most trusted lieutenants, the Secretary and General Manager of the Fairhaven Land Company, and an enthusiastic booster of Fairhaven. In the 1890s, it was considered that an up-to-date and thoroughly modern city must have two amenities, a fine luxurious hotel and an opera house. It was Cowgill's passion that since Fairhaven now had its hotel, it must soon have its opera house.

With the support of Bennett and the Land Company, he organized a bond subscription campaign to provide the necessary funding. An article in the *Fairhaven Herald* of December 29, 1890, tells it best.

> "Of the projected buildings, first and foremost is the opera house. A committee is now engaged in closing up the subscription for a bonus of $20,000. Once this amount is pledged, Mr. E.L. Cowgill will build a $100,000 opera house on his four lots at Harris and Thirteenth Street. A large portion of the amount has been raised and the work will be begun the moment the subscription is complete which will doubtless be in a very short time."

Raising the final $20,000 was not the only problem that the opera house project faced. Cowgill's residence sat squarely on the center of the four lots designated for the new building.

Undaunted, Cowgill determined to move his house to another location making way for the opera house. The better people in Fairhaven had begun to build their homes on the hill looking down on the city center. Local wags were calling it 'Nob Hill'. Cowgill decided to join them. He bought a lot at

Edgar Cowgill Home, 1889, Birdseye. Cowgill built his house close to the business district adjacent to the Fairhaven Hotel site. It soon became obvious that this was a commercial site, perfect for an opera house.

the northeast corner of 17th and Knox, high on the hill, and announced that he would move his house up the steep 14th Street hill, turn the corner and then up the even steeper grade on Knox from 14th to the 17th Street intersection.

That March of 1891, the house was lifted from its post-and-block foundation, the horses and wagons were assembled and the move began. The Fairhaven Herald wrote in a headline:

THE FIRST STEP
In the construction of Fairhaven's Grand Opera House

"Workmen were busily engaged yesterday in arranging for the removal of General Manager E.L. Cowgill's residence from the corner of Harris Avenue and Thirteenth Street. The building will be taken to the corner of Seventeenth Street and Knox Avenue. This is the first step taken towards the erection of Fairhaven's Grand Opera house, and as soon as the building is off the ground, excavation will be commenced for the basement and foundation of the building."

Each week its slow progress up the hill was noted in the weekly papers of the day.

"General Manager Cowgill's residence continues to climb the hill. Last evening it had reached the corner of Fourteenth Street and Knox Avenue. The incline on Knox Avenue is the steepest of any over which the house has been moved, but the contractor expects to have the building in its permanent place at Seventeenth and Knox Avenue by the latter part of the week."

The Forbes House at 1705 Knox Avenue. This large house replaced the Cowgill house which had been moved to Donovan Avenue. 2015, collection of the author.

By the end of March 1891, the house had reached its new location and been set upon its foundation. There it would remain through several ownerships. First Cowgill, then D.K. and Hattie Butler.

Then, incredibly, in 1915 the house was moved again. The Butlers sold it to Robert Forbes, Alaska manager for PAF, who built the large house which sits on that northeast corner lot at 1705 Knox Avenue today. Forbes, or someone that he sold the house to, chose to move the Cowgill house to its third location. The house began another epic journey, this time down Knox and 14th, and then all the way out to farmland at 2614 Donovan Avenue, in the center of Happy Valley where it became the home of the Frederick L. Schaefer family.

The story does not end there. The house still exists. After several generations as a farm home, it has been refurbished and serves as the Community Center building of the Bellingham Co-Housing community in Happy Valley. To honor the antiquity of the old house and preserve its charm, the Co-Housing originators chose to save it and restore it. They were not aware of its traveling history when they integrated it into their community building. Edgar Cowgill would be pleased and astounded.

Cowgill's dream of a grand opera house died with the Fairhaven boom and the 1893 depression, but not before Cowgill had begun excavation for its basement. The four lots were excavated soon after the house was removed. A deep pit remained on the site for generations. I remember it, C.X. Larrabee II remembered playing in it as a boy. The great pit was finally filled in 1972. Joel Douglas optioned the lots for $13,000. Douglas reports that the Sunset Building that had stood at the northwest corner of State and Holly streets was being demolished at that time, and the rubble from the demolition was used to fill the 'Opera House' pit. The lots were then sold to Ken Imus to provide parking for the Mason Block and his intended retail addition.

Presently the lots are being used for parking behind the strip shopping center on the former site of the Fairhaven Hotel. If you have parked there you will recall that the fill has settled in spots making for rather bumpy parking. Remember, the Sunset building was built of large pieces of Chuckanut sandstone.

The Final Destination? It is likely that the Cowgill house had made its last move, now permanently attached to the community building at Bellingham Co-housing on Donovan Avenue. Collection of the author, 2015.

The Empress Tree

For many years, Pacific American Fisheries employed several hundred Chinese workers each canning season. The Chinese were largely single men, many of whom had helped build the railroads across the continent, both in the United States and in Canada. Once the transcontinental rails were completed, the men were laid off. Chinese workers congregated in large numbers in the 'Chinatowns' of Vancouver, San Francisco, Tacoma and Portland.

The Chinese were excellent workers. They were willing to do the unpleasant jobs that the white man despised. They would work longer hours and for less pay than white people. In the canneries they were placed on the gutting line where the fish were cut open and eviscerated, and they were assigned to any other tasks that the white folks did not want. Illustrative of their specialty is the name assigned to the mechanical salmon gutting machine invented in 1903. It was called the 'Iron Chink'.

At most canneries, housing was provided for them in China Houses, large wooden bunk houses where the Chinese cooked for themselves. They were not always welcomed in the towns and cities in which they worked. Newspapers of the day, in unbridled racism, called them 'Chinks' or 'Celestials'. In Fairhaven they were discouraged from walking above 6th Street. There was a large China House at PAF located at the east end of the cannery buildings (see Joe Hansen's map, pg. 119). There was also a China House in Friday Harbor to service the cannery there. It was built partially on piling on the shoreline a quarter of a mile down the bay from the cannery.

The workers employed by PAF were organized by Goon Dip, a labor contractor and the Chinese Consul for the Northwest, located in Portland, Oregon. It is known that E.B. Deming, the President of PAF, considered Goon Dip one of the finest men he had ever dealt with, and that the two men had developed not only a respectful and successful business relationship, but a warm personal friendship.

Goon Dip, the respected Chinese Consul for the Northwest. Galen Biery
Photographs #0291, CPNWS.

To celebrate the completion of the new brick PAF headquarters building
in 1935, and as a token of his respect and friendship for Deming, Goon
Dip presented PAF with a sapling of the exotic Empress tree. The tree was
planted in 1935, outside the handsome brick building which now serves as
the Bellingham Amtrak railroad station and the Greyhound bus station. The
old tree stands there today, aged, its trunk reaching out in a grotesque lean to
the south, but still managing to display its huge purple blossoms each spring.

The dowager empress. The old tree is showing her age, but still stands beside the Amtrak station bravely sending out blossoms each spring. Collection of the author, 2015.

The Empress or Princess tree, is a native of China and Korea and was first brought to the U.S. in 1840. Its scientific name is *Paulownia Tormentosa*, named for Anna Paulownia, Queen of Holland, and the daughter of Czar Paul of Russia. *Tormentosa* is latin for having soft matted hair. The old tree stands as a monument of community history. The Port of Bellingham, which now owns the property, cares for it with proper respect for its provenance.

Edward Eldridge's Review

This article, written by one of the earliest settlers on Bellingham Bay, was published in the first edition of the *Whatcom Reveille* on June 15, 1883. The newspaper was published by T.G. Nicklin and W.D. Jenkins. It was printed every Friday and advertised a subscription price of $1.00 per year.

The article so eloquently describes the hopes and history as seen through the eyes of a early resident that we have included it in this history. It is slightly edited for length.

WESTERN WASHINGTON TERRITORY

by Edward Eldridge

"Indented by one of the finest seas in the world, and situated in the very center of the commercial belt that surrounds the earth, western Washington is destined to become a great commercial state. The time will come when the Pacific ocean will be as thickly dotted with the bearers of commerce as the Atlantic is now. It is evident that there will be one or more great commercial emporiums on the shores of Puget Sound. Where these emporiums will be it is folly to surmise. Every man who has sound reasoning faculties can easily discern where Nature designed they should be, but self-interest often induces humanity to attempt the designs of Nature.

"Commerce and manufacturing foster each other. Western Washington has great stores of natural wealth. It is a vast coal and iron field and the world does not contain its rival for forests of timber of different kinds. The development of these sources of wealth will give employment to thousands, and form a home market for tillers of the soil. There is but little land in western Washington fit for raising crops, in comparison with the whole, and consequently that little will become very valuable. And at the rate at which it is passing from public into private hands it will only be a short time before all the public lands will be absorbed in this locality. North of Bellingham Bay is the finest tract of agricultural land in western Washington. It is a level plateau, well watered and capable of maintaining a large population. For years the only coal shipped into San Francisco from American ports came from Bellingham Bay.

"Bellingham Bay is one of the finest harbors in the world. Very few places can be found completely land-locked, where a hundred square miles of anchorage exists, in any part of which a ship can safely ride out the heaviest gale. It is the central point of commerce for that portion of the mainland bordering upon these waters, both of Washington territory and British Columbia. And when the American and Canadian transcontinental lines of railroad now building to these waters are completed, a line connecting the two systems will skirt the shores of Bellingham Bay and the probabilities are that one of the through lines will terminate here.

"The first settlement in this county was made in 1852 by Captain W. Pattle about two miles south of Whatcom Creek, followed closely by Messrs. Roeder and Peabody, who built a sawmill at the mouth of that creek, where there is one of the finest waterpowers that can be found. This creek flows from a lake nearly twelve miles long and averaging two miles wide and more than three hundred feet above the level of the Bay. The mouth of the lake is not quite three miles from the bay in a straight line and along the creek are upwards of a dozen first class water-powers at which great manufacturing establishments can be carried on, all of which will some day be utilized.

"The county seat was located at Whatcom in 1854 where it has remained since that time. During this period Whatcom has met various vicissitudes, at times bidding fair to become a great city and again lapsing into insignificance. During the gold excitement of Fraser River, in 1858, for nearly three months there were more people at Bellingham Bay than in all the rest of the territory put together, but as the gold excitement died out, the people disappeared as fast as they came, and in a short time things went back to their former condition. Again, during the terminus excitement of 1870, 1871 and 1872 Whatcom bid fair to attain preeminence, but the French and German war nipped her prospects in the bud and again she sank into obscurity. Within the last two years people have steadily flowed into western Washington , and the advantages of Whatcom county becoming known, much of that population has reached here. A sawmill has recently been erected at Whatcom (the original one having burnt down many years ago) by a colony from Kansas, and Whatcom has again assumed an upward course which we may safely say will be permanent.

"The shoreline of the harbor proper in Bellingham Bay extends from Poe's Point to the mouth of Squalicum Creek, a distance of four miles This tract comprises the donation claims of Poe, Harris, Morrison, Pattle, Vail, Fitzhugh, Peabody, Roeder and the writer. The claim of Poe is owned by A.A. Denny and Bell of Seattle. Harris still owns his; Morrison's is owned by W.E. Bartlett of Maine; Pattle's by same Bartlett and Eldridge; Vail's and Fitzhugh's by the Bellingham Bay Coal Company; Peabody's by his heirs; Roeder still owns his and the writer still owns his. During the gold excitement of 1858 the town of Sehome was laid off on the Vail claim and a number of buildings erected thereon; after the excitement died out some of these buildings were removed and after the claim became the property of the B.B. Coal Company, it endeavored to repurchase all the lots that had been sold and succeeded in obtaining most of them, but as they could not get them all the town plat has not been vacated. Last winter Mr. Harris laid off a town on his land, named Fairhaven, and a number of buildings have already been erected thereon. This claim is completely sheltered from the prevailing winds, and is a good site for a steam sawmill. The mill site has been purchased from Mr. Harris and a mill is to be erected this summer.

"Recently the front portions of the Pattle and Morrison claims, which is the deep-water portion of the shoreline, at some portions of which large vessels can lay within fifty feet of the bank at low water, has been laid off as a town.

"A difficulty presented itself to the owners in selecting a name for the town. The idea of four names to a locality which will soon be all one town is absurd. We did not fancy calling it an addition to either Sehome or Fairhaven, and to call it an addition to Whatcom, while Sehome intervened, was out of the question. So we named it after the Bay which has been well-known for many years, and we leave it to those who will be here at the time when one name will have to do for all to determine what that name shall be. The proprietors of Bellingham will erect a steam sawmill capable of cutting 50,000 feet per day on what is known as Pattle's Point. The mill will be ready to cut in October. Other branches of industry will be established and to those who wish to locate homes and reside thereon liberal inducements will be offered, but we hold out no deceptive allurements either to induce persons to purchase town lots or to come here to live. Every person ought to have intelligence enough to be able to judge for themselves and those who allow other people to do their thinking for them need not be surprised if they often find themselves deceived.

"As the main portion of the town site should a great city arise here, belongs to the Bellingham Bay Coal Company, much will depend upon the course of that company relative to their property here. Possessing almost unlimited capital their influence can bring a railroad here and soon cause a great city to rise.

"Being one of the oldest settlers of this locality and thoroughly conversant with all its past history, and judging the future by the past. I seriously and earnestly commend the principle of harmony to all who intend to cast their lot here. With one of the most pleasant and healthful localities in the world to live in, and surrounded by natural sources of wealth which few localities can equal, it will be mainly our own fault if prosperity fails to attend us."

>—¡ ‹›•⊙•‹›¡—<

The Tin Rock

In February of 1898, the *Fairhaven Herald* announced that a tin can factory would be built at the foot of Front Street to make cans for the emerging salmon canning industry. This exciting news ushered the town out of its economic doldrums and into a heady period of investment, construction and employment. The three-story red brick building was indeed built as predicted by the Pacific Sheet Metal Company, with its first story at the level of the railroad track. With the construction of Ben Seaborg's cannery at Poe's Point, rapidly followed by Roland Onnfroy's Italian American Cannery beside it,

the can company had to rapidly increase its capacity and production space. They constructed two frame buildings on piling out over the water as production increased. A 'can way' conveyor over the Great Northern track consolidated the operation. Eventually they would build another warehouse building outside the new Bellingham Bay and Eastern trestle.

Each day after the last shift, the clean up crew would load wheelbarrows with the tin scraps accumulated in the day's production and take them to a large door on the northerly building. Sliding the door open, they would unceremoniously dump the scraps into the sea.

The Tin Rock. Kate Weisel photo.

The Tin Rock. Kate Weisel photo.

Day after day, shift after shift, for many years the wheel barrows were dumped and the scraps of tin dropped to the sea floor. The metallic refuse fused together as it rusted. Eventually the pile of rusted metal began to show above the surface of the water at low tide. Year after year, shift after shift, the wheel barrows continued to deposit their burden. Before long, the pile could be seen well above even the highest of tides, almost reaching the floor level of the building. Tin cans were made at that location until 1907. Pacific Sheet Metal Company had sold to the American Can Company, who in 1907 sold to PAF who set up their own can-making facility nearer their cannery. Thereafter the buildings were used for warehousing.

Surprisingly, the great tin heap that we now see was built entirely in the nine years between 1898 and 1907. This was, of course, long before environmental laws which surely would have prevented the scraps being dumped out of that door. The huge pile stands there today looking for all the world like a brown rock protruding from the sea. Its very bulk is defying the oxidation of its contents. Local residents have long called it the 'Tin Rock', and that is exactly what it is, just a great pile of industrial waste. Tin-plated steel!

The buildings built by the Pacific Sheet Metal Company were converted into warehousing in 1907 by their new owner PAF, and operated as a subsidiary company, Bellingham Warehouse Company, until their purchase by the Port of Bellingham in 1966. They were all demolished soon thereafter.

Second Trestle

The Great Northern Railroad bought the Fairhaven and Southern Railroad from C.X. Larrabee in 1902, and they immediately began building their Chuckanut Cutoff. The new track would avoid the steep grades and longer miles of the original track past Lake Samish and Alger that J.J. Donovan had built in 1888-89. The 'cutoff' began at the foot of Harris Avenue and followed the shoreline to the Skagit flats. The GN engineers built long wooden trestles across a number of indentations in the coastline along the way. The 'first trestle' crossed what became known as Garland's Lagoon, behind which is now sited the City of Bellingham's sewage treatment plant. Not surprisingly the locals called it 'first trestle'.

'Second trestle' was built to straighten the track at the shoreline indentation in front of Larrabee land, just below what would become the Edgemoor residential neighborhood. Both were typical railroad trestles of the day, a single track built on a heavy wooden structure set on wooden pilings driven into the sea bottom. As the years passed the cost of maintaining a wooden structure embedded in the marine environment caused the railroad to replace the wooden trestles with causeways of large stones.

By the 1960s, the gradual replacement of trestle with stone had created a tidal lagoon at second trestle, a mostly rock trackway with a small amount of wooden trestle which allowed the tidal waters to cleanse and refresh the waters of the lagoon.

Sam and Kate Peach purchased a waterfront building lot on Bayside Road in 1961. The home that they built sat high above the saltwater lagoon. Sam, a devoted salt water swimmer, installed a 104-step pathway from the house down to the sandy beach. Every sunny day Sam would navigate the stairs and revel in a swim in the waters of the lagoon. He also took great pleasure in rowing out under the trestle into the bay to set his crab trap, baited to lure the tasty Dungeness crab that abounded there.

Then one day disaster struck. The railroad company crews and equipment arrived and they tore out the remaining wooden trestle. They replaced it with huge boulders upon which they re-installed their rails. Deep under the rocks at the lagoon bottom, they installed a 30-inch steel pipe to allow the lagoon to drain and to allow some tidal flow. Sam was outraged. The entrapped waters of the lagoon soon became brackish and stale. He could no longer enjoy his swims in clean seawater replaced twice daily by the tides of the bay. He could no longer row his crab pots out into the bay.

Sam was an attorney. He sued the Great Northern Railway claiming that their impenetrable causeway had deprived him of his rights of navigation.

Sam won his case! At great expense the Great Northern was required to pull out a section of the rock causeway and its underlying pipe and replace it with a wooden trestle high enough and wide enough for a boat to pass under the track. With the new trestle a strong tidal exchange daily renewed the waters of the lagoon. Now the exultant lawyer was able to row under the track to tend his crab pots, and of most importance to him, now he was again able to enjoy his frequent swims in the clean waters of the lagoon.

Sam Peach died in April of 2005. His grieving family held a ceremony on Memorial Day of that year. On an outgoing tide they spread Sam's ashes on the waters of the lagoon and watched as they floated out under the trestle into the Salish Sea beyond.

The hand-grooved Harris Avenue pavement between 11th and 12th Streets, note the differing distances between the grooves. Photo by the author.

FAIRHAVEN, A HISTORY

The Wake Up Road

When I was a boy in the 1930s growing up on Bellingham's South Hill, the welcome tire sounds made by the grooved roads of Fairhaven were a familiar part of life. The loud hum made by the tires on those deep and irregular grooves, impressed into the concrete so long ago, signaled to my young ears that we were headed up the hill and were almost home.

My family celebrated Christmas at Grandma's in Seattle in those early years. Invariably on the long three-hour drive home I would fall asleep, tired from the exciting Christmas activities. We always returned via Chuckanut Drive. The scenic road would bring the family car onto Fairhaven's 12th Street with me sleeping soundly in the back seat. Then my father would turn the family auto uphill at Harris Avenue, and the car tires encountered those deep grooves in that venerable concrete street.

The sound the tires made on the first two blocks seemed to accelerate as we rounded the corner at 14th Street and headed up the very steep hill towards the Sacred Heart Church. The familiar vibrating sound was a certain wake up call. Without fail I would awaken to the warm knowledge that we were almost home. It signaled to me that we were on the 14th Street hill, and just another few blocks would find us at 432 15th Street and my warm bed.

Those grooved roads and the sounds our tires made on them are with me now as I write, so many years later. But alas, most of the experience has been silenced. A decade ago residents along the street complained to the City that the tire sound on the grooved road was annoying and excessive, even to the point of keeping them awake nights. They demanded that the 'Wake Up Road' be silenced. A single coat of asphalt did the trick. The 14th Street hill went silent. Past generations of South Hill residents are left with only the modest hum of a few blocks on Harris and a distant memory of the raucous drive up the steep 14th Street hill.

Fortunately, some of the history is still with us. There remain three full blocks of the original grooved-concrete streets of Fairhaven between 11th and 14th Streets. They preside there with their irregular grooves separated by a seven-foot strip of bricks and asphalt where the old trolley used to run. This short section of the street is preserved as part of the historic ambiance of Fairhaven and is zealously guarded by devoted members of the Historic Fairhaven Association. In fact, just four or five years ago repair of an under-the-road sewer line threatened the antique look of the street where 12th Street crosses Harris. John Servais and Stephanie Johnson were able to convince the city not to simply asphalt over the intersection, but to preserve the antique bricks and the reminder of the old trolley line.

Harris Avenue below 12th is rough and bumpy and is the bane of sports car drivers and car guys who worry about their shock absorbers, but to those of us who value Fairhaven history the old street is charming and warms the heart. May it be preserved forever, for it reminds us that at first, in 1890, Harris Avenue was simply a graded road in the dirt. In the rainy season, which was a good part of the year, it was a sea of mud. Then Harris Avenue was planked. Huge four-inch-thick planks of old growth Douglas fir were used and provided the utmost in luxury and modern streetscape.

In 1891 when the electric trolley line was completed, the planking had to be cut and rebuilt to accommodate the rails and the brick median was installed. Even old growth fir was not indestructible and after a period of years needed replacing. By 1915 the street was a sorry affair and badly needed work, so on July 19, 1915, the Bellingham City Council let a contract to K. Sauset for a permanent two-course concrete pavement to be laid on Harris Avenue from 4th Street to 14th Street. It had been bid and accepted at $11,148 to be paid by a local improvement district, whereby the property owners benefiting from the improvement would pay for it over a 12-year period via a property tax increase. The job was to be completed before December 1, 1915.

A *Fairhaven Herald* article dated November 15, 1915, states that "twenty four foot pavement is now being laid on Harris Avenue."

The article entitled "South Side Asks For Additional Paving" reports a petition, carrying signatures of 53% of owners of the abutting properties, asking the city to add a 9.5-foot strip of pavement be added to the pavement currently being laid. Their petition also asked for concrete curbs and planking connecting the curbs to the plank sidewalk.

If you measure the street today you will find that the strips on each side of the trolley tracks measure 12 feet apiece and the two side strips reaching to the curb are seven feet each.

1915 was still the era of the horse and buggy. Horses had trouble getting traction on snowy or icy streets as did the narrow-tired automobiles of the day, so the steep hills of Fairhaven received concrete streets hand-scored with deep grooves. It was, of course, those grooves which gave the pavement its distinctive sound and provided the wake up call for a sleepy little boy.

Old trolley tracks on 11th Street. A few of the rails of the Fairhaven and New Whatcom Street Railway Company remain in place. They were installed in 1891.

The Spanish Battle
and Other Harris Bay Legends

The early Spanish exploration of the northern coast over the years has spawned a number of impossible to prove, but intriguing stories. Perhaps first was the very old story told by an Englishman named Lok. Lok claimed that he had met an old sailor in Venice named Juan de Fuca, who told him of finding, in 1592, a great strait leading to the east at approximately the latitude at which the Strait of Juan de Fuca was finally found by Barkley in 1787. Did Juan de Fuca really find the strait that Barkley endowed with his name, or was the tale told so long ago in Venice simply a sailor's tale. No one will ever know.

Fairhaven has a legend of its own. The tale of a great battle between the consolidated tribes of the area and an unnamed and undocumented Spanish force. The story first surfaced to modern eyes in an 1883 article in a local newspaper. The story gained great traction when in 1991 local historian, Tyrone Tillson, devoted much of two issues of his *Fairhaven Gazette* to the story, complete with illustrations of a purported Spanish fort and armaments claimed to be found locally. The story has several different permutations depending on the source, but it goes something like this:

The oral history traditions of the local Indian tribes include the story of three Spanish ships sailing into Bellingham Bay, 300 years ago and anchoring in the protected waters off the mouth of Padden Creek. The Spaniards went ashore and built a stockade on the sand spit at the mouth of the creek, digging a moat on the shoreward side so the fort would be surrounded by water. The local Indians, objecting to this invasion of their lands, gathered the tribes and attacked the Spaniards. A great battle ensued with many slain on both sides. The battle ended in a victory by the Indians. The surviving Spaniards boarded their ships and sailed off, only to perish in a storm in the Straits.

Tillson's *Gazette* quoted the newspaper article from 1883, citing "the mouldering earth works behind which the early Spanish navigators fortified